Dear Tom James Partners,

While many of you knew him well, those of you who joined Tom James since 2011 did not have the pleasure of knowing the gentleman whom Spencer Hays credits with the success of Tom James. In the forward of this book, Spencer says Tom James would not exist today without Jim McEachern.

When I think of Jim McEachern, I think of someone whose love for Tom James and unwavering commitment to principles formed the fiber of his very being. When I faced tough decisions in my career or even in my personal life, I first picked up the phone to call Jim. It was Jim's advice and counsel that I sought - and for good reason. Not only did his faith serve as the foundation for all his actions, but he lived a life that demonstrated that no matter what your situation in life, success and victory are possible. He was a living example that there is a suitable, win/win solution in ALL circumstances and I should strive to find it.

Even though Jim is not here for us to pick up the phone and call, it is my desire that this book provides you with a glimpse of the wisdom and love which Jim bestowed upon his Tom James family. Reading it will not only help you better understand our company, it will also help you to see how Tom James can change your life, through the person you can become, the goals you can reach, and the lives you can impact.

It is my hope that you seize the very same opportunity that Jim had: to realize the very best for your life and to use every gift within you to become more than who you ever thought you could be. And when you do, trust me, there are people within Tom James who saw that success in you long before you ever made it your own and who will celebrate with you as you achieve it!

We are delighted to provide this invaluable insight into Jim's life. Please enjoy this book. May you find new treasures of thought and inspiration. May it 'Change Your Life!'

Todd

Also by James E. McEachern

<u>Plan to Win</u>, Co-authored with Bill Glass

Today *is* My Favorite Day *and* Right Now *is* My Favorite Time

The Autobiography of James E. McEachern

Jim McEachern

With Caleb Pirtle, III and Dr. Michael McDowell

CONTENTS

Epigraph

You don't have to be a
"person of influence" to be
influential. In fact, the most
influential people in my life
were probably not even
aware of the things they've
taught me.

--Scott Adams

A person should never doubt
the influence he or she has
to give hope, confidence,
expectations, love, and
happiness to others.

I want to live my life in a
way that I can influence
others long after I have gone.

--Jim McEachern

DEDICATION

For Spencer Hays,
who gave me a chance,
and for my wife Arlene,
and children,
Karen
Mike
Lynda
and Angie
who made it all worthwhile.

FOREWORD

Without Jim McEachern, there wouldn't be a Tom James Company.

That's a strong statement but one I believe to be true. He was the first person I hired for the new company in 1966. From then until his death in 2011, he always said he had three priorities in his life—God, Family and the Tom James Company.

In 1970, he told me his vision for our company--$100 Million in sales. He never lost sight of that goal. He made it real to hundreds of sales professionals and worked side by side with them to make it a reality. He asked me to give him 20 years to reach it but it took 25. When we reached it in 1995, Jim knew we could do more and we have. Last year we had over $330 Million in sales.

In all of the years we worked together I watched him make thousands of decisions always based on what was best for everyone in our company and not just best for one or two people. He never made a decision where he put himself first. He was the most unselfish person and by his actions and deeds exemplified the life we should all lead.

More than anyone I have ever known, Jim practiced the important principles of gratitude and of appreciation. Jim never missed the opportunity to express to others how grateful he was for the chances God had given him. He never failed to both say and show his appreciation about what he felt was his good fortune to be born and live in this great country of ours. He appreciated every day that God had led him to the love of his life, Arlene. He was appreciative of his four children Karen, Mike, Lynda and his youngest Angela Jeanne Hays McEachern.

This book chronicles Jim's struggles from his early life in Texas; through his years as a high school drop-out who went on to become a college graduate; to his failures in business; and his triumphs in building the Tom James Company. It provides all of us the opportunity to learn from a great man. He shares the simple principle that guided him.

"I would do my very best to influence the lives of others in a positive manner while I was on earth and hopefully long after I had gone."

In July, 2011, I stood before a huge crowd gathered to memorialize Jim. Like so many who were there that day, I wasn't ready to say good bye to my dear friend and colleague. Yet knowing Jim and his deep and abiding faith, I was comforted and I shared this about Jim. Many attribute it to Ralph Waldo Emerson but it was actually written by a woman from Kansas, Bessie Stanley, in 1905.

He has achieved success who has lived well, laughed often and loved much (*that was Jim McEachern*); who has gained the respect of intelligent men and the love of little children; who has filled his niche and accomplished his task; who has left the world better than he found it (*that was Jim McEachern*); who has never lacked appreciation of earth's beauty or failed to express it; who has always looked for the best in others and given them the best he had (*that was Jim McEachern*); whose life is an inspiration; whose memory a benediction.

Spencer Hays
January, 2013

PROLOGUE

July 12, 2011 started off much like every other day in a blessed life for my family and I. It was summer time and, as a college professor, I was not teaching but had gone into the office to do some writing when I received word that James E. McEachern had passed from this world to see His Lord. Indeed, it was a shock. One of my greatest friends and mentors was gone. Perhaps the single most influential person in my life (to use the biblical euphemism) had "fallen asleep."

Of course, whenever someone so beloved passes there is a wide range of emotions and a certain amount of chaos of the mind that takes over during the early days. After some days and the reality of the loss had sunk in, we were reminded by an author that Jim had been working with that his biography was in the final phases of completion. The writer, Caleb Pirtle, who is a gifted and talented author, had been working with Jim to help him write an autobiography of his life and experiences. This book which had been a work in progress for some months prior to his death would be Jim's "swan song" for the world. It was his attempt to tell his story first person in a way that only he could.

Jim had talked with me on numerous occasions about his goals for this book. It seemed to have become a focus for him since 2006 when he had his first brush with cancer and the realization of his own mortality. He wanted to write a book that would tell the truth about his life but not in the way that many autobiographical works do. He wasn't merely interested in telling his readers stories of his early life, his circumstances, and his later successes, failures, trophies, victories, etc. He wanted to tell his readers why he was successful and embed that into the story of his life. This is the Jim McEachern that I knew, the great teacher. If Jim had to use one phrase to describe the goal of his own life it would have been "to be a positive influence on as many people as he possibly could." Even now as you are about to read his life story he is attempting to influence you from the afterlife. Oh how I think he would be laughing with us all right now about this.

A couple of alterations to his original plan for the book have been made in order to more fully honor his life. The original manuscript did not include anecdotes from family, friends, and colleagues. This was something that was added in (after his passing) as a way to present others' perspectives of this great man. The hope is that these will produce a richer experience for the reader as well as increased understanding of Jim's life and times. Second, questions were added at the end of each chapter in order to help the reader focus on the big ideas of the chapter. Finally, an epilogue was added as a way of bringing in some other details of Jim's life that took place during the final years of his life after he was diagnosed with cancer. In some ways these may have been some of the richest days for him and so the family will tell some stories about his last years. The McEachern family wants you as the reader to understand what Jim desired most in publishing this book. He desired for anyone who would look through the lens of his life, to understand the possibilities within theirs. May this happen in your life.

Dr. Michael McDowell
January 2013

CHAPTER 1

Choosing to Become a Positive Influence

She was the lady I never met, the lady whose voice I never heard, the lady who used others to speak to me, the lady whose wisdom built the man I was to be, the lady whose face I only saw in a faded, black and white photograph, the lady who never knew I was even destined to walk the face of this earth, the lady who died almost six decades before I was born. Yet, she made a difference. She paved the way for me. It would be her footprints that I followed through life. When faced with critical decisions to make, when coming to a crossroad and not quite knowing which way to turn or which road to take, it would be the strength of her wisdom, passed down from one generation to mine, that gently led me onward and almost always in the right direction.

Her name was Nancy Green. She became a McEachern. She was my great grandmother. Her life and the words she left for those who knew her, the values she ingrained in her children, became my own. She was there, always there. I only wish that I had known her. Then again, maybe I did.

Looking back, I realize that it was not the easiest of times, but when a boy is four years old and has never known anything but difficult times, life doesn't particularly seem to be unbearable at all. It was all I knew. It was all I expected. It was certainly more than I had

1

ever been promised. In those days, if the promises weren't somewhere in the Bible, then we hardly ever paid any attention to them. Promises had hope. Not a lot of hope had found its way to West Texas. I didn't know we were on the verge of being broke because I didn't know anybody on the verge of being rich. Every time we were down to our last dime, it seemed as though my grandfather would find another one. I don't know how he did it, but he kept our world intact and our lives from unraveling. We all had each other and didn't need anything else. Our happiness did not revolve around getting what we wanted. It was being thankful for what we got, provided we got anything at all.

Perhaps, my parents had thrown me away. Or maybe I had just been abandoned. I did not really know or think much about it at the time. At the age of four, I looked up one morning, and they had gone, leaving my little brother, my younger sister, and me behind. I did not miss them, not at first anyway. I did not realize they were gone for good. Day after day, I would see an old car kicking up dust in the distance and think that the road out front was bringing them home again. The dust came closer. The motor kept whining. The vehicle would pass and never slow down. I watched as the dust faded far down the road, and after awhile, I no longer paid any attention to the sound of an approaching car. Let it come. Let it go. No one was stopping for me. I could not remember if my mama had even kissed me or my daddy had told me goodbye. The pain of loneliness must have cut deep. But I shoved it down inside, tried to ignore it, refused to think about either one of them, and, over time, the pain didn't hurt so bad anymore. By the time I started to school, it didn't hurt at all. I knew I had a mother. I knew I had a father. But I had lost them. It was as though they had died. They no longer existed. My brother, sister, and I did not talk about them anymore, and I did the best I could to forget them. They had not wanted us.

My grandparents did. There is a lot that a small boy doesn't know or understand. Only later in life can he stand aside, look back with clear eyes, and, with the wisdom of years gone by, begin to put all of the scattered pieces together. Neither my mother nor my father ever had a chance. Their marriage was probably doomed from day one. My father had been only eighteen years old, my mother fifteen, when they said their wedding vows. In those days, people did grow up a lot faster – time, fate, and circumstance forced them to grow up a lot quicker – but still they were so young to take on the difficult burden of marriage and the responsibility of raising children.

My father found a little farm work, but that was about all. He had only been to school a few years and could barely read. No one worried about an education until the crops were harvested, and by then, it was usually too late to catch up.

My mother had left school after the sixth grade. There were no jobs for them. No money. No education. No hope.

My parents did not have a life together. It was only a fight for survival, and they were losing. My father, at least, was free to come and go as he chose, and mostly he was gone. At home, he was in bondage. On the road, he was free. Spend a dollar on his family. Spend a dollar on somebody else's daughter. The money, what little of it there was, didn't last long.

My mother must have felt as though she were shackled inside the little shed we called home. It was ten feet wide, sixteen feet long, and had one room where we ate and slept. There was one bed. The children had pallets on the floor. We didn't know it was hard. We had never felt soft.

It was cold in winter and suffocating in summer. The chill came through the same cracks as the heat. The shed had originally been built against my grandfather's barn and utilized to house migrant workers when they came across the South Plains looking for cotton to pick and vegetables to harvest.

It was not fit for them. It wasn't fit for us either.

But after the wedding ceremony, which I doubt was much more than a country preacher reading a few sacred words, a nervous boy and a frightened girl making a few sacred vows, a father and mother smiling and praying it would work and knowing all the time that it probably wouldn't, my grandfather placed a couple of skids under the

3

floor of the shed, hitched it up to his tractor, and dragged it a quarter of a mile on down the road.

They considered themselves quite fortunate. Not everyone in those days got married with a roof over their head. It kept the rain out of our eyes and our feet out of the mud, but that was about all. I never minded the old shed. It wasn't much. But it was home. Its wooden walls were wrapped around almost everything I loved.

Then suddenly and unexpectedly, it was empty. Dark even during the light of day. No laughter. No tears. No words spoken in anger. No words spoken at all. Nothing but silence. Nothing at all. My parents simply didn't live there anymore. Everything I loved had been torn apart, and nobody told me why.

My grandparents simply moved us from the old shed to their farmhouse, bought us some new clothes, kept the old ones washed and patched, made sure we felt safe in the storms, gave us a place at the table, and told me that they loved us. For a four-year-old who had little and lost it all, that was enough.

The farmhouse wasn't big, but it had three more rooms than I had ever seen before. I could see no future past tomorrow, and tomorrow was never much different from the day before. I just lived a day at a time. My grandparents always made us know that we belonged, but somehow I realized that a part of my life was missing. Maybe I needed something else. Maybe I needed someone else. Even the face of my mother, the sound of my father's voice began to fade. Don't think about them, and it doesn't hurt so badly. Out of sight, out of mind. That's what I thought anyway.

When I was in the third grade, I was riding home one afternoon on the school bus. I was staring out the window, probably daydreaming, and that's when I saw it – a sight that I had never thought I would see again. It was a car sitting in the driveway of my grandfather's farm. It wasn't just any ordinary car. It was special. It was sure a sight for sore eyes. It belonged to my daddy.

I yelled to the bus driver, "Mr. Fain, that's my dad's car out there." That's when reality hit me again. And it hit me hard.

I was excited because my dad's old car was parked beside the house. No one else on the bus could understand. Every day, they rode home from school knowing that a car would be parked in the driveway. Every day, they came home knowing their father would be waiting for them. But I was different. The thought stunned me. It unsettled me. It was the first time I ever realized that my situation and my life were different.

The words had barely escaped my lips when I felt embarrassed. I was the only one on the bus who had been thrown away. Then I grew mad, and I couldn't remember ever feeling mad before. I clenched my fists and looked away and hoped nobody was staring at me. I closed my eyes. I could feel my eyes burning with tears of anger and frustration. My dad was home. My mama wasn't.

I was mad at him for coming back and tearing up my life again. He had ripped a hardened scab off of an old wound. I was mad at her for not coming back and picking up loose ends, knitting them back together the way they should be, the way she should have. I stayed mad for a long time.

My mother and father did come back to see us from time to time. But only once were they at the house at the same time. She was with another husband. She would have nine of them. And he was with another wife. He would only have three but manage to collect a lot of girl friends along the way.

I should have been glad to see them. I only sought to punish them. I ignored them. I lashed out at them. I never had a kind word for either of them. When one came into the room where I was sitting, I would get up and leave. I tried to pick a fight with one of my mama's husbands. The bitterness swelled up inside me like bile. If I had been older, I would have slugged him. If I had been older, he would have probably whipped me. He said he would have, and I think he meant it. There were never any goodbyes or goodbye kisses. The door would open, and all was right with the world. Then it closed, and all I could hear was the sound of their footsteps walking away again. They did not reach out for me. I did not cry out for them. I was in the midst of a silent war. I wanted them to hurt as badly as I did. I had begun to resent the very ground they walked on.

It was better if I removed them from my mind, buried any memories that might be lingering around, and acted as though I had never had a mother or a father or been left alone when they drove away. No resentment. No anger. No regrets. It didn't work.

I turned my attention to the farm and trailed along behind the only man who really cared about me. I dogged every footstep my grandfather took. He was already too old to raise any more children, but he raised us with kind words, a stern voice, and his own interpretation of what was right and wrong. It differed very little from the Bible. He was already in his sixties. I saw him sweat a lot and heard him pray a lot, but not once did I ever hear him complain. He prepared for the worst and expected nothing better. He loved his land, and he loved his family. God, he said, had been extremely good to him.

My grandfather always wore khaki pants and a khaki shirt to the field. When he dressed up, he wore khaki pants and a khaki shirt that was freshly starched and ironed. The shirt was always buttoned to the top. He had a broad-brimmed straw hat on his head in summer and a felt hat when the seasons changed and the days turned cold. He always had three pairs of lace-up work shoes – one for church, one for town, and one when he headed back to his crop rows. He had one suit and one pair of black shoes he kept clean and shined for funerals. He was a man of character and dignity. He could hold his head high, and he never met a stranger. I wanted to be just like him.

By the time I was eight years old, I was in the sun-blistered fields of West Texas, doing the work of two boys, simply because my grandfather was doing the work of two men, and I was trying to keep up with him. It wasn't easy. But then, I don't recall ever being told that any part of life would be easy. I respected every dirt row he plowed, planted, and picked in cotton fields where the weather could either break us or keep us fed for another day. With a good crop, the food might last all year. I learned a lot from my grandfather. Mostly,

I learned how to work, and it may have been the most important lesson of all.

Malcolm McEachern's family had journeyed from Barber County in Alabama a year after the twentieth century began. His father and brother settled down amidst the piney woods in East Texas, but Malcolm kept moving farther west toward the plains. He could buy land there, and it was fairly cheap. He farmed a hundred and sixty acres he had bought in 1922, gambling on his cash crop of cotton, maize, and other grains, always able to find room for a big vegetable garden out behind the house. Every year, it was always the same. Plant the seeds and pray for rain. On a harsh, dry landscape that was seldom touched by much more than fifteen to eighteen inches of rain a year, it was a constant and a bitter struggle for survival. We would wait as long as we possibly could in the late spring before putting the seeds in the ground. If they didn't have rain soon, they would lie there in the dust and the sun and die. If it rained at all, the skies opened up in the spring. We owed our souls to the Good Lord and the Farmer's Almanac.

The winds blew hot in dry weather, and I've seen gusts come roaring across the fields hard enough to kick up dust devils and knock the bolls off the cotton stalks. Just when we thought we might make a good crop, here came the hail. It hammered the just and the unjust alike. I've walked out across the land plenty of times after a storm and found only a few battered and barren stems in the ground. All of the hard work had been for nothing. Often it was too late to start again. My grandfather sweated to grow a good crop, and all he received for his troubles was dust plastered in the sweat.

I watched my grandfather. He remained stoic in good times and in bad. He never quit. He always fought back. He didn't blame anyone for the hard times. He squared his shoulders and endured them. Even in the midst of a drought, he always knew he was one day closer to rain than he had ever been before.

We had two cows, and my grandfather turned them over to my brother, Charles, who was four years younger, and me. We milked them. We churned butter. We gathered eggs from our two to three

7

hundred laying hens every day, cleaned them good with water, sorted them by size, and packed them up in crates that held thirty-six dozen eggs each. My grandfather would haul it all to town, selling the butter and eggs to the Piggly Wiggly grocery store. He took the cash and bought the flour and cornmeal, salt and seasonings my grandmother would need in the kitchen. Charles and I usually wore shirts she had made from feed store sacks, and my little sister Peggy wore feed sack dresses. They were bright and colorful, but we didn't feel as though we were different from anyone else. Almost every child on the South Plains was dressed in feed sack clothes. The colors faded rather quickly, but the material was strong and sturdy and would last for a long time.

My grandmother fed us biscuits made from scratch most mornings, and we piled them high with butter and syrup. She hardly ever fried, scrambled, or poached eggs for breakfast. She didn't need to. Biscuits kept us filled, and the eggs brought good money. Eggs were served only by those who could afford to buy them. Lunch was always beef or chicken and plates full of vegetables, most grown just beyond our back door. We had leftovers for supper, and nothing ever went to waste. During the week, we could find peanut flavored cookies in the jar on the counter, and Sunday was never Sunday without a pie or cake or banana pudding. She talked to me hour after hour as she worked in the kitchen preparing meals. Her recipes for life were just as important as her recipes for Sunday-go-to-meeting meals.

With my grandmother around, I never felt any sense of desperation, even though I somehow knew how desperate our plight in life had become. She made us feel loved with every meal she made, every shirt she washed, every biscuit she rolled out of flour, every egg she sold, every hymn she sang, and every prayer she whispered. At night, I could see my grandmother and grandfather standing by the window, their arms wrapped around each other, holding each other tightly as they watched the rain and lightning dance across the plains, and I knew all was right with the world. All was right with me.

On Unrecognized Blessing

My dad loved to tell this story from his childhood to his kids and grandkids. It was about his failure to truly see the blessings that he had in his life when he was a kid. Since he lived on a farm, they had many benefits in plentiful supply including foods that many others rarely had at the time including: beef, eggs, vegetables, and milk. As he told this story, he would take on a child's persona and begin to speak in a high pitched whiney voice. "Grandma, why do I have to eat these steak sandwiches every day at school? The other kids don't have to eat steak sandwiches. Why do I have to eat steak sandwiches? They all get to eat (pause for effect) . . . bologna sandwiches." (He would then laugh uproariously). "Grandma, do I have to eat steak sandwiches?" As told by Lynda McEachern McDowell (Daughter)

My grandfather and I were inseparable. If he was in the field, I was there right along beside him. If he worked until the sun went down, I was standing alongside of him when the last rays of daylight touched the earth. If he had a sack full of cotton slung over his shoulders, I had a feed sack filled with cotton as well.

We never worked in silence. He talked a lot about his mother. She had meant so much to him. She had instilled in him the values of life, and she taught him well. He would think of her with a faraway mist in his eyes. He missed her dearly. She had died when he was only six years old. She had died at the age of twenty-four, only days after the birth of a child. So much of her still lived within him

We walked down one crop row and up another, and my grandfather spent his days telling me the same stories she had told him, and they all had a moral that he believed was worth my remembering. Honesty. Integrity. Always do your best. Never quit. Never give up. Be respectful. When someone is down, lift him up. Be a friend to those who have no friend. Believe in God. Believe in yourself. Strive to be the man God wanted you to be. Don't be wasteful. Have courage. Be optimistic even when the world seems to be the darkest. Even black clouds have silver linings. Do the right thing. Take care of your fellow man. And I love you. Always, he said, I love you.

I heard his words. It was though I was listening to my great grandmother. Her voice had been silenced for so many years. Her influence on him and therefore on me settled down forever in my mind and in my heart. To my grandfather, those weren't just words. They were places on a map that would guide him throughout his life.

Even though he had only been six years old, he never forgot her final words. His mother called him into the bedroom. It was growing late, but he could see her smiling at him in the dim light that fell through the windows. He sat down beside her.

She touched his face with her fingers and whispered, "Malcolm, I'm so sorry, but I am dying. I just want you to know that I'm going to Heaven, and I want you to promise me that you'll meet me there someday."

He sat in silence, weighing the enormity of her words. He had never thought he might wake up someday without her. He thought that his mother would be there forever.

"Promise me, Malcolm. It's important to me," she said. He leaned down and gently kissed her face.

"I promise, mama," he said. It was a promise made in earnest and a promise he kept.

Farming was a hard life, and neither he nor my grandmother had a lot of money to spare. But they gave what they had to the little Baptist Church to support missionaries in the field. They did not have a lot of books, and those on their shelves talked mostly about mission work in Africa and in China. I read them time and again and realized that a world did exist beyond the last knoll on the distant horizon of the South Plains. I would sit with my grandmother and look at the photographs of the people living in those countries, and I realized that a lot of them were much worse off than we were. It is difficult for a boy to feel sorry for himself once he has viewed the troubles and tribulations facing others in far corners of the globe. It never bothered me that I might be poor. My grandfather gave me a sense of gratitude because I had been allowed to live in a country where life might be bad today, but we had the opportunity to make it better for ourselves tomorrow.

My grandmother, with her books and her wisdom, opened my mind and fired my imagination. She was the first to tell me it was all right to dream. Nothing ever happened unless you dreamed it first. She had been born only fifteen years after the War Between the States had ended at Appomattox, and she grew up in south Alabama, the fourth of six children. Tough times were a way of life, and the Bible was the only book that mattered in her home, as a child and with children and grandchildren of her own. When I was a young boy, she regularly sat me in her lap and sang hymns to me. I've gone to sleep on many occasions with the words of *Amazing Grace* running through my mind. She never talked about her family. She never missed a chance to talk about God and tell me Bible stories. As she explained it, the love of God did not seem mysterious at all. It was plain. It was simple. It was meant for me.

If anyone in the farming community needed someone to pray for them, they came to call on my grandmother. She was a godly woman, and they believed she had a direct line. Others might kneel and pray. But God listened to my grandmother. That's what they said anyway, and no one dared to doubt them.

On the Importance of Faith

"One of the things that I think about several times a day is the fact that Poppa led me to faith when I was seven years old. He is a spiritual giant in my eyes. He was relentless in his pursuit of drawing closer to the Lord. He taught me that this was the most important thing and how this aspect had to be right or everything else in your life was meaningless. It carried over in his personal life in how he treated people, his

11

> *thought processes in decision making, his interaction*
> *businesswise in leading Tom James, his leadership of*
> *our family and everything else he had his hand in. He*
> *had completely integrated his faith and practice into*
> *every area of his life." As told by Jonathan Snow (Eldest*
> *grandchild)*

As I grew older, I became more aware that, in reality, *my great grandmother* was living through them and the way they treated those around them. The Golden Rule was gospel. She was having a great impact on us all. It often felt as though I grew to manhood with her watching over my shoulder.

When I had a decision to make, I immediately thought of her and wondered, "What would Nancy Green McEachern do? How would she act? What words would she use? Which direction would she take with her life? What move would she make? How successful would she have been if she had been given the chance?"

She never had an opportunity. I did. I didn't want to waste it, and I would have loved to be able to sit beside my great grandmother and let her tell me what to do, what decision to make, which turn to take, which road I should travel, and which turn to avoid. She would have known. I often had no idea.

I was in my early thirties, had graduated from Howard Payne University, had a wife and three children, worked at a few jobs, was still searching for a career, had no idea what that might be, had my share of ups and downs, found a measure of success and more than a handful of disappointments.

I wasn't sure what my next step should be. Too many roads had dead ends. Then I knew what I should do. Without a doubt, I knew. Maybe I had known it all along. I loaded my wife, Arlene, and children, Karen, Mike, and Lynda, in the car, turned down a highway heading east, and went to see my great grandmother. I didn't know exactly where she was. I only knew that I would find her.

In my pocket, I carried the names of some of my father's relatives in Nashville, Tennessee. When I parked in front of the house, I was aware that I was nothing more than a common stranger, knocking on the door of family. I didn't remember ever meeting them. They did not remember ever seeing me. Most never knew I had been born. In those early days of the twentieth century when my father headed west, it was though he had driven to the edge of the earth and fallen off. People had a tendency to take a road out of town, and they hardly ever had time or a reason to take the same road back home. Leave a life; begin a new one. Miles separated more families than disputes, arguments, or bad blood.

A distant cousin said he knew where my great grandmother was buried. And, yes, he would go with us and point the way. No, it was no trouble. Yes, he had the time and would be glad to ride with us down to the little cemetery in Barber County, not far from Eufaula, Alabama. Sure, it was several hundred miles away, but the road was pretty good. At least it had been the last time he saw it. And, besides, he had nothing better to do.

We left Nashville early in April of 1967, and it was late in the afternoon when we finally found the little white-frame country Baptist Church where a young lady named Nancy Green McEachern had no doubt witnessed two of the most important events in her life: her wedding and her funeral. They had been only a few years apart. Out back, we saw the tombstones, the silent monuments of those who had been returned to the earth. A few trees cast their scattered shadows, and the two acres had been cleared of all grass and weeds. It was bare ground but well kept.

I walked down the rows, moving quietly from one grave to another, reading the names, checking the dates. No one had been buried there for a long time. My cousin had known the location of the cemetery. He could not remember where the grave might be. It was just as well. I was close. I could feel it. And I knew I would find her. The memories of my grandfather trailed after my every step.

Her name on a simple slate headstone reached out and grabbed me. I stopped.

Nancy Green McEachern.
Born: January 1859
Died: February 1886.

That's all. Her life had been reduced to a name and two dates, the beginning of her life and it's ending, and yet she was so much more than that. I stood there silently beside her headstone, and it seemed as if I were reflecting on someone I had personally known all my life. Because of my grandfather, she had played such a vital role in life. And she would never know. A melancholy sadness swept over me.

The loss of her life had been a loss in my life, but I had not really lost her at all. Her stories lived on. Her words lived on. Her calm assurances lived on, even though my great grandmother had died almost sixty years before I was born.

A curious thought struck me with power and emotion. I thought it over once, then again. As I stood beside the grave of Nancy Green McEachern on that April afternoon, as those final shards of daylight fell among the trees, I was rocked by the realization that she had been dead for eighty-two years. And still she was influencing my life. Still she was making a difference.

I wondered what would be happening eighty-two years after my death. Would anyone remember? What could I do to make a difference in someone else's life?

The sun was slowly falling behind the little church. Darkness had begun to slide like shadows across the land. I silently made the decision that would guide me for the rest of my days. I vowed to myself and to the memory of Nancy Green McEachern that I would live in such a way that my deeds, my thoughts, my values, my advice, my actions, and my compassion might influence others and perhaps have an impact on their lives even if I was already gone, even if I had been gone for eighty-two years.

The sun departed the sky. Darkness fell on the grave of my great grandmother. But the night didn't seem dark at all and it never would again.

Takeaways From the Chapter

- *Every human being has the possibility of having a positive lasting influence well beyond their own lifetime.*
- *Nancy Green McEachern was still influencing Jim's life 125 years later as he wrote this book.*
- *It was his grandparents who taught him to love God and that nothing happens "unless you dream first."*
- *What will be the legacy of my life?*

CHAPTER 2

Choosing to Overcome Life's Obstacles

I looked into the face staring back at me from the mirror. The eyes had life and little else. They looked as worn, as haggard, as troubled as I felt. My life, by the time I was fourteen, had experienced its share of ups and downs, but mostly it was down. And just when I thought that I had finally settled down to a hard but peaceful existence on a small West Texas farm, I felt it all begin to turn upside down again. It wasn't my fault. It wasn't the fault of either my grandfather or my grandmother. Nobody was to blame. Not really. It's just that life, once again, had taken a sudden, unexpected, and unforeseen turn, and it wasn't for the better.

For the past ten years, my brother, sister, and I had lived on my grandfather's farmstead. We planted a lot of crops. We plowed a lot of crops. We harvested a lot of crops. It was all work. There was hardly any chance for us to be kids. Not in those days anyway. I often felt as though I had become a man by the time I could walk and put on my jeans one leg at a time. We had a good and a loving home, and I thought nothing would ever change. My mother did come around from time to time. But only for a day or two, an hour or two. I occasionally saw my father, but I wondered if he was really coming to see us or simply visit with his father. And I wondered what he wanted or what he needed, since I knew for sure that he didn't want or need us.

He may have sought a little help financially now and again. Those were hard times, a lot of tables were bare of food, too many farmers were down to their last dime and still owed somebody a dollar, maybe two, more boys hit the streets without a high school diploma than with one, and my grandfather was never the kind to turn anyone away, especially not his own blood kin. I never bothered to ask why my father drove back to the farm, and no one ever mentioned a reason, either good or bad. Maybe he loved us. Maybe he felt guilty because he didn't love us. Maybe he just wanted to show off his latest girl friend or newest wife. My father didn't impress me, and, after awhile he no longer tried.

I shut the rest of the world out, stuck to my chores on the farm, and knew that I was losing ground in school every time one day was exchanged for the next one. For a time, it bothered me, then I began to ignore the fact that I hadn't walked into a classroom for a long time. I didn't miss the smell of paste or glue or crayons or the cheap perfume dabbed on some teacher's neck.

One fall, I awoke and realized that my grandfather was no longer the strong, sturdy man he used to be. Time, I guess, had a way of catching up with everybody. Ready or not, here it came. I had never worried about my grandfather's last birthday or his next one. He had never been a big man, seldom ever weighing more than a hundred and thirty-five pounds, but he was always full of life and energy with clear eyes and a bold stride to his walk when he crossed the plowed fields. No hardscrabble farmer on the South Plains could outsmart him or outwork him, and I had tried. His health was virtually gone before I realized he was sick.

He was my rock. Always had been. He was my strength. I relied on him when there was no one else for me to depend on. I could not figure out what had happened to him when I wasn't watching or had looked the other way. In early September of his seventieth year, my grandfather underwent surgery for a gall bladder that didn't work like it was supposed to anymore. I was saddened to see him in the hospital, but I had no idea that Malcolm McEachern, the defiant one, was facing the end of his years on the farm. He had never talked of quitting or retiring or leaving a West Texas field that had soaked so much of his sweat over the years.

He came home, but his back was a little more bent, and his shoulders more slumped than I had remembered them. He stayed inside where it was cool and dark. He did not seem to have the raw ambition to face a field white with cotton, wanton from the lack of work. He would in time, he said, but not now. He would wait awhile. He would wait . . . forever.

His mind was convinced that he could work as hard as always. His heart knew better. For whatever reason, he could not bounce back. He tried to fight the good fight, but his energy ebbed, and I believe he knew that he would never plant another seed or harvest another crop. He lost twenty pounds. His clothes hung on his bones as though he were nothing more than a skeleton in a straw hat and work boots. He could not lean on my grandmother for strength as he had done before. Her health had been on the decline for years.

I didn't even bother to start school that year. I couldn't. I looked around to see who would be out harvesting the crops, and there was nobody but me. Both my brother and sister were still too young to help much. Of course, we had itinerant cotton pickers who followed the changing seasons from farm to farm, and we were paying a man to bring in his combine to gather the acres of maize and milo grain. But as far as running the farm and making sure that everything was picked clean and on time, it was just me and the dirt and a tough west wind from sun up to sundown.

Mostly, my grandfather wanted me on hand to weigh the sacks of cotton dragged in by every picker who signed on to earn two cents a pound. They were strangers. Most were good, honest, hard-working men. But their faces were new. So were their names. And we had no idea who among them treated the field as though it was their own and who might be tempted to bury big stalks, rocks, and clods of dirt beneath the cotton in their sacks. Work less. Earn more. It was easier to make two cents a pound on heavy rocks than cotton. So I weighed the sacks. And emptied them.

Men and women earned an honest dollar for an honest day's work. They learned in a hurry that they could not bluff a fourteen-year old boy. Some tried. They were off the farm by the time darkness spread across the plains.

Other kids were in school learning higher mathematics. I was becoming pretty good at multiplying two pennies a pound. Others would pass their tests and move on to the next grade. I didn't bother to pass any tests, darken the doorways of any school, and watched a year of my life pass by. I would never get it back. School was beyond me now. I tried. I really did. I could never catch up.

Unfortunately, that was the least of my worries. Autumn turned to winter, and the farm I called home began to crumble around me. For the past ten years, my grandparents had sheltered us, fed us, made sure we had clothes to wear, and did what they could to soften the hard times that crept across the plains. Overnight, it was all coming to an end.

The decision was made for them to leave their farmstead on the South Plains, turn their backs on farming altogether, and move to Channelview, down near Houston, to live with a son and his wife.

They were too weak and too tired to fight the land anymore. The hard work had not beaten them. The years did. My grandfather never expected to grow old. He never planned to retire. He had no idea that the day would ever come when his calloused hands could no longer hold the hoe or chop the weeds from the cotton. Age was the grim reaper.

My grandparents drove away from the South Plains. I waved at them. They waved back. I smiled. It felt like a tear. They were gone. We weren't.

The miles that separated us were long and tenuous, and Charles, Peggy, and I walked into the house of a stranger. The woman waiting inside should not have been a stranger, but she was. She was our mother and probably no happier to see us than we were to see her again. She had thrown us away once. Now mother had no choice but to take us back. She watched us walk into the house with the same love she would have reserved for a passel of stray dogs. My siblings and I would now live in Abilene, Texas.

I guess I can't really blame her. We had, more or less, been out of her life for almost a decade. She had a new husband, number four if anyone was keeping count. She was working as a waitress in a cheap café from early in the morning until late at night. We were nothing more than an obligation she did not need. Mostly, we tried to stay out of her way, and she was either out of the house, out of sight, or sleeping. My mother put a little food on the table, and we found a place to sleep; sometimes in a bed, sometimes on a sofa, but usually on the floor. We had her blood and DNA. I would have traded both for her love. She was always too tired to pass out hugs. Then again, maybe she just didn't want to. Even when we lived with her, it seemed as though we were always on the outside and looking in.

Her husband was a pretty good guy when he was sober, but whiskey was the best friend he had. He may have loved mama. He spent most of his time trekking across the West Texas oilfields and the rest of his time with a bottle. He was a driller and lived a fairly sober life when he was out on the rig and coaxing that drill bit down into the rich oil sands of the great Permian Basin. But during those times between bringing in one oil well and starting another, he made life bitter and painful for us all. He drank whiskey until he went to sleep, and he didn't wake up until he was thirsty again. He was a mean drunk. Hostile. Always looking for a fight. I was too young. Charles was too small. So, filled with rage and alcohol, he found some solace in cursing my mother. He did not hit her, at least I never saw him take a swing at her, but his language consisted of one four-letter insult after another. She should have left him. She certainly knew how. Mother was barely thirty years old and had already left three no-good men. Now she had tied herself to another. Maybe she loved him. Maybe she loved the fact that he made good money in the oil patch. He may have been worthless, but he and a steady paycheck offered as much security she had ever known. Then again, he had a filthy habit of taking his hard-earned money and gambling it all away. He had a lusty passion for cards that ran as deeply as his passion for whiskey.

My mother would wait for him on payday. On numerous occasions, he did not bother to come home, and neither did his money. Time and again, mother would haul me out to the street, and would walk down one sidewalk and up the next, checking down black alleys in the darkness of night, looking for his car. He was never hard to find. We knew the pool halls and beer joints where he liked to hang out. We just never knew which one would be taking his money on any particular night. So, we worked our way through those two-bit, honky-tonk neon jungles, cold or hot, wet or dry, until we found him.

Mother must have been afraid of him. She did not want to confront him. Maybe she was only ashamed and embarrassed. Hers was not the best nor the easiest of lives. She managed to fall in love with the dregs of the earth, attach her name to theirs, and only realize her folly sometime after the honeymoon had ended.

She never darkened the doorway of a pool hall or beer joint. She stood nervously outside in the shadows and closed the anonymity of night in around her. She sent me inside alone, a fourteen-year-old boy face-to-face with a grown, hard-boiled drunk who had five cards in one hand, a bottle in the other, and a mean streak of hell running down his back. My job was to persuade him to leave and let me take him back home before he lost all of his money and was too drunk to drive alone. We lived from payday to payday. The bills added up. Without his earnings, we were always a dollar or two away from being jerked up and thrown out on the streets. Mother did her best to keep the bills paid. The debts kept her awake at night. When the money was left on a poker table, it was the crying that kept her awake.

It wasn't long before I knew my way around the backrooms of those honky-tonks pretty well. I didn't like going in. I was as ashamed and embarrassed as my mother must have been. I sometimes had to stand behind him and beg and plead for thirty minutes or more before he finally grabbed a handful of money off the table, pushed back his chair, and headed for the door. It was never easy. He was never rational. He thought he was always one face card away from being a rich man. The trouble was; the face card was always tucked away in somebody else's hand. A drunk can't read cards, cut cards, or play the ones he's dealt. He would stagger out into the night. I would follow right behind to make sure he did not hurt my mother. He cursed her on the way home, and he probably hurt her deeply on the inside, but I made sure he did not hit her as long as I was around.

He never threatened me until we got home. Life's most unpardonable sins take place behind closed doors, and no one ever sees or knows. No one ever wants to know.

He only swung at me once. He was too drunk to hit me. I walked out of the door thinking, "If he ever hits me, I'll kill him." Even a fourteen-year-old could figure out a way if he was mad enough.

It became so bad that I did everything I could to keep from going home after school. I would sneak in at night after everyone had gone to sleep, then leave early the next morning before anyone had awakened. I delivered bundles of the *Fort Worth Star-Telegram* to hotels and drugstores in downtown Abilene, and at night, I set pins at the bowling alley. It didn't shut down until almost eleven o'clock at night, which meant that I only had to get lost for another hour before going home. I had schoolwork and homework to do but never got around to it. After awhile, I don't think my teachers even expected me to finish it. I was falling farther behind and had absolutely no interest in catching up. My only ambition was to have a little food to eat, a shelter during cold or rainy weather, keep from being killed or killing anybody, and survive to live another day. The odds were long and hardly ever favorable.

What do you want to be when you grow up? That was the question everyone asked. I kept the answer to myself. All I ever wanted to be was alive.

I was caught in a vicious cycle. Go to school. Forget my homework. Watch my grades drop. Figure I just wasn't smart enough to ever catch up. Work late. Deliver those newspapers. Set those bowling pens. Trim trees around back alley power lines. Stay out late. Leave home early. Dodge the drunks. Break up poker games. Eat a little. Eat a little less. I was in a hurry, trapped on a dead-end street, and going nowhere. When life doesn't get any better, it just seems to get worse.

I longed for those peaceful days when I worked on the farm with my grandparents. It had been a hard life but a comfortable one. When a boy knows he is loved, he never minds the hardships in his life. The love had moved far away to Channelview. I often thought of them but only saw my grandmother one last time before she died. On a cold January day in 1951, I was notified that she had suffered a stroke and had been taken to the hospital in Galena Park. And there I was in Abilene with no money and no car. I walked down to the side of the highway and hitchhiked my way to Houston. A lot of miles. I made it by the time the sun went down. Day after day, hour after hour, I sat with my grandmother in her room even though she no longer recognized me or probably heard my voice. One evening, the family came into the room and asked me to leave.

"Why?" I wanted to know.

"It's best," they said.

I touched her and walked away. By the time I reached the end of the hall, no one had to tell me why I was leaving. By then, I knew.

Fifteen minutes later, she had died. Goodbye, I whispered. Goodbye again.

And I turned back toward Abilene. It was a lonely world, an empty world. I stuck out my thumb and waited for the headlights of an approaching car. No one turned down a fifteen-year-old boy with a sad face who looked homeless and probably was.

By the summer of that year, I finally gave up on my mother and Abilene. Frankly, I couldn't take it anymore. I washed my clothes, packed them up even though they were still wrinkled, and left for my Dad's home in Albany, thirty miles away. My mom and her husband drove me. He was glad to get rid of me, and she did not say she would miss me. I'm sure she was relieved to see me go. When she returned home, there would be one less problem in the house.

I'm sure my father wasn't too thrilled about my moving in with him, and neither was his third wife. In reality, they had no place for me but didn't turn me away. Families did what they had to do even if they were firmly against it. I never had a chance to be a bother to his wife. In a few weeks, she loaded up their two children and was gone. My father may have missed her. I don't know. He never said.

My father had little education and less ambition. He took odd jobs, bad jobs, dirty jobs, and would work for anyone who hired him, regardless of the pay. By now, he had become a cement finisher in the oilfield, and I was working with him, throwing gravel, water, sand, and concrete together in a little cement mixer.

Against my better judgment, I enrolled in high school and, for the first time in my life, went out for the football team. I was a sophomore and never played for the varsity. I didn't have any experience, and Albany certainly didn't need another hundred and forty-two-pound lineman. I was shifted over to the JV team as a linebacker. There wasn't a big demand for a hundred and forty-two pound linebacker either. It was probably a waste of time, but I was trying to fit in. I never knew whether I was a round peg in a square hole or a square peg when the board was run amuck with round holes. There was no place for me. I was an outsider at school and at home both.

My father did not worry about my problems. He had troubles of his own. His wife and children had left, and he had not yet gotten around to paying child support. A letter from a Big Spring attorney reminded him. He borrowed two hundred dollars to hire his own lawyer in Albany, and a tight financial situation became even tighter. He could either support her or us. The attorneys cared nothing for us.

One night we sat at the table, and the only food we had in the house was two cans of hominy. We scraped the cans clean. The cupboard was bare.

I looked at my father and wondered what he was going to do about suddenly coming face to face with the first hints of starvation. He had no idea. His eyes were empty. He had one too many mouths to feed. Mine. I walked out the front door, hit the streets, and found a restaurant that was willing to put me on the payroll. I washed dishes and cleaned up after the last customers had left for the night. The pay wasn't very good. It was only a dollar an hour. But I was given two meals a day, and that's all that mattered. I had a few dollars in my pocket, and there was no chance of my ever going hungry again. Life had turned around and was about as good as it could get. I may not have been on top of the world, but I was a long way from the bottom, for a change, and had my priorities in order.

On Hominy

Jim was not a picky person when it came to what he ate. During the later years of his life he became more cautious about what he ate but it wasn't because he didn't like all kinds of foods. He was simply being health conscious. There was one food that he would not go near, however. You may have guessed it: "hominy." I heard him tell the above story many times and when he would tell it, he spoke of that night and how disgusting that food was to him. This single meal is what drove him out to find a job so that he would never have to eat hominy again . . . and he never did. As told by Michael McDowell (Son-In-Law)

Of course, I had to give up football, which was no great loss for either Albany high school or me. In reality, I had already given up on school. No time to study. No reason to study. No hope even if I did study. English grammar was impossible for me, and I read only books that didn't have questions at the end of every chapter.

It seemed that I was always on the run and undecided about which way to go. I kept going back and forth, always hoping for a better chance and never quite finding it. I couldn't figure out whether I was running toward something or away from something. By 1952, I was back in Abilene. My mother hadn't wanted me. My father didn't want me. I tried to find peace with one, then the other, and finally realized that it might be better to return and help raise my brother and sister, if nothing else. My mother was still working the early shift and the late shift at the café. She was up early, slept during the middle of the day, and didn't come home until after midnight. We never saw her. It sometimes seemed that she was a ghost who didn't really exist. Her husband was drilling for oil wells or pouring hard whiskey down his throat, and we left him alone. If he were too drunk to realize we were around, he couldn't cause us any trouble.

My life felt as though it had been shattered like a broken jigsaw puzzle. I kept trying to put it all back together again, but the pieces that had to do with school were no longer part of the equation. I had lost confidence in my ability to learn, pass any test, or advance from one grade level to the next. After awhile, I would crawl out of bed in the morning, put on my clothes, head out for school, and find something better to do along the way. I hung out on street corners and wandered from one side of town to the other. I had nothing to do and plenty of time to do it. I didn't miss school, and I'm sure school didn't even realize I was gone. I trimmed trees during the summer and found a job with Rose Construction Company. We tore down, gutted, and refurbished the insides of a dormitory at Hardin-Simmons University, and I figured that would be the only time I ever walked across campus or spent any time at a college. I was a failure at high school. College was out of the question. It was hard, strenuous work, and not once was I required to open a textbook, which was fine with me.

School continued to be a stop and start and stop again venture. I knew that I was trapped and lingering at the bottom with no way of ever rising to the top. I thought that my life could not get any worse. I was wrong. Early the next year, my mother decided to move to Midland. She packed up Charles and Peggy, but I was left behind. I probably had a choice. For the time being, however, I preferred being left behind. I didn't wallow in my own misery, but I was aware that misery was a constant companion. I moved in with a couple who had a little two-bedroom rent house and no children. The arrangement offered a measure of solace, if nothing else. No longer was I keeping a wary eye on a man who liked his whiskey much better than the children who had infringed on his life. No longer was I walking from pool hall to beer joint in an effort to rescue my mother's husband from a sport that required him to throw his money away in a poker game.

I was pretty much alone and told myself that I liked it that way. I didn't, but I had become pretty good at trying to find the bright side of a dark situation. My calm and undisturbed existence did not last for long. I came home one afternoon and found the couple moving to California. I was on the streets again, but by the time they crossed the New Mexico line, I had bedded down on a cot in a boarding house. I had a place to sleep and two good meals a day, and it was only costing me fifteen dollars a week, which meant I needed a job much worse than I needed an education. That was my thinking anyway. So, I hired on as a checker for a supermarket. Maybe, I thought, if I showed up on time and worked hard enough I might become a manager someday. It wasn't so much of a goal as a hope.

For years, my life had been in constant turmoil and chaos. It had neither structure nor supervision. I was always moving from one town to another, from one little house to another, never quite feeling as though I belonged anywhere, not at home, not at school, not even on the streets. I was forced to face up to my own emotions that ranged from loneliness to fear. I awoke each new day without having any idea about what would happen before sundown. I lived a minute at a time, an hour at a time, a day at a time, a paycheck at a time. Nickels and dimes were a fortune when a boy's pockets were empty.

I had never lived on the straight and narrow path to anywhere, except to church. In Abilene, the Corinth Baptist Church was my one constant, my one fragile hold on security. Sunday morning. Sunday night. Whenever the doors were open and I wasn't working, I was sitting in a pew. I didn't read a lot in school. I read a lot in church. The Bible was history, and I loved history. I wore the cover off every history book I could find. No assignments. No tests. Just stories of the past, and I clung to them as though they were my own.

Pastor Elbert Peake was in his early thirties, but he took an interest in me. So did the lady who worked with the youth. She was divorced, lived with her parents, and I was always welcome in their home, especially at dinner time. Billy Webb was my best friend, even though he was a year older, and his parents treated me as though I had an important place in their day-to-day living. No one since my

(margin handwriting: GODS HEART for widow & orphans)

grandparents left had bothered to go out of their way and make me feel as if I were worth their time and attention. They took me out to eat at a steak place, which had always been too rich for me to ever dream about. I didn't frequent cafes with high-dollar menus. The steaks, I'm sure, were probably only a couple of dollars apiece, but that was high dollar as far as I was concerned. Mr. Webb actually paid for my meal, and he would have not spent that much money on a stranger in his house if he hadn't genuinely cared about me.

Billy's mother talked to me as though I was her son, too. She listened to me, and, with a smile, tried to ease my mind when I mentioned that going to the picture show or, God forbid, swimming down at the pool in mixed company, where you could see more flesh than cloth, was sinful and no doubt leading me straight downhill to hell. She and the youth minister of the Baptist church, for the first time in a long time, gave me a sense of stability, emotional support, and a belief that I might be loved, or at least appreciated, after all. Maybe my life wasn't a waste. Then again, maybe it was.

During the Christmas holidays of 1953, I broke down and went to Midland to see my family. My mother probably didn't need me. My brother and sister did. Since I was a prodigal always adrift on a new road, a different road, and usually a bad road, I decided to move back into her house and enroll in school. Nothing ventured, nothing gained, I guessed. Back in Abilene, for the past year, I had received no schooling, no grades, and no credit. I was always walking into schools and then walking out just as quickly. Now I was starting all over again, even though speech was the only class I cared about. I greatly admired people who could stand up in front of a group and speak clearly and concisely with something important to say. I wanted to be able to do that, too.

I still remember that morning in elementary school when each student was asked, "How did you spend your summer vacation?" I arose when it was my turn. My mouth was dry. My throat locked up. My mind went blank. No words came from my mouth. It happened every time.

Maybe a genuine speech teacher like Mrs. Verna Harris could help me gain a little confidence. She tried. She really did. Mrs. Harris treated me as though I were special. She complimented me even when I messed up, and I messed up a lot. She almost convinced me that I could do it, but, in my heart, I knew better. However, I worked hard in speech, and I read every history book I could find even though I didn't take or pass any exam on any of them. The school didn't have a library, but the bookmobile came regularly, and I would check out three books at a time, and then read them all twice before turning them back in again. I read new newspapers, old newspapers, and even the want ads.

When Mrs. Harris gave us a test on current events, I earned the highest grade. I knew what was happening around the country and the world but wasn't concerned at all about anything happening in Midland, around town, or down the street. The rest of my schoolwork was no more than an afterthought. Going to class was little more than killing time, and I had become a self-trained expert at killing time.

I worked at a supermarket, dug a few ditches in the oilfield, farmed some acreage with my mother's brother in Lamesa, and before school started again in the fall of 1954, I simply ran out of steam. I quit school for good. Might as well, I figured. I hadn't gone to class that often anyway. In fact, the only course I passed the year before had been speech, and I knew I would never get a paying job making speeches.

I didn't see a lot of choices for myself. I had dug a deep hole, and when I couldn't find a way out, I just kept digging deeper. During November, I walked into the recruiting office in downtown Midland and announced my intentions to join the Army. World War II was behind us, and the troops had come home from Korea, but the military was still out looking for every able-bodied boy it could run down. If nothing else, I was able-bodied. Digging ditches could keep a boy physically fit and in shape.

"You'll have to take a test," the recruiter said.

"Why?"

"To see if you qualify to get in."

I nodded. I knew all about taking tests. I didn't know anything about passing them. I turned in my test. The recruiter studied it for awhile, made a stray mark here and there, and then told me, "You have made the highest score I have ever seen in all of my years in the army." He looked surprised. I was dumbfounded.

He filled out the proper papers, and I took them home to sign. I set them down on a table and left them there. I had every intention of scratching my signature on the bottom line and heading back down to see the recruiter in a few days. I never made it.

Christmas was only a few weeks away, and I decided that I didn't want to leave home for the holidays. The Army could wait. The Army was always waiting. At church one evening, a gentleman approached me and said, "I hear you're going to enlist."

I nodded. "Yes, sir," I said.

"The Army could be good for you."

"Yes, sir."

"College would be even better."

I started to laugh but thought better of it. "I don't think I can get in," I said.

"What?" he asked.

"College," I said.

He smiled. "You might be surprised," he told me.

I shrugged. "I've never finished high school."

"I've watched you," he said. "I think you've got a pretty good head on your shoulders."

'My teachers didn't think so."

He smiled again. "I'd like for you to go down to Brownwood and visit Howard Payne University," he said.

"I think it's a waste of time."

"Do you think it would hurt anything if you at least went down to see the school?" he asked.

"I guess it wouldn't."

By Monday, I was on the bus to Brownwood. It was a long way from Midland. Maybe, I thought, it wasn't far enough. I walked across campus, beneath the shadow of the trees, across the green quadrangle, and into the registrar's office.

"I'd like to talk to somebody about attending college," I said.

She smiled. "Do you have your high school transcript?" she asked.

"No, ma'am," I replied. "I'm a drop out."

"You haven't graduated?"

"No, ma'am."

She frowned.

"Is that a problem?" I asked.

"Have you taken a GED?" she wanted to know.

"No, ma'am."

"Would you like to?"

"I guess so. Where can I take it?"

"We'll let you take the first part today and the rest of it tomorrow, if you'd like," she said.

I had gone to the trouble of making the trip. I was on campus. I might as well, although I had no expectations about achieving anything close to respectability, much less a passing grade.

Generally, tests and I didn't get along. I had left a handful of schools and several dozen teachers behind who would admit the same thing. I did not have a stellar performance in high school; why in the world did I think I belonged in college?

I took a deep breath and sat down with the GED exam. For two days, it was just me in the middle of questions I had never heard about or imagined before. There were all kinds of questions, all kinds of subjects, all kinds of reasons to flunk, very few reasons to pass. I plowed my way through – it felt as if I was sinking in a quagmire of confusion – wondering about the sanity of it all.

I was sitting alone in the room when the registrar came in with the results. I didn't ask how I might have fared. I didn't want to know. Failure and I were old friends by now. It was time to say thank you and goodbye and hit the road again. She was smiling. But then, she always smiled. "You scored in the ninety-eight percentile," she said. It sounded like Greek to me.

"What does that mean?" I asked.

31

"It means you can go to college if you want," she said.

I grinned. Either I was smarter, or perhaps luckier, than I had thought, or Howard Payne was not nearly as discriminating as I thought a university would be. Howard Payne actually wanted me.

Why Every Single Person Has the Potential to Change Someone's Life

Jim would regularly tell of individuals who impacted his life for the better. I heard Jim tell the above story on a number of occasions. He felt like a failure. He was, in fact, a failure and a high school dropout. The registrar at HPU in 1954 was Mrs. Doram Mae Herring. After he had taken the test, the registrar told him that he had scored higher than anyone she had ever seen who had taken the test at HPU. When he would tell this part of the story he would get emotional and begin to get tears in his eyes and shake with emotion. He said after years of believing that he was below average in intelligence and capacity with no hope for success in school and/or life, this kind woman said "you are one of the brightest people to have ever taken this test and I believe that you could be very successful at HPU." These words changed the trajectory of his life. While many people contributed to his life after this and he was grateful for their contribution, he seemed to be keenly aware that there was always those first links in the chain. For him it was a registrar who saw in him potential that he could not see prior to their conversation. As told by Michael McDowell (son-in-law)

I walked out of the room, headed to Midland to pack my clothes, and couldn't wait to get back to Brownwood. I hadn't even bothered to ask how much a college education would cost me, or if it would cost anything at all. I don't remember if the sun was shining, the rain was falling, or whether the cold December winds had yet begun to blow down the big hill from the nearby town of Bangs, Texas. It didn't matter anymore.

All of the detours I had taken in life suddenly came to an abrupt end in Brownwood, and no one was asking me to leave.

Takeaways From the Chapter

- *Life is full of twists and turns and other people can help me navigate these. Who are the people who are currently helping me navigate? Are they experienced and wise?*
- *Big influences in Jim's life were Christian adults who loved him and/or had encouraging words for him when his own family failed to do this. Who are the people in my life that I could have this kind of influence on through my actions and words?*
- *As humans we may be down because of circumstances but we are never out. There is a principle of continuing to move ahead in the midst of great turmoil. We really don't know what is around the next corner.*

CHAPTER 3

Choosing to Recognize Unexpected Opportunities

I had been given the gift that so few people receive in life: a clean slate and a fresh start, a chance to walk away from the frustrations of my past and head down a new road not yet pockmarked with ruts or chuck holes or dead ends. I could forget all of those missed exams and leave the missed classrooms and days of truancy behind me. No longer would I simply be condemned to hang out on street corners, usually by myself and never really wanting to be alone, always moving from town to town, from one home to another and caught somewhere in the middle, or be satisfied with a bleak career of odd hours and hand-me-down jobs, requiring little knowledge, few skills, and low self-esteem known only to a high school dropout. That was then. Now was different. A clean slate. A fresh start.

And nothing would ever be the same again. The compass connected to my life had abruptly changed and was pointing me in another direction. It would begin in Brownwood.

High schools may have wanted me or been required by law to teach me, but they had not kept me. When I wasn't in class, no one came looking for me. They made it easy for me to move on, and I kept moving on. It no longer mattered. I was a college man.

During the rest of the holiday season and until the spring semester began in late January, I grabbed every odd job I could find and had two hundred dollars tucked in my wallet when I returned to the Howard Payne campus. Tuition, at ten dollars an hour, and the cost of textbooks took it all. I may have been flat broke, but that didn't bother me. I had faced the world without a nickel to my name before. Empty pockets were a feeling I knew well. But this was the first time I had ever settled down into the safe and secure confines of a college dormitory, blessed with the chance to receive an education, earn a degree, be handed a diploma, and perhaps even make something worthwhile of myself. I was raw material, perhaps, but maybe someone could polish it up a little. Besides, money was only another odd job away, and, if nothing else, hard work and I had a long-standing relationship, and we had always gotten along together pretty well.

Before the first week ended, a man from a downtown bakery walked through the dorm hallways early one morning, looking for somebody to unload sacks of flour from a truck.

"How big are they?" I asked.

"What?"

"The sacks."

"Fifty pounds is what the label says."

"What does it pay?"

He told me.

"When does the truck get here?"

"This afternoon."

I grinned. "I'll be there," I said.

The baker would come into the dorm two or three times a week. He was always looking for help. He was always looking for a boy either strong enough or foolish enough to haul sacks of flour for a few hours.

He never had to look any farther than my room. After awhile, he came to me first. He had no business and no use looking for anybody else. It was just a waste of time.

Those were trying times for me. I had always viewed myself as a tick or two below average, and it seemed to me as though I possessed the high school grades, the unfinished homework, and the incomplete class work to prove it. For me, it was just a wild streak of blue luck that I was in college, knowing all the while that I probably did not belong nor even deserve to be attending Howard Payne. I looked around me and saw a never-ending parade of students moving briskly across campus. They had come from a lot of places, from a lot of towns both big and small, and had all walked across the stage on graduation night, had a principal shake their hands, received a diploma, and took the high road to Brownwood.

I felt as though I had come sneaking into town and into college, holding on for dear life to the back of the proverbial "turnip truck." At least, it seemed that way. I was the odd one, the interloper, but I kept my secret to myself. No one ever treated me any differently. No one ever guessed my secret, knew it, or even cared that I had one. I simply crawled out of bed on the morning of my first class, dressed, walked out into the quadrangle, crossed my fingers, and hoped I could make it. Time would tell. Time told a lot.

My goal was to graduate with a history degree and maybe even find a job as a schoolteacher somewhere in West Texas. It was an honorable profession. It was a chance to help some young man or woman along the way. We all stumbled. We all fell. Only the fortunate had someone pick them up, dust them off, and tell them everything would be all right. More than anyone on campus, perhaps, I realized the importance of reaching out to those students who might be lost or misplaced or in the midst of wayward and awkward circumstances.

We all want to make a difference. So it was with me. There were, I thought, only two kinds of people who actually went to college. Those who wanted to be teachers and those who had a burning desire to be preachers. I decided that I might have a better chance in a classroom with a handful of students. I did not care about their age. I might not know a lot, but chances were I knew more than they had learned. I deeply admired those who wanted to become ministers and lead a church congregation. My strong Christian views, my most important possession even when times were hectic, frantic, and growing worse with every passing day, had been my salvation. Even though I was hardly ever in one place for very long, I always had a church to lean on, a Bible to read, and some man or woman who was willing to sit down, talk with me, and help guide me through an assortment of tough days, relentless trials, and restless nights. None of them ever judged me right or wrong. They simply shined a new light on the darkness that came and went from my debilitating day-to-day existence. They might not have known all of the answers, but they cared enough to hear the questions.

However, I could not escape one simple and undeniable fact. I would have loved to become a preacher. I had even considered it from time to time. But the thought of standing up before a large crowd on Sundays, morning and night, and actually delivering a sermon out loud and with my own voice was absolutely terrifying. I lost my nerve just thinking about it. A classroom would be bad enough. A pulpit was out of the question.

I still had trouble with my mouth growing dry and my throat locking up even when I stood to answer a teacher's question in class. Some people had the gift, I believed. It had not been passed on to me.

My mind was made up. A good teaching job carried a decent payday. It offered me security and stability, which I had never experienced before, and my summers would be free so I could travel, which I had always wanted to do. Growing up, I had felt like a swinging door, always moving, back and forth, always in somebody's way, and never quite getting anywhere. I never gave my decision a second thought. Teaching was the natural track for me to follow, and I knew that I would never regret it.

I began that spring semester with classes in history, English, math, speech, and Spanish, but history intrigued me the most. My professor, Dr. T. R. Havens, was among the elite historians in Texas, possessing a close friendship with such legends as J. Frank Dobie and Dr. Walter Prescott Webb. He would stand there in front of the class, look us squarely in the eyes, and make history come alive. I could hear the rusty rattle of wagon wheels, smell the smoke, hear the distant sounds of gunfire, watch men turn themselves into warriors, and finally statesmen. His stories seared my soul. They weren't merely dates, places, and names to remember. They were events to experience. And I was out on the battlefield and in the halls of Congress with them. Their words became my words. Their courage, duty, loyalty, and honor became my creed. Their lives helped shape the man I would become.

Coach Bob Wright was the man in charge of Physical Education, and he made sure that everyone knew he was in charge. He was the line coach for the Howard Payne Yellowjacket football team and believed that PE should be a rough and tumble kind of conditioning class with hard, demanding calisthenics. He would work us until we wanted to drop, and then work us until we did. And somewhere between the first jumping jack and the last pushup, we played one of his own homespun versions of dodge ball with a little football thrown in. Throw the ball. Throw it harder. Dodge. And if anyone dared to pick the ball up, knock him to his knees, face in the grass, spitting dirt, sweat, and sometimes teeth and blood.

I was only about five feet, nine inches tall and weighed a hundred and sixty-five pounds, dripping wet and with my shoes on. But I liked Bob Wright's idea of physical education.

When we did pushups, his goal was to outlast us. My goal was to outlast him. He hardly ever gave out. On more than one occasion, I beat him.

I was not as big or as strong, but I never quit. As long as I had a breath to breathe, I could force myself to do one more pushup. Forget the pain. Ignore the strain. Sixty pushups. Seventy.

He and I would keep on going, only the two of us. My muscles quivered, my breaths came in short bursts, my eyes were bulging, and my arms were shaking, but I kept pushing the earth away from me, one more time, one last time, never a last time until I collapsed.

Coach Wright even taught me the technique for one-arm pushups, then challenged me to beat him and laughed when I did. After P. E. one afternoon, he asked me to try out for the football team. "I think you're good enough," he said.

"Where will a hundred and sixty-five pound player play?" I asked. I didn't know. Neither did he.

So, I became Coach Wright's student assistant and, for the next four semesters, I was handed the task of running his physical education classes for him. He came in the first day and the last day. He left the rest of the time in my hands. I had the responsibility for three classes a week and was paid fifty dollars a semester. Well, I wasn't actually paid fifty hard cash dollars to put in my pocket for walking around money. The school simply took it off of my tuition bill. I never saw the money. I never missed it. I was just glad that somebody who counted had it.

What Coach Wright gave me was more valuable than money. He made me feel good about myself. Out of all of those students in P. E. at Howard Payne University, he chose me, and he treated me as though he might have been my big brother. I may not have been any older than the rest of the students – I was probably younger than most of them – but those who had enrolled in P. E. treated me with the same respect they usually reserved for a coach. At the end of each semester, I put on a display of "fighting tooth and nail", but the students ganged up on me and hauled me down to the H-Pond and threw me in. I would have been disappointed if they hadn't. I was part of something. I was part of something special. It was a whole new awakening for me.

However, the pressures of college did take their toll. Paul Butler, who lived two doors down the hallway from my room, was a big old, rawboned boy who stood six feet, five inches tall, and probably weighed over two hundred pounds. He was a mountain of a man and full of mischief. Often, he could be downright ornery in a fun-loving sort of way.

Just before the Thanksgiving holidays, Paul Butler brought out an old air horn and started blowing it wildly while I was frantically studying for the three tests I had the next day, the last day before the break.

I asked him to stop making the noise. It was loud. It was distracting. Cramming for a test was hard enough. With the harsh sound of the air horn ricocheting off the walls of the hallway wall, it was bordering on impossible.

Twice, I asked him to stop. He didn't argue. But he didn't stop with the air horn blasts. The third time I asked, Paul sneered and said, "Make me."

I was street smart, but I wasn't a fighter. I never threw my weight around. I hardly had any weight.

He was eight inches taller than I. He was broad and thick in the shoulders. He was still sneering when I hit him.

Paul Butler didn't blow the horn anymore that afternoon. He was in the hospital emergency room having a broken nose wired back together. He felt terrible, but not as badly as I did. The next day, I apologized, and Paul became one of the best friends I had in school. I don't recall, but I think he may have decided to retire his air horn from public use or display.

In an effort to become further engrained at Howard Payne and overcome my fear of speaking in front of crowds, I joined the University's Mission Band, and we drove to different Baptist churches on the weekend, performing with piano, organ, guitar, drums, and voice. We hardly ever missed a Sunday in those towns within striking distance of Brownwood, and our travels took us as far away as Houston, Corsicana, and even Mount Pleasant on the way to Arkansas. There were almost forty of us in the Mission Band, but we only carried six or seven who could cram themselves into an old station wagon. Some went this week. Others would go the next one. I crawled on board every chance I had.

I didn't play a musical instrument. I didn't sing. I had a dramatic reading.

I was still scared and still stricken with butterflies in my stomach, all of them in a near state of panic as they fought with nervous wings to free themselves. But I was there on stage, eyeball to eyeball with the congregation, forcing myself to speak loudly, speak slowly, speak with fire and passion, leaving behind my own version of an inspirational message that someone else had written. I was merely passing it on second-hand.

During my first semester at Howard Payne, a gentleman named Rose, who owned a construction company brought a new Ford

Station Wagon to the campus and gave it to the University. He handed President Guy Newman the keys and the title, and I knew that his was a face I had seen before. I had worked for Mr. Rose in Abilene, helping with the renovation of the dormitory at Hardin-Simmons. His donation made a deep impression on me. I thought it was amazing that someone had made so much money he could afford to give away a new station wagon like that. Someday, I told myself, I would like to be able to do something like that.

Someday. I laughed. We all dream of somedays. Too often, they never come.

On Gifting Cars

Jim did buy many cars for a variety of people over the years. Some of these were strictly between him and that individual. He would see a need and out of his abundance provide a gift of a vehicle to that person or ministry. He also bought numerous cars over the years for family members as well. He didn't buy family members a new car every year or anything like that. He often said that cars were best utilized if replaced every ten years. When his children were in high school he bought them each a brand new car. He decided when his grandchildren started to hit driving ages that he would buy them each a car as well. He would research the safest cars on the road that year and then go with the grandchild and buy one of those cars. He would always buy ONLY the cars that had a five star safety rating. He wanted his grandchildren to be safe. He would always tell the grandchild that the new car should last them all the way through college and he expected them to take care of it. He also would warn them that if it got back to him that they were being foolish with his gift that he would take it back. As told by McEachern Family

The students filed their way into chapel every Wednesday morning, and President Guy Newman usually provided us with a message aimed to inspire us for the rest of the week and often the rest of our lives. Some studied while he spoke. A few slept. It paid to pay attention. I hung onto his every word. I was searching for the key to a better life, and I was convinced that Guy Newman possessed a lot of keys. Maybe one of them would be just right for me.

Every now and then, an outside speaker or successful businessman would drive or fly to Brownwood, speak during chapel, and meet with us afterward. James Jeffries had been a star football player at Baylor, and he gathered with a number of us in the lobby to answer whatever questions we might have. He was an insurance sales person, forceful but polite, polished and professional. He exuded confidence and success. He inspired me to dream larger dreams. He was spellbinding when he spoke and influenced me to become a good speaker in spite of my fears and trepidation before a crowd. I still had a long way to go. It never dawned on me that, perhaps one day years ago, he may have had a long way to go as well.

During those first five semesters, I developed a lot of friendships and experienced a sense of quiet and peace that I hadn't known since the days I lived on the farm with my grandparents. I no longer felt anxiety or stress. Howard Payne had surrounded me with the kind of atmosphere that once again triggered the dreams I had dared dream so long ago, the dreams that had faded when I believed they were no longer possible. The dreams that had taken root when I was a child but had lain dormant for so many years. They weren't specific or nearly as expansive as they had been when I lay in my room at night and looked out my window and watched the stars fill the sky above the farm. At Howard Payne, however, I caught a glimpse of life being good again. Maybe I could achieve a measure of success after all. All I had to do was hold on. I had no idea how fragile my grip had become.

I had enveloped myself in the comforting and tranquil environment offered by Howard Payne. I wasn't anybody particularly special, but the school and the professors made me feel as though I was. I was immersed in my studies, performing whenever I could with the Mission Band, running a P. E. class for Coach Wright, and living a good but simple life in Taylor Hall.

The administrators looked at me in a different light. A new business manager, A. C. Garvin, had walked on campus. He was smart, straightforward, aggressive, and always focused on numbers; not bothered by the fact that a few boys were trying to rise up and escape the hindrances of their past. He kept a critical eye on the bottom line. Money was a precious commodity. Money was the lifeline of the University. Money kept the doors open, the lights burning, and the professors paid.

Without it, the University was destined to fall on hard times. His mission was to make sure that Howard Payne not only survived, but grew. He did not care about sad stories. Every student in school had one.

Mr. Garvin called me in one morning. His face was grim.

I wasn't feeling too good myself.

"Mr. McEachern," he began, "I believe you have run up a rather substantial debt at the school."

His words did not surprise me. I had tuition to pay, textbooks to buy, meals to eat, a dorm room to keep me off the streets at night. All of them cost money. A little here. A little there. It kept adding up.

I had been steadily working every odd job I could find. Didn't earn a lot. Saved what I could. Didn't save nearly enough. By the time I had managed to scrape enough scattered dollars together to pay off one bill to the school, another invoice suddenly showed up. And I kept falling farther behind. It felt like déjà vu all over again.

I just couldn't catch up. No matter how hard I tried, I couldn't catch up. After awhile, just the hope of breaking even seemed to be a formidable task.

"How much do I owe?" I asked Mr. Garvin.

"Right at two thousand dollars."

The number staggered me. It seemed like an impossible amount of money. As far as I was concerned, it may have been only a dollar or two short of all the money in the world.

"I don't have two thousand dollars," I said softly.

My heart was in my throat. My pulse was pounding. I felt sick. No. I was sick.

"Son," the business manager said as gently as he could, "I'm afraid that you won't be able to enroll at Howard Payne for another semester until your bill is cleared up and paid in full."

I walked out of the office.

There was nothing left for me to say and no hope in my returning to school the following fall. Howard Payne would go on and go on quite well without me.

Generosity to Students

My relationship with Jim McEachern began in 1994 when I arrived at Howard Payne University. What I realized after just a very few minutes of conversation was that he had a passion for the education of students. A lot of people speak passionately about wanting to help students but he actually did it. He recruited many students to HPU . . . into the hundreds. I believe his love for HPU runs deep because he was so impacted during his time here. He believed that HPU could change the trajectory of student's lives much like it had changed the trajectory of his own. He believed that "possibility was something worth investing in." He wanted to remove as many barriers as he could to helping students get an education from HPU. This is why he set up endowed scholarship funds that would make it possible for many students to pursue their education into the future. Through these scholarship funds given by Jim and Arlene students will be helped in perpetuity. As told by Louise Sharp at HPU

Here it came again, an old feeling, one that I had not felt for a long time. Fear. I could taste it when I swallowed. Fear. It had found me again.

I rode out of Brownwood on a Greyhound Bus headed in the general direction of Houston. I had an uncle, on my father's side of the family, who worked for a chemical plant down in Baytown, and my aunt, his sister, had a nephew employed by International Harvester. Maybe I could find a job with one of those companies. That had been my plan anyway. If not, however, Houston was a big town. It was booming and electric. Surely somebody would want to hire a young man with two years of college under his belt. My uncle said that I could stay with him and his wife until I found a job. I knew I would not be living with them very long.

One door had been shut behind me. Houston had a lot of doors for me to kick open. I immediately found a job in the truck division of International Harvester, working in the parts department. Steady work. Steady income. A promotion now and then. A chance for advancement. Maybe a career. It wasn't the big dream I had, but, unlike the first few times I had faced a stumbling block, I refused to let the big dream wither away.

Within a week or two, my mind had it all figured out. Work hard. Save as much money as I could. And when fall rolled around, I would head back to Brownwood, pay off that two thousand dollar debt weighing heavy on my shoulders, and head back to the classroom. I didn't doubt it. I didn't doubt it for a moment.

I didn't fully understand it at the time but I now believe it was ultimately divine providence.

It did not take long before I settled down in my own regular pew at the Second Baptist Church in Channelview. I glanced across the sanctuary one Sunday morning, and my eyes happened to sweep across the face of a lovely young lady. I had not seen her before. I would certainly like to see her again. I quickly discovered that my fascination with her may have been a noble cause, but it was no doubt a lost one. I was twenty-two. Arlene was a high school senior. Either I was too old, or she was too young. I never did quite figure out which. Still, when I was in church, I could not take my eyes off of her.

In January of that year, in 1958, I was dating another young lady, more my age, and asked if she would like to accompany me to the Dairy Queen.

"Sure," she said, "but I have one question."

"What's that?"

"Would it be all right if my friend went with us?"

I certainly had no objections. Little did I know that her friend was Arlene. It was the "right" Arlene.

We all crawled into my '57 four-door, light gray Ford. It was the economy model: no heating, no air-conditioning, and no radio. But it would run. At least it ran well enough to get me to my job, back to my apartment, and to the Dairy Queen on Sunday night as soon as the preacher said *amen* and the choir sang the invitational hymn one final time.

While we were in the midst of a cheeseburger, hamburger, or a hot fudge sundae – I don't remember which – Arlene leaned around her friend, cocked her pretty little head to one side, looked at me, and smiled.

"Jim," she said, "I could just listen to you talk all night."

I smiled back, and a sudden thought struck me hard and would not go away. "Just maybe," I silently told myself, "she's not too young after all."

When Valentine's Day rolled around, I asked Arlene if she would like to be my date for a banquet at the church. I had been chosen to emcee the event, and I knew that the microphone would not be nearly as terrifying or as intimidating if she were sitting at the table with me. She said she would. She did.

We spoke on the phone at least once every day during the rest of February. I took her to the Houston Rodeo on Saturday night, March 2. The next day was Arlene's birthday. I proposed.

It was about time. After all, we had been dating all of two and a half weeks, and on the ferry boat ride across the bay to the San

Jacinto Monument, she had turned to me and said, "I think it would be a good idea if we spent our whole lives together."

I gave her that chance. She did not flinch. Arlene accepted.

And my life, which had almost always been embroiled with turmoil, picked up speed at a dizzying pace. On April 12, we went down and picked out a wedding ring. She graduated from high school in late May. We were married on June 28.

My draft notice arrived a month later. Uncle Sam wanted me. Besides Arlene, he may have been the only one.

Takeaways from the Chapter

- *There is a beauty to fresh beginnings. Jim viewed HPU as a new beginning. We can always change the direction of our lives. What am I doing that allows for me to grow and leave the past behind and begin again?*

- *The people who shaped Jim's life were in his life for brief periods of time but they became a part of his formation as a person. He was interested in what made people successful and wanted to be successful like them. Do I recognize that I am always being watched by someone? Who is impacting me at this very moment?*

- *Acceptance: Crucial to Jim's change of trajectory was his acceptance into the HPU community. His self regard began to change through people who helped him to believe and feel that he was somebody significant. What communities do I belong to? Are they providing the acceptance that alters my self-perception? Who am I affirming in my own sphere of influence?*

- *Providence: While this part of the story seems tragic, it actually demonstrates the principle of divine providence. Jim has to leave college and go and find a job in another city. It is through this negative life event that he meets the single most important person in his life, Arlene Norris, his beloved wife of 53 years. How am I looking for God's providence in all circumstances for life?*

CHAPTER 4

Choosing to Finish What You Start

On my eighteenth birthday, I had practiced the same drill required of every other red-blooded American male while we were all trapped in that awkward age separating boys from men. Most had walked out of high school with a diploma. A few were already on the job and working long hours for a fistful of dollars, no longer possessing any far-fetched ambition of nailing a certificate of graduation on their walls. Didn't need it, they said. Too late to get it, they said. I would have been one of those on the outside looking in if the Good Lord had not led me down to Brownwood and a schedule full of classes at Howard Payne University.

Still I had a duty to perform. I drove up to Abilene, saw my mother, made sure she was as happy as she could be under a myriad of ill-fated circumstances, and, without any fanfare or trepidation, signed up for the draft. We had all been given two options: sign our name on the dotted line or take our chances with a government not known for second chances, especially not with draft dodgers. The military did not mess around with slackers. The room was packed, most of the boys had a nervous twitch, and none of us knew what to expect next. There we were, high school graduates wearing football letter jackets, high school dropouts, day laborers, and a few believing that Uncle Sam just might be offering them the best job they could find anywhere between Buffalo Gap and Bangs. Long, but steady hours. Plenty of food. A good bed. Clean sheets. Enough money to buy a little beer and a few cigarettes on the weekend. Lots of travel. No chance of war. Little chance of dying. America, for the time being, had made peace with the world. So many of them wondered if the next bus leaving town would be hauling them off to some Army base. They fretted. They hadn't taken time to pack or say goodbye to mama. The sergeant merely smiled and said, "Thank You. We will be in touch."

"When?"

"When it's time."

A few wanted to raise their right arms and join on the spot. Being a soldier, they figured, would have scattered moments of intrigue, bravado, and possibly even danger, which was a lot more provocative than hanging around the outskirts of Abilene or Cross Plains, running after the same flirtatious girls they had been chasing since the second grade. The military just might give them a chance to fire a rifle even when they weren't out in the rock ravines hunting rabbits and rattlesnakes. New towns. New places. New hope. The brochures made the Army sound a lot more captivating than it probably really was. Girls liked men in uniforms. At least they had read that somewhere.

As the weeks and months passed by, any worries or fears I might have had about being drafted began to fade away. Frankly, I was too busy to give the military a second thought. After all, by then I was hurrying from classroom to classroom at Howard Payne, working hard to make grades good enough to keep me in class, working at nights and on weekends to keep a few loose coins in my pocket. America was no longer at war. The troops, years ago, had marched home from the battlefields of Germany, the Philippine Islands, Japan, and Korea. We weren't mad at anybody. No big country was marching across a bunch of little countries, trying to rule the world. We were at peace, which was a good place to be.

Besides, college students had been given automatic deferments. The draft chased down those who wandered the streets and usually made their way from one lackluster job to another. Farm awhile. Pump gas for awhile. Fix a few flats. Throw a few newspapers. Sack a few groceries. Their time was running short.

By the time I walked away from Howard Payne and began working in the parts department at International Harvester, the threat or promise of becoming a soldier never entered or crossed my mind. Life seemed to be working out pretty well for me. I had been promoted to a shop clerk, which meant I mostly handled bookkeeping chores, calculating the cost of repairs on a truck, keeping track of a mechanic's time, and preparing invoices.

The job paid better. But it was dull, and every passing hour of the day was filled with drudgery. It was the same job done over and over. Nothing ever changed but the numbers. I liked the idea of moving up the corporate ladder, even if it was a slow and laborious climb. I did not like the job. I dreaded waking up every morning, knowing the kind of boredom that awaited me at work. I was caught in a web. I wanted to leave. I had no place better to go. I liked the money. I doubted if any company would pay me more. I wanted to quit. I could not afford to.

The Army gave me an unexpected way out. Uncle Sam was calling. Uncle Sam did not take no for an answer.

With draft notice in hand, I walked into my supervisor's office and placed the piece of paper on his desk. The notice had a written statement, mostly in fine print, that said International Harvester was required by law to keep my job waiting for me, and I could not lose what little seniority I had. Serve my country for two years. Come back to Houston as soon as the hitch ended. Start calculating truck repair invoices again.

We shook hands. He said he hated to see me go. I said I was sorry to go. I may not have been entirely truthful. He said, "Good luck."

I closed the door behind me when I left. I knew I would never be coming back to either Houston or International Harvester. Good city. Good company. It was my goal in life to do better. I may have been chasing smoke, but I thought I could catch it.

In August of <u>1958,</u> Arlene and I drove to Sweetwater to spend a couple of days with my father. Everyone liked to see us coming when they realized we wouldn't be staying for any length of time. For us, those next few days on the road and on our own were as close to a honeymoon as we would have. We had been married one day, and I was back at work the next. A sojourn in Sweetwater may have lacked the usual romantic accoutrements, but we were together for awhile and mostly alone. We knew when I climbed on board a plane heading for parts and Army posts unknown, our lives, at least for the short term, would unravel and be torn asunder. I didn't mind being a soldier. It was a new adventure. It was an honor to serve my country, and I believed that I was tough enough to endure any physical training or torment some drill sergeant could throw my way. However, the thought of leaving Arlene behind left me feeling empty, helpless, and heartbroken. For so long, I had possessed a hole in my heart. She had filled it. We were together, at least for the moment, but each tick of the clock was slowly pulling us apart. I held her and wondered how I could survive when she wasn't there and I couldn't feel her breath touching my face anymore.

"I love you," I said.

"I love you,' she said.

Three words. That's all. They would be strong enough to hold us and keep us together, regardless of the miles separating us. I didn't sleep much that night. The clock kept ticking, and each tick brought us closer to morning.

The whirlwind began early that Monday. I rode the bus to Abilene, walked to the post office, raised my right hand, and agreed to make the Army my home for the next two years. As soon as the swearing in ceremony ended, we were herded on board another bus and headed for the airport. The flight took us to Fort Carson in Colorado Springs. There wasn't a lot of talking along the way. We were lost in our own thoughts, and one newly born soldier looked as nervous, as lost, and as lonely as the next. I sat there thinking that this would be my life for the next two years. It did not matter whether I liked it or not. But my life would be either good or bad, depending solely on my own attitude. I vowed to do the best I could from the time we landed until the day I walked away with my discharge papers in my pocket.

The flight did not take long, but when we stepped on Colorado soil, we were a different lot from the boys who had left Texas. Reality began to work its way into our souls like a thorn. I felt the mood of excitement ebb away before I knew why.

The Army offered a lot of intrigue and expectations until a sergeant climbed on board our bus at the reception station and told us, in no uncertain terms, that we were the lowest, most useless, miserable, insignificant, and worthless human beings he had ever seen. God help us all. He had better things to say about the gum stuck on the sole of his boots. Don't worry, he said. He would shape us up. We came to Fort Carson as boys. We would leave as men, provided we survived and, from the looks of us, he had his doubts. Serious doubts. He knew what to expect. We had no clue. Inside he was laughing. We had not yet seen anything humorous. We were at his mercy, and he knew it, and he knew that we knew it. He laughed again.

The sergeant was in a rush. We were in a rush. Run here. Run there. Always on the run. No time to stop. No time to slow down unless you were standing in a line, and one line always led to another. Shots, mostly to prevent diseases I knew nothing about. Haircuts. Buzz cuts. If the barber could find patches of brown on our head, he kept right on shaving until the patches had turned the color of our skin. Uniforms. Boots. None of them fit. We could strap on our helmets no matter how large or small they might be. A good helmet could keep me alive. I felt a deep attachment to my helmet.

The Army had one mission when we walked onto the base of Fort Carson. Break us down. Then build us up. Ruin us. Then resurrect us.

Physical training was tough. It threw us in the middle of a rough and unforgiving regimen, no quarter given. Push-ups till we dropped, and then more push-ups. Muscles strained. Muscles ached. I smiled. Nothing to it. Back at Howard Payne, my P.E. had been just as hard. You think you hurt now? Just wait till morning. The pain reached to places most of us didn't know we had.

They packed all five hundred of us into a room and tested us one day. The officers brought the top five percent back the next morning and ran us through another battery of tests. On the third day, only five, the top one percent, were again assigned to the testing room. I was one of them.

"You scored pretty high," I was told.

I nodded.

"The top ninety-eight percentile," the officer said.

I nodded again.

"We would like to interview you for the counterintelligence corps," he said in hushed tones that made the position seem mysterious and confidential. I waited for him to continue.

I learned early that you should never form any kind of judgment on the first set of facts. Wait until you hear the details and read the fine print.

"You will be investigating spies," he said.

I nodded.

"And catching them."

"Sounds important," I said.

"It is."

"What happens if I'm accepted?"

"Well," the officer said, leaning back in his chair, "all you have to do is extend your training to three years."

"Instead of two."

This time, he nodded. "Only the elite are chosen," he said.

I weighed the two options.

Spies?

Or Arlene?

There was no comparison.

"What else you got?" I asked.

A shadow of disappointment swept over his face. He turned to the table behind him and picked up a list of schools and handed them to me. My choice. No pressure. It was my life.

I chose the Neuropsychiatric Section of the Medical Service Corps. I don't know why I did. I had no reason. I had never even been intrigued about diseases of the mind. I just figured that everyone had fits of schizophrenia or depression from time to time. For most of us, our straight and narrow paths always took a lot of unexpected turns. My own life had just taken another one.

Basic training was nothing more than days on the rifle range with my M-1 rifle and tossing fragment and sometimes handling phosphorous hand grenades. Place one under the hood of a car, and it would burn through the engine. We marched from daylight to sundown, sometimes into the night. We double timed whenever the drill sergeant grew tired of marching. He loved running, mile after mile, hour after hour, up in the high country, up in the thin air. So did I. Could we keep on going when our legs wanted to quit and collapse, when our chests ached badly enough to crack; when we were sucking air for our next breath? He thought running would tell him a lot about our intestinal fortitude. I had an interest in finding out about my own.

Our unit was broken down into fifteen squads, and two weeks later, I was chosen to serve as our squad leader. My life didn't change a lot. I was just allowed to march at the front of the squad. That's all. Still, the honor was quite a boost to my confidence and self esteem. Life wasn't kicking me around anymore.

At the end of basic training, everyone was anxious about the dreaded endurance test. Pass or take the arduous training all over again. Pass or be left behind. I placed third and looked at myself with a whole new set of eyes. A strange phenomenon was in the midst of occurring. Until that moment, I had never thought of myself as a soldier. But suddenly and unexpectedly, I felt as though I was mentally and emotionally prepared to go to war. I was ready to go to war. Here or on some foreign shore. It did not matter. And the realization surprised me.

We had been given one canteen filled with water. It had to last all day. Water on those long, forced marches was a precious commodity. It was the stuff of life. I walked out of a lecture one morning and saw another soldier dropping gravel in our canteens.

I yelled for him to stop.

He smirked. "Make me," he said.

I was small. I was not a fighter. I had never been a street fighter. I looked at him with a pair of incredulous eyes. He stared back. His eyes glazed over when I hit him.

The scuffle only lasted for thirty seconds, maybe less. It didn't amount to a lot. The sergeants must have been too tired to watch a good or a bad fight, so they broke us up. Back in the barracks, we were asked, "What happened?"

We told our stories. The sergeant sighed. "Don't get into any more fights," he told me. "Now get out of here."

The culprit guilty of messing with our canteens was given three days of extra duty. On the surface, his crime probably didn't amount to much. But in the Army, in the heat of a long, hot summer, if a man didn't have a canteen of water, the circumstances could be sickening and devastating.

We had one young soldier who must have been afflicted with deep problems that the rest of us could only imagine. Better put, he was "absolutely nuts."

When we all rolled out of our bunks in the morning, he remained asleep. Had no intention of waking up. Had no intention of getting up. When we answered roll call, he was absent. Always absent. We could all do quite well without him, he thought. The drill sergeant yelled at him, berated him, and cursed him.

The young soldier merely yawned. He disdained discipline and authority and had no use for anyone who had the audacity to give him orders. He marched insolently to his own drummer, and the drum was beaten by his own demons. They never stopped.

We would return from the field at night, and he would crawl into the upper cot above me still dressed in his uniform and boots. He never took them off. He did not talk to anybody. He did not listen if any of us tried to talk to him. He was a loner. He preferred it that way.

We were up early, the dawn only a distant crease in the sky, and headed to the grenade range when he announced to no one in particular that, given the chance, he just might kill somebody that day. Not a bad day to die, he said. Everybody had a last day sooner or later. He grinned. It was devoid of humor.

"Don't let him touch a grenade," the sergeant said.

I nodded.

The young soldier was standing right next to me. The sergeant didn't want him to have a grenade in his hand. Neither did I.

One afternoon, he just wasn't around anymore. His bunk was made. He was missing. Don't know what happened to him. But whatever did, it did not happen with a grenade in his hand. I made sure of it.

It would be a subtle introduction to my venture into the Neuropsychiatric Section of the Medical Service Corps. But first, I spent four weeks of advanced training at Fort Sam Houston in San Antonio, being schooled in battlefield first aid and learning how to keep the wounded alive until they could be evacuated. I was taught to give shots, which are never painful as long as you have the needle in your hand, and I spent untold hours watching graphic film of battlefield doctors fighting to save lives during the bleakest of days. It was a gut-wrenching experience. A lot of guys, on a lot of occasions, ran madly out of the theater, looking for someplace out of the way to throw up. I doubted if they had long careers in the medical service corps. The scenes were often horrifying and always terrifying. I was beset with sympathy for the wounded and empathy for the battlefront medical team. But I was having trouble taking it all seriously. There was no war being waged anywhere, at least none that demanded American troops and were littered with American casualties. And Vietnam was only a distant rumor. None of us even knew where Vietnam was on the map. The newspapers called it Indochina, and the country seemed so far away.

We hadn't gone far, just down the street to Brooke Army Hospital, and every instructor was either a psychiatrist M.D., a psychologist with a Ph. D, or a nurse with a degree in psychology. All of them were officers. We might as well walk down the hall, saluting everyone we saw. We were surrounded by bars and stars. They were, however, much more interested in being doctors and nurses than military officers. The information they gave us in class was demanding, critical, and to the point. We could stay current or stay lost. There would never be any time to catch up. The class work and the schedules were daunting.

When we settled down to take our first exam, there were forty-three of us. The average IQ of everyone in the class was 128, the captain said. He expected a lot of us. The exam expected even more.

The next morning, the captain began handing our papers back. "We had seventy-two questions," he said. "The highest score had 69 correct answers.' I waited. I looked down at my graded exam. Seventy-two questions. Sixty-nine right answers. I may not have been at the head of the class, but I was sitting on the front row.

By the time I arrived at Fitzsimmons Army Hospital in Aurora, Colorado, I was only an E-2, a PFC, but I realized immediately that I was at home in the country club of the Army. That's the way it appeared on the outside. On base were three thousand Army personnel, one thousand officers —all of them doctors and nurses — and three thousand civilians employed for cooking, janitorial, and maintenance work.

It would be the best of times. I was convinced of it. The appearance from the outside had lied. Once through the doorway, I discovered the demons that lived on the inside, demons lurking deep inside the troubled minds of men and women.

Divine providence followed me to Fitzsimmons. I was selected by a psychiatrist to be his assistant, which gave me the privilege of attending his group therapy sessions. He did not want to take notes or use a tape recorder, believing that it might inhibit any of the discussions. He wanted the conversations to be open and flowing freely, straight from the heart and twisted recesses of those disturbed minds.

I never spoke. I never expressed an opinion. My job was simple.

He asked me to remember everything that everyone said. We met later, rehashed the sessions, and he dutifully wrote down every word I could recall. After awhile, I could recall them all. The power of concentration is an impressive and a potent tool. We met on a daily basis with the depressed, the schizophrenic, the troubled, the demented – soldiers who had obviously experienced more mental anguish and trauma than they could handle. To me, it was as though their brains had unraveled with ragged edges and gone awry. The study of the mind was and will always be on the cutting edge of science, a precarious and unpredictable place that no one understands, full of riddles and mystery.

During my sojourn at Fitzsimmons, experimental science had begun treating some mental disturbances and behaviors with electric shock therapy. We had a dozen patients who, once a week, would be rolled into the procedural room on a gurney. A hard rubber mouthpiece was placed between their teeth to keep them from chewing their tongues. A physician held down their arms and legs when the electric shocks triggered convulsions. And my assignment was to place my hand beneath their chins to hold their mouths shut as the electrodes on their foreheads sent shockwaves for thirty seconds – for thirty, long, unending, unforgiving seconds – through their brains.

Afterward, the patients would be confused for an hour or two. Then they would sleep a peaceful and unconcerned sleep while scientific debate tried to figure out if or why electric shock therapy could be used as an effective and practical tool. I only knew that patients did seem more normal for a day or two, allowing us to better communicate with them. I'm not for sure it was ever a cure. The demons did not stay away forever or seldom a week.

Doctors tried. That's all they could do. Still, the human brain remained an unexplored and uncharted territory.

During the daylight hours, we worked among the psychotic and delusional. One soldier was convinced that all corpsmen, doctors, nurses, and patients were Communists and out to get him. He had nowhere to turn. He had no one to comfort him. He was afraid that he would be unable to protect himself when he was the only person in the hospital not committed to the doctrine of Communism.

A red-headed Irish girl believed she was Jesus. But then, that wasn't particularly uncommon at all. A great majority of delusional patients thought they had a good chance of either being Jesus or Napoleon. Nobody has ever known why.

She was led into the ward. She looked around and quietly counted the twelve patients staring at her. Twelve. It was the right number. They must be, she thought, her disciples, and she feared greatly that one of them was Judas. No. She was convinced that one of them was Judas. She waited day and night, in a virtual state of panic, wondering when she would be betrayed.

A sergeant from the Korean conflict had fought hand-to-hand combat in the cold and the mud and the trenches against overwhelming odds. His unit was overrun, with the first wave of North Koreans charging down upon them with clubs. No rifles. Just clubs. There had been so many of the enemy, and he had fired his rifle so often, it heated up and froze. No bullets. No firepower. He was out of luck. And still they came, out of the night, a never-ending onslaught, shoulder to shoulder, leaping into the trenches with American troops in a last desperate fight to the death. The sergeant had killed one Korean soldier in close quarters by biting his throat, and he lay with a man's blood soaking into his uniform and the mud beneath him.

He had nightmares. He had flashbacks. Close his eyes and the last desperate fight to the death began all over again. The sergeant would go wild. The past had become his present.

He lived in a padded cell, was given shot after shot, and gradually improved until the doctors, probably against their better judgment, took a chance on him. They gave him an outside pass for the night, and he might have done quite well if he hadn't gotten drunk and wanted to fight again. It took several corpsmen to hold him down long enough for another shot to sedate him.

The ward was like a jail, walled off with heavy doors. The men trapped behind those doors were our patients. They could just as easily be criminals. It began to dawn on me that their view of themselves and of the world at large was distorted, maybe out of focus, and their behavior had nothing to do with reality. Their perception was the only reality they understood, and their perception came from a dark, peculiar, and puzzling place in the recesses of a shattered and fragmented mind.

Some threatened you even though they had no idea who you were. One had shot and killed his sergeant and company commander in Korea long after the battlefield wars had ceased. He didn't think he was through fighting. Even now, his mind was little more than a scarred war zone. One believed that he was being secretly poisoned. I gave him a cigarette one afternoon. He threw it down and stomped on it. The smoke was poison, he said. He didn't know me. I didn't know him. Why in the world was I doing my best to poison him, he wondered.

The odd thing was, most of the patients seemed normal a great deal of the time. They were nice, friendly, and easy to know. They could have been the boys next door, the boys in my squad; the boys on their way home from a trip. Then something happened, out of the blue but not out of the ordinary, and the evils of the mind would explode. So many of them heard voices. Day and night. Sleeping or awake. The voices never left their heads. The voices were killers.

Theirs' were miserable lives and sad cases. But I learned a lot from them. I began to better understand how people interacted with me as a human being. Whether they liked me or not quite possibly had nothing to do with me, what I had said, or what I had done. Their actions were based solely on the thoughts tumbling around in their minds. In that respect, they were no different from anyone else.

Later on in life, when I ventured into sales, I could take *no* as an answer, not a rejection. The word *no* simply meant that, at this particular moment, on this particular day, they did not want the product I had to offer. I had learned to accept such an answer without becoming defensive, upset, irritated, or frustrated. I became more analytical and thoughtful about the data or information I was presenting to people. I now had the ability to anticipate what made me mad, so I didn't allow it to happen. I could anticipate what others might think or feel because of my words or my actions, which made it possible for me to become more effective in anything I did.

Life, I believe, would have been a lot different if I had not spent those sixteen months in the neuropsychiatric section of the Army hospital. Because of those days in that ward, I was able to look back on the trials and tribulations of my early life and realize that no one – neither my father nor my mother – ever did anything negative toward me on purpose. None of it had been premeditated. It was just an entanglement of time and circumstances, the worst of circumstances. All of those angry regrets that had tormented me for so many years began to slowly fade away. I could love the past again. I could forgive the past. I prayed that the past would forgive me.

I have so many to thank in life. Some of them heard voices in their heads. They would never know I had passed their way. But I would never forget them.

On Listening

Anyone who knew Jim could almost immediately recognize that listening was one of his greatest strengths. He seems to have honed this skill while in military service. Arlene, his bride of 53 years said "when he was with a person, it was only you and him." She believes this is one of the reasons that so many over the years became so close to him. "He was able to block everything and everybody else out and in those moments of conversation you felt like you and your thoughts were significant. He listened very intently and affirmed the person and their ideas as much as he possibly could. He inspired many people by listening first and then encouraging." As told by Arlene McEachern (wife)

When I packed my uniform away for the final time, I was faced with the rest of my life, which could be a sobering experience. What now? What next? I was not the man I had been. That was not the man I ever wanted to be again. I had witnessed a lot. I had experienced a lot. There were many roads on which I could travel, and I was only sure about two of them. One led me home to Arlene. The other would carry me back to Brownwood.

I had managed to be frugal and save some of my earnings from International Harvester. I had at least two thousand dollars stacked up in a Houston bank. I withdrew the money and gave it to the business manager at Howard Payne University. He smiled. He had no doubt that I would be back someday. I smiled. Neither did I. I had unfinished business, and I never liked to leave anything unfinished.

Takeaways from the Chapter

- *Embrace unchosen circumstances as opportunities, not obstacles, and determine to have a good attitude about it. There are many things in life that we would not choose on our own but are somewhat dictated by our circumstances. The real question is "how will I approach those unchosen circumstances?"*

- *Jim recognized that his preparation at HPU in Physical Ed prepared him to do well in the military. This idea comes up over and over in this book. One part of life is always preparation for another part of life. Sometimes we are aware of this and other times we aren't but it is a truth. What I am doing today, is preparation for tomorrow. What can I do to remind myself of this regularly?*

- *Every opportunity should not be taken. We have to weigh out what is most important to us. In Jim's case, even the intrigue of being a spy could not overpower his desire to return to his wife and normalcy? What have you said "no" to recently? Are you saying "no" enough?*

- *Listening is a skill that all of us could develop more. Jim, during his military service, had to learn to listen carefully to other people. How important is it to learn to listen carefully to others' thoughts? Do I really believe the answer I just gave? What can I do to become a better listener?*

- *Jim made peace with his family of origin. Forgiveness is a huge part of moving on in life. Am I at peace with my family and/or others who have wronged me in deep and substantial ways? Have I realized that quite possibly the reason they damaged me was because they were severely damaged themselves?*

CHAPTER 5

Choosing to Confront a Fear

As far back as I could remember I had envisioned a good life for myself. It would not be easy, I figured, but I had an unwavering faith in myself and in God's reasoning for placing me on earth, even during those early days when my confidence had been severely shaken. Back when I was walking the plow furrows with my grandfather, I had thoughts of grandeur running rampant in my mind. I caught images of myself becoming a big-time farmer someday. A lot of land. A lot of cattle. Tractors running wide open and in almost every direction. Cotton fields stretching from one end of the horizon to the other. And I would be in charge of it all.

I greatly admired the man who owned the Dean Ranch only a few miles from Borden County, out where the plains dropped off into the rugged country of the Texas Caprock region. He ran cattle, of course, but his raw land was thick with oil and gas wells that pumped trucks full of money. It was said that Mr. Dean, who was dressed in the khaki shirts and trousers of a working man, wore hundred dollar hats and expensive boots. He may not have been the man I wanted to be, but I could see myself riding his ranch lands and driving his big, fancy cars.

Then again, there were some days when I wanted to own a big grocery store, not unlike Mr. Coleman who lived in Ackerly, only eight miles away. He had a big farm and an even larger ranch, but what impressed me was the fact that he was also the proprietor and owner of a lumber yard, a gas station, a locker plant, and a grocery store. If he could do it, then I could too. Well, that was how the idea started anyway. I planned to build a single supermarket, work long and hard hours to make sure that it became the cornerstone and the life of the community, and then begin developing stores just like it in a minimum of ten towns, burgs, or hamlets that lined both sides of the highways straightlining through West Texas within an hour's drive from Lamesa. The stores would have my name on top, and I would be somebody important, somebody like Mr. Dean and Mr. Coleman. They were so important and, in my mind, so rich that I never knew their first names or thought I needed to. They didn't dress any differently from anyone else. The horses they rode weren't that uncommon or out of the ordinary. I might never be among the big rich, the men like they were, but even though my circumstances were tough, I did believe I could climb my way to a respected status within the little rich. The dreams of a boy had no limits and knew no boundaries. Then life gets in the way.

By the time I finished hanging out on the backstreets of Abilene, Albany, and Midland, my aspirations were not quite as grandiose as they had once been. Still, they were just as real. By the time I enrolled in Howard Payne, I was convinced that a man with a good education, a man who wasn't afraid to work and had a little ambition, could accomplish just about anything he tried. At the moment, I only had one problem boring a hole in my outlook on the future. I did not yet know what I really wanted to try.

I loved the written word, and I had a habit of reading everything I could get my hands on – magazines, books, the Bible, and even newspapers, from the front page headlines to the want ads in small agate type on the back page. I was smitten with the idea of soaking up every scattered scrap of information I could find. All of it was important. There were no wasted words, particularly if they had anything to do with recent or distant history.

I had a deep fascination for the past and for those men and women who struggled to overcome so many odds during difficult periods of their lives and accomplished so much. They kept going.

Knock them down, and they would get up and keep going. They made their own opportunities because life gave them so few. They became the difference makers. They may not have built cities, but cities were built in the prints of their footsteps. I wanted to be a difference maker.

On Validation and Authentication

Jim was a voracious reader (for more information on this, see appendix 2). Jim's intellectual capacity was widely known throughout Tom James Company and certainly to all who met with him. I observed him many times computing data in his head when bank officers and executives were using devices for the answers. However, in our one-on-one conferences and in meetings he rarely shared a truth or concept without validation and authentication from many sources. He read incessantly. In my last joint one-on-one with Jim and another Tom James colleague, I listed 17 different references and books he used to help us gain valuable understanding of the information he was sharing. This has been one of the greatest leadership traits I learned from Jim. I saw it modeled throughout his career. This was a personal discipline he used to prevent his comments or suggestions from being polarizing or offensive. Since I am a Christian, he freely shared Biblical truths to explain principles of life and business. With groups, however, his breadth of reading gave him a multitude of ways to couch truth. Much could be written about this as it relates to his wisdom and discernment in dealing with people. Bob Sherrer (former Tom James CEO)

During my first sojourn on a college campus, Howard Payne had given my life a boost. The university was known as "the school where everybody is somebody," and the students went out of their way to make me feel that I was indeed somebody after all. Not just a name. Not just a number. Not just some boy sitting in the third chair of the second row. But somebody who actually had a reason for walking this earth. As the days passed, I no longer felt inferior or someone wallowing around below average. I believed I was on an equal footing with everyone else. I could make it on my own now. I was sure of it.

I had chances to sit down with any of my professors and talk about school, my class work, or life itself. Those things didn't matter to them. I did. They gave me their time when I needed it, and that made me feel worthwhile for a change. They apparently saw some value in me, so I began looking for some value in myself as well. Listening to the inspiring and motivational messages of Dr. Guy Newman at chapel each week rekindled the fire that had once burned within me. I lost any sense of desperation that might have been gnawing at my innards and regained touch with a comforting sense of security. I thought I had misplaced it along the way.

I no longer merely thought about my existence on a day-to-day basis. Again, as I had done on my grandfather's farm, I began thinking long term and understood that life had something far better waiting for me than the mundane prospect of loading flour sacks for a paycheck. There was no reason for me to go back to the past. I had left it. I should go ahead and forget it. Those mistakes would never hold me back unless I went back and picked them up again. Maybe it was time to give them to a power greater than I.

During one of my early Bible Classes, Dr. Nat Tracy looked out at us, leaned forward, and said quietly: "If we could see ourselves the way God sees us, we would be tempted to fall down on our knees and worship ourselves." His words stunned me. They sounded blasphemous. I glanced around.

Everyone else looked as astounded as I did. I knew lightning must be on its way. I just didn't know how soon it would get there and where it would strike. I shuddered and waited for the worst.

Dr. Tracy let the shock wear off, then smiled and told us, "Instead of worshipping ourselves, we should be tempted to fall down on our knees and worship God because he had made us all with such awesome potential."

Of all I would learn in school and elsewhere, those words would forever mean the most to me. For the first time I realized that God had given me enormous potential. If I ever did happen to become successful one day, I would never be able to take credit for anything I might have accomplished. God would be the one who did it. I made up my mind right there. If God had gone to the trouble of bestowing on me all of that potential, I should do my best to live up to it. I realized that I could never out grow my potential. After this lesson, I vowed to have a greater impact on the future than I had on the past.

In the back of my mind, I had already decided that I would no doubt graduate, nail my diploma to an office wall, and wind up as a high school teacher, preferably a teacher of history. It seemed like an obvious choice. It would be a good job, a steady job, one that offered, I thought, decent pay and the kind of security I had never really known before. It was a time of my life when security was the brass ring I was striving to capture and hold on to. Besides, maybe I could actually be a difference maker and make a difference in the life of some students. That's where my ambition came to an end. Earn a diploma. Find a school. Find a job. Walk into the classroom. It would be my finest hour. I had it all figured out. Or so I thought.

Once again, here came "life." Once again, "it got in the way" or perhaps "got me in the way."

I awoke one morning as the spring semester was drawing to an end and realized that I needed to start looking for a place to work during the summer months. I obviously needed rent and meal money while school was out of session, and it certainly wouldn't do any harm to start putting away a few dollars to help cover tuition when the next year rolled around, I knew that I was only weeks away from again patching together another assortment of odd jobs. The oilfield was waiting for me back home. So was a checker's job at the supermarket. Get up early. Work late. Cash a paycheck. Cash two if possible. They were jobs and nothing else. Make it a day at a time, then a week at time, and look forward to the classroom again. I didn't have to plan ahead for anything but breakfast. But I knew full well the constant frustration and turmoil that was in store for me if I lived in the house with my mother once more. It was as though she and I lived in a different but parallel universe together. We might share the same roof, but she went her way, and I went mine, and, for the most part, neither one of us had anything to say or do with each other. I knew her. I'm not so sure my mother was even aware I existed. We were just two people passing in a darkened hallway.

During April, Lloyd Conner approached me with an idea. He and I both lived on the west side of Taylor Hall, but we never socialized with each other. We hardly ever had a reason to speak. He was a junior, and I was a freshman, and our paths never crossed. On this particular afternoon, they did.

He mentioned to me that, during the previous two summers, he had worked with a big company up in Nashville, selling books door-to-door. The work hadn't been hard. The pay had been fairly decent. Living in another part of the country, even northern Alabama for a few months, had been quite an adventure. He had done it twice. He would probably do it again. The company was looking for college students to recruit. The whole program was set up to help people like us supplement their incomes and help pay for another year of college. Lloyd wondered if I would be interested. I wasn't.

It all sounded pretty good on the surface, but I knew immediately that the position would not appeal to me. Not now. Not any time. Even though I realized God had blessed me with enormous potential, my greatest fear had not changed over the years. My potential did not include standing up before a crowd, large or small, and giving a presentation. I even felt awkward, uncomfortable, and uneasy to open a conversation with a stranger. I didn't mind work and didn't care how difficult it might be. But knocking on doors day after day, always new doors, always meeting new people, always trying to sell them some kind of book, having doors slammed in my face, being told *no,* being rejected, all represented the kind of life that terrified me. I couldn't do it. That's what I told myself. My potential lay elsewhere. I was sure of it.

"No," I told Lloyd. I wasn't interested.

"Okay." He grinned. "You'll miss a good chance to make good money," he said.

"How much?"

"The average student makes about fifteen dollars a day."

His answer hit me squarely between the eyes. Here was a chance for me to earn fifteen dollars a day even if I was average, and, after arriving at HPU and some early success I had ceased to think of myself as average. I was used to earning a dollar an hour. And that was hard labor.

My mind did a sudden tailspin. Maybe I wasn't interested. Maybe the job didn't appeal to me. Maybe I didn't want to knock on doors. Maybe I would rather read books than sell them. Maybe I couldn't sell them. Maybe I would never overcome the fear of talking to crowds or strangers. Then again, I wasn't totally disinterested either.

A few days later, against my better judgment, I talked myself into sitting down with <u>Fred Lan</u>ders who had been sent to Brownwood by the Southwestern Company to recruit college students.

I was nervous and unsure of myself. I already had the bitter taste of fear lodged in my throat, my mouth was dry, and the interview had not even begun. Don't let yourself be fooled by a slick sales person, I warned myself. The job wouldn't be nearly as good as it sounded, and I did not want to face any disappointments. You can't do this. That's what I told myself. You may be able to teach, but you'll never be able to sell. Don't get your hopes up. Lloyd told me that a lot of students quit during the first three weeks they were on the road. I might be one of them. In my mind, I began searching for a few words and hoped I could find a few. The fear had the sour taste of bile, and it was nauseating.

All I knew about the Southwestern Company were a few basic facts. It had been founded more than a hundred years earlier by a Baptist minister named James R. Graves. It was located in Nashville, Tennessee. It was a publisher and a direct sales company, and it might even want me to go to work for a few months. Student sales were its' lifeblood. Fred Landers smiled. We shook hands. So far, so good.

He asked a few questions about my work experience. He found out, if nothing else, that I might be afraid of a lot of things but never hard work.

"Exactly what is the job?" I asked.

"If you're chosen to work for the Southwestern Company, we will bring you to Nashville for a week's training at our expense," he said. "We'll teach you everything you need to know. We will provide you with sample products, and you will be taught a sales presentation that has proved to be quite successful over the years."

"What kind of books?"

"You'll have a Bible reference book, a dictionary, some cookbooks, and some children's Bible story books," Landers said. "These are the kinds of books that appeal to a lot of families and rightfully belong in everybody's home."

I nodded. It made sense.

"Where will you be sending me?" I asked.

"That will be determined after your training."

"When it comes to selling books, what am I supposed to do, and how am I supposed to do it?"

"I would suggest starting out on one side of the street every morning, knock on as many doors as you can, make your presentation to as many people as possible, and try to get down both sides of the street before you go home at night."

"How much money should I expect to make?"

"It all depends on you," Fred said.

He called Lloyd over to the table. Lloyd was an old pro by now. He had been out knocking on doors for two summers now. He knew all of the right verbiage and all of the tricks.

Fred Landers asked him to make a presentation about the family Bible just as if he were sitting down in somebody's living room and talking to a customer.

Lloyd did. He wasn't great. But he did just fine. He had his pitch memorized. He didn't miss a beat or stumble over a word. It was fairly smooth, precise, and short. I listened intently to everything he said.

When Lloyd had finished, Fred Landers asked, "Can you learn to do that?"

I nodded. "I believe I can," I said.

"Fifteen or twenty times a day?"

"I think so."

Then came the key question as he began to set the trap.

"If you do," Landers said, "how many books do you think you can sell a day?"

I shrugged. "At least three or four," I answered.

He nodded thoughtfully.

"Let's do a quick calculation," Landers said. "The family Bible sells for twenty-five dollars, and you earn twelve dollars from each sale. The other books sell for twenty-two dollars and ninety-five cents, and you earn ten dollars. How much will you have at the end of the day if you sell the three or four books as you say you can?"

It was quick and simple math: at least thirty dollars and maybe even more.

"But I thought the average sales person makes about fifteen dollars a day," I said. I was not yet ready to believe the earning potential he had outlined for me.

Landers agreed. "That's the average," he said. "But some earn more, and some make less. It's really up to the individual. With us, you will be running your own sales company while selling our products. You can work a lot or a little. You can sell a lot or a little. Mr. McEachern, it's really up to you. Whether you are successful or not lies solely in your hands."

I mulled over the numbers. Whether I made thirty dollars a day or forty dollars a day or proved to be average and went home each night with only fifteen dollars in my pocket, I would be earning a lot more money than some job in the oilfield or supermarket would pay. Even if the position wasn't nearly as good as it sounded, working with the Southwestern Company might well be far better than any other line of work I could find for the summer. Besides, I was intrigued by the thought of spending a week in Nashville. I liked the idea of settling down for three months in a town I had never seen before. It was another chance with another fresh start. Life had more than a few of those.

Deep inside me, whether I wanted to admit it or not, I realized that I was tempted to accept the offer Fred Landers was extending me for one plain and simple reason. Deep inside me, I wanted to confront my fear. I wanted to meet it face to face and conquer the fright I experienced when dealing with crowds and strangers. This was my one chance. I would be new in town. I would be unknown. If I failed, I could leave without anyone ever remembering my name or knowing I had walked down their streets. But if I succeeded, a whole new world would open up for me. I would rise to the occasion or fall a thousand miles from home. There would be no one to help me. No one to demand more of me. No one to console or comfort me when I failed, if I failed. It would be me against the world, and I would meet it on my own terms.

It was disquieting. I was scared. I had butterflies in my stomach. One side of my brain was urging to go forward while the other side of my brain was telling me that the smart thing for me to do was stay home. I did not listen. Nor did I worry about the consequences. I could not wait to knock on the first door.

Takeaways from the Chapter

- *People who are successful don't give up too easily. They keep going. As Jim studied great and successful people of the past he realized this. What is it that is keeping me from doing something great? What opportunities am I missing right now because of "life"? What can I do to change that situation? There are always things one can do. We simply have to get over the inertia that keeps us locked into our current trajectory.*

- *Jim's professor stated: "If we could see ourselves the way God sees us, we would be tempted to fall down on our knees and worship ourselves. (Pause) Instead of worshipping ourselves, we should be tempted to fall down on our knees and worship God because he made us all with such awesome potential." If I allowed this idea to penetrate life, my life could change as dramatically as Jim's. What gifts and potential am I presently not using or failing to properly use?*

- *Taking a chance- Jim decided to take a chance and confront his greatest fear. This is a laugh out loud story to anyone who ever knew him: fear of public speaking. <u>What are you afraid of professionally?</u> Is this fear the obstacle that is keeping you from having increased professional success?*

CHAPTER 6

Choosing to Do What's Right

I have always possessed a sense of adventure, the interest in traveling different highways in different directions to places I had never seen before, an unabated curiosity of what I might find at the end of or around the next bend of the road. I have never been able to forget that summer of 1952 when I packed up a few clothes, crawled into the car with my grandfather, and rode west to California. The road was long. The miles seemed endless, and I was fascinated with every one of them. We stayed six weeks with Uncle Ben and Aunt Mary Shumake, and I spent most of my time on their dairy farm not far from Escondido.

From the time the sun came up until the day grew dark, I rode with my uncle while he cut alfalfa, then grabbed a bucket and unloaded the grain into his cattle troughs. On many afternoons, however, I hitchhiked my way into San Diego, once even traveling as far away as Los Angeles. It was a glorious era when no one was afraid to hitch a ride with a passing motorist, and people were not uneasy about picking a boy up from the side of the road. We all trusted each other and depended on each other and went out of our way to help each other. For those six weeks, I woke up every morning in the midst of a grand adventure. I often doubted that I would ever experience another one; never one so memorable. But I never stopped searching for another chance to explore a faraway part of the country where every passing day brought even greater expectations.

The Southwestern Company plucked me from the plains of far West Texas and placed me in the midst of Galax, Virginia. Once again I was a new face in a new place, walking new streets and wondering if I belonged or had chosen another wrong turn. I was stricken with mixed emotions, and they fluttered like misguided butterflies in my mind. Would anyone open a door when I knocked? Did anyone want to hear my presentation? And when I offered my line of books, would anyone actually say *yes*?

I felt that old fear knotted in my stomach again. Would any words come out when I opened my mouth? Would I talk too fast, too slow, or for too long? In the back of my mind, I kept remembering the year I turned fourteen. I had discovered a great, sure-fire, can't miss opportunity for selling magazine subscriptions door-to-door with the hope of making enough sales to earn a new bicycle. It all seemed so simple to me. Head up one street and down another. Knock on every door I found. Make my sales pitch. Sign the folks up for a new magazine, maybe two. And I would have a new bicycle beneath me by the time the summer ended. It didn't go quite as I had planned.

I knocked on three doors.

"No," said one lady.

"Not interested," said another.

"Not today," said a third.

That was my last door. I quit and threw my magazine subscription forms away. Sales might be for some people, but it certainly wasn't for me. Being rejected was not a good feeling. My confidence and self-esteem took a severe blow. I doubted that either would ever recover.

Yet I had been told that Southwestern book sales people generally sold enough books to pocket about fifteen dollars a day, and not all of them were great sales people. I might not be the company's top book peddler during the summer, but I was convinced that I could do as well as the average sales person. Three books a day should not be difficult to sell. After all, these weren't magazine subscriptions. These were an assortment of well-crafted, high quality Bibles, cookbooks, and reference books. No home should be without them. That was my pitch anyway.

However, I knew quite well that none of the money was guaranteed. As I stepped off the bus in Galax, I was already facing the reality that I was responsible for buying my meals and paying my rent, and I had not yet sold my first book. I had not yet knocked on the first door. All I had done thus far was stand tall and straight in front of a mirror and practice my presentation. The words all sounded plausible to me. The pitch was short, to the point, and quite powerful, just the way Southwestern had written it. I was on my own, however, and there would be no one around to help me.

Selling books might be a great opportunity, but it was also a risky venture. As far as I could tell, the ability to earn commissions was the only way a man or woman could achieve financial success. Work hard. Do well. Work harder. Do better. All of my life, I had disliked the thought of working for a fixed income. Now, other than the fear that kept churning in the pit of my stomach, there were no limitations confronting me. For once, I was in charge of my own failure or success. I could not blame or credit anyone else.

I had spent a week undergoing extensive training back at the Southwestern home office in Nashville. I had learned a lot. I realized that a door-to-door book sales person had much greater earning potential than an oilfield ditch digger or a grocery store stock boy. But, in the end, when it was all said and done, whether I succeeded or failed depended strictly on me and on my ability to match wits with my customers. I shoved those knots of fear aside, and by the time the sun was high on that first Monday morning, I was ready to face the great unknown.

I didn't waste any time. I promptly knocked on my first door at nine o'clock on a Saturday morning. The family must be fairly affluent, I decided. The house was large and probably the nicest one I had ever seen.

The door opened. The lady was smiling. Her appearance and mannerisms reflected a genuine Southern gentility. So far, so good, I thought.

"I'm selling books," I said.

"What kind?" she asked.

"Family Bibles," I said.

"Come in," she said.

So far, so good, I thought.

We sat in her living room, and she thumbed through the Bible once, then twice. Her smile had not yet faded. I held my breath.

"I want two of them," she said.

It only took two or three minutes to write up the order. It only took two or three minutes for me to earn as much money as I would make working two full days, digging holes in the oil patch.

It might not be a career, I thought. But it was a real good beginning.

The second house I visited that morning was not as profitable. I only sold a single book for three dollars and eighty-five cents, but a dollar-sixty of the sale belonged to me. Again I had spent a couple of minutes and earned more than I could make working a full hour with the blistered end of a shovel out beside a West Texas oil rig. The good beginning was getting better.

I decided that anyone could be a book sales person. I was wrong. My roommate and I were sharing a room in a little tourist home for six dollars a week. It wasn't much, but the price was right, and we only needed a place to sleep at night. All rooms, big or small, fancy or drab, looked the same in the dark. The bed was old, but the lumps weren't bad when a man's asleep. But then, it was difficult to sleep at night. I was too excited. My roommate didn't sleep a lot either. He was disgruntled. Too few doors. Too few hours. Hardly any sales at all. At the end of the first week, my roommate quit. He decided he had better things to do with his life, packed up overnight, and headed home.

I now had to pay the whole six dollars worth of rent each week. Yet, I had the whole town to myself. Every house in Galax belonged to me, and I had more doors to knock on than ever before. I decided I had wound up with the best part of the deal.

Every morning I would stand at the far end of a street and let my gaze wander from door to door, wondering which one I should knock on next. They all looked alike. I soon learned that the ladies who opened them were not the same. Some were glad to see me. Some regarded me as a nuisance. On occasion, I had a door slammed in my face. I met rejection head-on. It hurt. It wasn't fatal. Some were intrigued with the books. A few were intrigued with me. My accent was different. It was definitely western, not southern, and they wanted to hear everything I could tell them about Texas. In those days, Texas was still a place of mythical proportions. They asked if we still rode horses to town and if we tied them to parking meters when we went inside the stores to shop.

I became acquainted with people whose backgrounds were far different from mine. I knew about farming and small towns that depended on farmers to survive. Galax had tied its past and future to a furniture factory and a hosiery mill. We possessed lives with different experiences from different parts of the country, and a single knock on the door brought us together. It was not unusual at all for some of the ladies to invite me in for lunch if it were almost noon, so I made it a point to always knock on somebody's door when the clock was nearing noon. During those days when I was carefully counting every spare nickel and dime in my pocket, a free meal from time to time went a long way in keeping the expenses down.

I saw life up close and on both sides of the track from the most affluent families in town to people who were struggling as hard as I was to make ends meet. A lot of them bought books and were proud to show them off in their little ramshackle homes. There were times when I walked out the front door wondering if I should have called on them at all. They didn't have a lot of money. What if the cost of a book took the last dollar they had? And what if they didn't really want or need the book but was just trying to help an old country boy like me? Southern families, rich or poor, would do that sometimes.

One man drove a cleaning and laundry truck all over town, making his regular pickups and deliveries. He would see me walking down the sidewalk on my way from one neighborhood to another, pull over to the curb, and take me wherever I happened to be going at the time. If it wasn't on his route, it wasn't far out of the way. He and I would cross paths two or three times a week. He made distances a lot shorter for me, and, more than anything else, I think, he was glad to have someone to talk to. He never bought a book. I don't recall ever trying to sell him one. But he made it a point to make life easier for me when he didn't have to, and I would never forget him. He made a difference. He instilled in me the need to make a difference in the lives of others. Sometimes it doesn't require a lot. Sometimes it's nothing more than helping someone along the way when we have no idea how far he needs to go.

On the Value of All People

"My dad realized more than anyone I've ever known how important every person that we interact with is. He was grateful for every person who impacted him whether it was large or small. He never had the idea that he was a self-made man. Of course, he recognized his own personal investment in who he had become but he also understood that many people had poured into him over the course of his life. I believe this is one of the reasons that he invested so much into people. He always viewed himself as possibly changing the trajectory of someone's life by his encouragement or affirmation."
Lynda McDowell (Jim's daughter)

Not everyone was glad to see me. Not everyone was an old-fashioned portrait of genuine Southern gentility. But I was averaging as many as twelve demonstrations and selling books to three or four customers a day. Not once did I head back to my little room without at least one order in my pocket. Before the month ended, working from early morning until sometimes after dark, I was earning anywhere from eighty to a hundred and twenty dollars a week – three and often four times as much money as I would be making back home. I discovered that all I had to do was present my line of books in a way that made people want them. The books were beautiful. The price was right. They filled a void in any home, and every Southern home had a deep affection for the Bible and for cooking. My cookbooks had both new and time-honored recipes, and, sooner or later, I wanted every cook in every kitchen in town to be preparing the same recipes, preferably from the same cookbooks I had sold them.

Each summer, while attending Howard Payne, I would head back to Nashville when my spring semester ended and enroll for another assignment with Southwestern. The sales kept me solvent. They helped me put money aside to pay my tuition, board, and books in college. And they helped me overcome my fear of speaking in public, speaking to strangers, and asking someone to buy a product I was representing. Whether I realized it or not, those summers with Southwestern were preparing me for a future that I had not even dared to envision. I liked the business. I was fairly good at it. My presentations were getting better every time I knocked on a new door. I enjoyed my interaction with other people. I liked the challenge of having to think fast and on my feet. I was making good money. But to me, selling books was just another summer job. As much as I thought about it, there was no way I could make a career out of a business that began in June and ended the last of August. That left nine dry, empty months without a job or a paycheck, and I had no idea what to do with them.

After graduation from Howard Payne, I endured the best and the worst of times. I tried one job and then another. None of them worked out. Selling books, I felt as though I had made a success of myself. With a diploma tucked under my arm, however, my search for a rewarding career left me disillusioned and in debt, and this, I knew, was not the way life was supposed to be. I jumped from one job to another, from bad to worse. I taught. I unloaded trucks at a grocery store. I clerked in a beauty supply company. I even lowered myself to selling snow cones.

I felt as though I had reached the bottom of a bottomless pit. I was married. I had two children. I was broke. My confidence was shot. My self-esteem had been shattered. I was terrified.

I was no longer a college student, but, with no other options, I applied again to sell books for Southwestern during the summer months. The job wouldn't last long. It never did. At the moment, I was struggling to keep the bills paid and falling farther behind every time another invoice hit my mailbox. It was like trying to catch wayward straws in a strong wind. They were always just beyond my grasp.

After my week-long sales training school in Nashville – I had attended the classes so often I probably could have taught them – I was assigned to Gallatin, Tennessee, on the Cumberland River. I was alone and as lonely as I had been in a long time. Arlene and my two children, Karen and Michael, were back in Fort Worth, and thus far, I had done little more than fail them; I felt guilty. I was afraid. And the fear was stifling.

Morning came, and I wasn't ready for it. An old familiar dread began to knot my stomach again. Arlene was depending on me. But what if no one in Gallatin would let me in the house? What if no one would listen to my presentation? What if no one wanted to buy books? I had asked all of these questions before. Last year's answers weren't doing me any good this year. I drove up one street, didn't particularly like what I saw, and set out to find another, looking for a good place to start. I could not find one. At least, I could not decide on one. The sun was beginning to depart the western sky when I realized that I had driven all day without knocking on a single door.

I pulled the car over to the curb and stopped. I grabbed my satchel of books and walked up the sidewalk of the house closest to me. I knocked. The door opened.

A lady smiled. Her appearance and mannerisms reflected genuine Southern gentility. I grinned. It suddenly seemed like old times. I showed her the books, and she bought a comprehensive analysis of the Bible. I would be able to pay the rent that week.

I was back in business.

After seven days, I had made enough money from sales to buy bus tickets to Nashville for Arlene, Karen, and Michael. I would drive down and pick them up at the bus station. They had not yet begun their journey north, but I didn't feel quite so lonely anymore.

For the next six weeks, I averaged eight to ten sales a day. It was the best I had ever done, but somewhere deep inside me, I remained terrified that I would fail again. I wondered if each sale just might be the last I ever made.

Here I was with a wife, a five-year-old daughter, and a two-year-old son, working during the summer with no prospects and no hope for a job when the dog days of August turned to September. The pressure was suffocating and wearing me down.

It got worse.

I came home one afternoon in July, and Arlene gave me the news. "You're going to be a father again," she said. Number three was on the way.

I left our little basement apartment one morning and started knocking on doors. No one was home. No one wanted to see me. No one was interested in either cookbooks or the Bible. For the life of me, I could not make a sale. I had made dry runs before, but never this dry.

At two o'clock that afternoon, I watched the last door slam and gave it up. I was tired of banging my head against the wall. The magic had run its course. I turned my car around and headed home. Arlene was surprised when I walked through the door. She was not expecting to see me. I was never back this early and never back with such a disgusted and frustrated look on my face.

"What are you doing here?" she wanted to know.

"I quit."

"What?"

"I quit." I slumped down on the sofa. "I can't do this anymore," I said. 'I quit."

Arlene folded her arms, cocked her head to one side, and said, "Let me ask you something."

"Okay."

"Have you changed since yesterday?"

"No."

"Have the people out there changed since yesterday?"

"No."

"Have the books changed since yesterday?"

"No."

"Then go back out there and sell something."

I nodded, stood up, picked up my samples, and walked back out the door. I had not been inside the apartment for more than five minutes. I made nine more sales calls that day. I worked until long after dark. I sold books to all nine customers.

I came back to Arlene and the children with eighty dollars in my pocket. I was in a much better mood than when I left. So was she.

Normally, I knocked on twenty doors a day. I still did. But now I was geared and committed to make another nine sales calls, working until after nine o'clock each night. It became the best summer of our lives. We lived in a beautiful home built before the War Between the States. Of course, our little apartment occupied the basement, but we didn't mind. The accommodations were comfortable. The children played in a big yard. And the sales kept rolling in. The sales kept rolling in because Arlene refused to let me give up.

I wanted to quit. She did not quit on me. The summer could have been lost. My future could have remained in shambles. Arlene did not let it happen. She saved me.

As the summer faded away, we drove slowly back to Nashville. I did not understand it at the time, but Nashville would become the starting place for a whole new life for me and my family.

Takeaways from the Chapter

- *Behind every person who achieves great things, there is almost always a cheerleader, an encourager, a believer. If you have one of these people in your life don't ever let them get away. Don't take them for granted and make sure they know who they are. Be grateful. You have a greater likelihood of success than the person who doesn't have this individual. In Jim's case it was his beloved wife, Arlene. He says about her: "She saved me." He wanted to quit but he had someone who believed in him and refused to let him give up. Who do I have in my life that believes in me? Who do I believe in and regularly say so to them?*

- *It's the small things that add up. Jim points out that when we do small things for others it can make a big difference in their lives. I should never underestimate how important any assistance, no matter how small it might seem, is to another human being. Am I consciously and consistently aware of the people around me who I could help?*

CHAPTER 7

Choosing to Find a Mentor

It had been a long and arduous journey, but when I walked out of Howard Payne University clutching my diploma, I thought I was ready at last to conquer the world. I had an education. I possessed a degree. I knew how to work. I had worked all of my life on the farm, in grocery stores, bowling alleys, bakeries, and on the street, selling Bibles and cookbooks door-to-door. I had invested almost two years of my life in the Army, working side by side with neurological psychiatrists. And when I drove away from Brownwood, I already had a good job waiting for me. I had survived the bad years of my life, overcome the adverse circumstances that had threatened to derail my ambitions, and now I was free to go out into the world and forge my own success. There were no limits or limitations.

I had always harbored the thought of someday becoming a high school history teacher. I loved reading and studying about the past, whether it was in books or the Old Testament. The lives of men and women – their trials, their triumphs, their battles, their hopes, their accomplishments – had long intrigued me. I had majored in history with an additional thirty hours in secondary education, and I had been hired to teach in the high plains West Texas town of Post. Unfortunately, Post did not need or have an opening for a history teacher at any level. I had been gainfully employed to teach three classes of Spanish and three classes of sixth grade science. Nothing to worry about, I thought. I had my foot in the door. I was earning a paycheck, and when the need for a history teacher arose, I would be in place to step in. I had it all planned out. I was leaving nothing to chance, but, whether I liked it or not, chance or (from my perspective) providence would draw me in another direction.

On History and Longhorns

Jim always loved history. His library was filled with books on various persons and subjects of historical interest. He took a particular interest in his later years in the history of Longhorn cattle. This was no doubt spurred on by a close friend who was an expert on the subject. Frank Sharp would become a very close friend of Jim's after 1994 and they shared a particular passion for preserving pure bred Longhorn cattle. Jim had, over the course of his adult life, owned a ranch and property with sheep and other kinds of cattle, but He particularly enjoyed being with his Longhorns. He knew them all by name but also kept in mind that he bred them for food and/or profit. Family members would often go with him out to his property and he would want to walk on his property in the midst of these beautiful animals. Being with the cattle seemed to relax him in a therapeutic manner and he very much enjoyed talking about them to interested parties (and, as some grandkids report, uninterested parties). Even though he hadn't lived on a farm or a ranch since he was a small boy he always loved this environment. Frank suggested that what fueled his passion in particular about Longhorn cattle was a desire to preserve the pure Longhorn species that was slowly being bred out of existence. He believed something of great historical value was being lost. So the preservation of history was very important to him. As told by McEachern family and Frank Sharp

Post was a small town that had originally been built by C. W. Post, who had also invented such cereals as Postum, Grapenuts, and Post Toasties in a desperate effort to ease the constant pain that tormented a bad stomach. The town was isolated on the far edge of the Caprock, perched on land that had a regular acquaintance with sandstorms and was as flat and hot as a blistered tortilla. But the pay, as far as Texas schools were concerned, was exceptional. The average base pay for districts in Texas was forty-two hundred dollars a year. Post paid forty-four hundred dollars, and, what's more, I earned an extra sixty dollars a month driving a school bus.

I settled down, I thought, to a long career in education. Arlene and I had found a nice place to stay in Post. It wasn't much. It was a little shotgun house that had been part of an old Army barracks. The living room was at one end, the bedroom at the other, with a kitchen in between. Arlene made it a home. We were living comfortably but modestly and always within our means. I had a devout aversion to debt and was pleased that my paycheck and our monthly bills sort of crossed each other out. We didn't have a lot of money left over, but we didn't owe anybody either.

During the spring of 1963, however, our second child, Michael, was born, and the doctor presented us with a bill for one thousand dollars. It was fair. There was nothing I could dispute about the invoice. It's just that I did not have a thousand dollars. I was in the hole. I drove home from the hospital, excited about my baby boy, but realizing that, no matter how hard I tried, I would never be able to properly provide for my family with a teacher's salary. Arlene and the children deserved a lot more than I was able to give them. We began to exist even more frugally than before, and it cost every cent I earned to live out the semester. I was heartsick. I was doing what I had always wanted to do and knew that, on a meager fixed income, I would never get ahead in life. A definite financial barrier would forever be staring me in the face.

At the end of the year, the principal offered me a new contract. "Thank you, sir," I said. "It's been a good year."

"We certainly want you back."

"It's time to move on," I said and did my best to smile.

Indecision

It was during this time that Jim began to reconsider going into full-time Christian ministry. His future was uncertain. He had briefly considered that career path in college but now he was once again searching for God's will for his life. He knew that it wasn't going to be teaching students, so he sought the advice of a local pastor. He met with the pastor and told him his story, about his unsettledness, and about his belief that God might possibly be calling him to be a preacher. Jim said he expected the minister to tell him by all means to go into vocational ministry. The minister did not do that, however. He asked Jim if he had ever had happiness and success in any job that he had undertaken. Jim replied: "I've been very happy and successful selling books over several summers." The minister said, "That's it young man. God's not calling you to be a pastor. He's calling you to be a God-glorifying salesman." Jim said he left there upset with the minister because he hadn't told him what he wanted to hear but upon reflection he later realized that the minister had told him exactly what he needed to hear. As told by Michael McDowell (son-in-law)

When the four of us drove out of Post, I really had no idea about what I would do. I was simply on the road headed east, back in the general direction of civilization. It was that remote part of the West Texas prairie where you could drive for miles and miles and see nothing but miles and miles. Ahead lay Abilene, Brownwood, and Fort Worth. I had my choice. At the moment, I was unemployed in all three of them. I hesitated to go back to Brownwood. It was a college town, and I was no longer a student. I was familiar with Abilene, but the town had a lot of bad memories for me. I settled on Fort Worth. It was largest and should offer a lot more job opportunities.

I had worked in supermarkets. I understood how they operated. They did not have to particularly worry about customers. They offered products that everyone needed, and they all had to do with food. A man could work hard, receive a few promotions, and earn a good living while achieving a long-term career in the grocery store business. My mind was made up long before I reached the Fort Worth city limit sign.

It didn't take long to find a job with Buddy's Supermarkets, and I immediately started working as a management trainee in the chain's largest store in Fort Worth. The pay was disappointing. A year's wage was only slightly more than four thousand dollars, not quite as much as I had been earning as a teacher. But I wasn't concerned. I had my eyes set on a long-range goal.

Work a little while as a management trainee. Arlene and I knew we could make it on a small paycheck. We had done it before in Post. Work my way steadily up the chain of command, earn a few promotions over the next couple of years, and I could easily wind up as a store manager before I was thirty years old. Reach the top early. I had no doubt that I could do it.

It all made good sense to me. I had it figured in my head that store managers probably earned as much as thirty-five thousand dollars a year, which, during the late 1960s, seemed like the kind of salary that only rich men took home.

I took the dream I had long possessed about being a history teacher, wadded it up, and tossed it aside. I was on my way to becoming a rich man.

I dutifully handled the assignments given to a management trainee. I unloaded the trucks. I stacked the products. I sacked groceries. I cleaned up the aisles when something was dropped, knocked over, or spilled. There was nothing glamorous about it, but I didn't mind.

I was learning the grocery store business from the ground up. That was the only way I could look at it. Buddy's was a good company.

It treated its employees well. I knew, at long last, I had found a permanent home.

After several months, I was on a break one afternoon with both the manager and assistant manager of the supermarket. I knew them pretty well by now. They were good, honest, hard-working men, and I felt comfortable around them.

I casually said, "I don't want to pry, but I have a question to ask."

"What is it?"

"What's the starting pay for a store manager?"

The manager frowned as he thought it over, and then answered, "At a small store, the beginning manager makes about six hundred dollars a month."

I did a quick calculation in my head. That was seventy-two hundred dollars a year.

"What's the top pay a manager can ever expect to make?" I asked.

"About thirteen thousand dollars a year," he said. "Maybe fourteen thousand if he's there long enough."

Only one man, other than the family who owned Buddy's Supermarkets, was doing better. That was Mr. Berman. He was running half of the stores in the chain.

No one made more money than Mr. Berman. He was earning seventeen thousand dollars a year. I felt sick to my stomach. I had thought I was working my way toward a thirty-five thousand dollar a year salary, and now that dream had been shattered on the loading docks out behind the store. I had a job. I had a fixed income. There might be opportunity at the top. But it was a hard climb and certainly didn't pay a lot.

A few weeks later, I was sent to Weatherford as an assistant manager. It was a small store, only a two-man operation, and, being the low man on the chart, my job was to do pretty much everything that needed to be done.

I helped open a new Buddy's Supermarket in the north part of Fort Worth and promptly became the number three man in the store. I was moving around. My career was progressing. Each new store was looked at as a new promotion. None of it was ever reflected in my paycheck. Work more. Work harder. The money remained pretty much the same.

I knew that my attitude was beginning to change for the worse. I didn't like it, but there was nothing I could do about it. I let my bad attitude start dragging me down. I was not the dedicated, devoted, friendly, happy employee I had been.

My level of enthusiasm had dropped to zero. My confidence had been tossed out the window like trash on a city side street. My hopes were dimming. My ambition was running on empty. I had carefully prepared a road map for my life to follow. The road was full of twists and turns, detours and finally a dead end.

I woke up every morning and dreaded going to work. As long as I was running the cash register or sacking groceries, I was fine. What I didn't like was stocking and stacking, and every time I stood at the end of an aisle and saw another flat full of cans waiting to be arranged on the shelves, my attitude soured even more. I couldn't keep it hidden anymore.

One afternoon, the store manager called me to his office. He didn't beat around the bush. He spoke plainly, and his words left no doubt about the way he felt. He looked me over good and said, "It's obvious that you're not cut out for this job. I'm going to let you go find something that's better suited for you."

He didn't say it in so many words. But I knew what he meant. *You're fired.*

I had taught school and walked away after a year. Strike one. Now I was fired from the supermarket chain. Strike two.

It was the middle of summer. I had a wife and two children. I had bills to pay, groceries to buy, another month's rent coming due. And I was out on the streets. No job. No money.

I looked through the help wanted ads in the newspaper. I was no longer searching for anything long-term or a career. I was looking for somebody to hire me. I needed to go to work. Today if possible, certainly no later than tomorrow. I needed to find someone as desperate for an employee as I was desperate for a job.

The ad immediately caught my eye. There was an opening for a snow cone truck driver. I could start immediately. The company would give a designated route and hire a helper for me.

The pay was a dollar an hour. I didn't feel as though I had time to look for anything better. I needed every dollar I could earn, and I needed it in a hurry.

For the next forty-five days, I was a snow cone sales person. I drove slowly up one street and down another. The music played loudly. The children came running down the street to meet me. It was summer. It was hot. The ice was cold. The ice was sweet. I sold snow cones. Eight hours. Eight dollars.

I had fallen, I thought, as far as I could fall. If I weren't careful, I would have to reach up to touch bottom.

The summer abruptly ended. School started. I parked the snow cone truck. I was out of business.

Again I turned to the help wanted ads in the newspapers. It was becoming a rather common occurrence. Somebody must be hiring, I thought. The Southland Beauty Supply wanted to hire someone who could prepare orders for those daily deliveries to the beauty and barber shops served by the company.

By the time I pulled my car back into rush hour traffic, I had a job. I was back on somebody's payroll. The duties weren't difficult to perform. Anybody could have done them. But I found myself cornered and locked into a dull, dismal, wearisome existence.

The owner and his wife were wonderful people. The position did not challenge me at all. I could not envision myself sitting there and preparing delivery orders for the next twenty years. At the moment, however, I could not see myself doing anything else. I certainly didn't have any better prospects. I had a job I liked. And I quit.

I had a job I didn't like, and I was told, in no uncertain terms, that my job had run its course. It was definitely time to leave, and I probably shouldn't concern myself with ever thinking of coming back.

So, I wrote up the orders, and, on rare occasions, drove the delivery trucks. I thought I had disliked the grocery store business.

It was a cakewalk compared to my position at the beauty supply company. Every day was drudgery. The work was tedious and only a notch above menial labor. But I needed the income. And I could not stand the humiliation of being fired again.

I was able to keep my sanity because the owner subscribed to a business magazine published by the U.S. Chamber of Commerce. He allowed me to borrow the publication and take it home at night. Each issue contained articles on leadership and the character traits of successful businessmen. There was always an in-depth interview with some executive in charge of running a Fortune 500 company.

I had always believed that most rich men had probably inherited their wealth, or at least wound up as president or chief executive officer of the family business. Money wasn't earned the old fashioned way – with blood, sweat, determination, and sound decisions – as much as it had been passed down from one generation to another. And, in a lot of cases, that was exactly what had happened.

However, I was surprised to learn that many of the country's most successful and dynamic individuals in the business world had climbed their way to the top from down-to-earth, ordinary situations.

They built companies and wealth because they had better ideas and possessed the strength, the vision, the tenacity, and the resolve to give their ideas a chance to become a reality. It hadn't always been easy for them. In fact, it hadn't been easy for any of them. But they stuck to it. They never gave up. They sometimes defied tradition. And they stood tall even in the face of adversity.

They were my kind of businessmen. I could identify with them. I began to see myself following in their footsteps. They had sometimes overcome circumstances even more difficult than mine had been, and if they could reach the top of their profession, I reasoned to myself, then I could do it as well. If nothing else, those success stories of corporate executives had planted a new seed and instilled within me a new commitment for someday building a business to be reckoned with. I could envision myself sitting at the head of the corporate table, analyzing business strategies, planning for a strong, viable future; building a productive and prosperous company.

But I could never get it done while sitting at a little desk and writing up delivery orders for beauty shops. I had allowed a new dream to inch its way into my life. I knew it would lead me somewhere. I just didn't know which way to turn. So I reached over, picked up a new set of orders, and handed them to the delivery men. I was ready to try my hand in the world of business, the bigger, the better, and here I was stuck in neutral.

I wanted a better job. But I didn't have the time to look for a better job or even another job. I was chained to my clerk's chair by the desperate need for a steady paycheck.

I had my dreams all right, some old, some new, some always changing, but they were nothing but illusions and most of them had long been fraying around the edges. I had always been told that "time waits for no man." Neither did opportunity. I was frustrated at the world but mostly at myself. Life was like a carousel passing me by. I didn't know whether I should jump on or jump off.

My life was filled with inner turmoil and disappointments. I had never felt so exasperated in my life. However, during those days when I fulfilled my tedious duties at a tedious job, I was searching for a way out and not being able to find one.

In order to earn a little extra income, I painted the inside of a neighbor's house. It gave me time to do a lot of thinking, and I began to have a better understanding of the plight my parents had faced almost three decades earlier. For the first time in my life, I was able to place my feet in their shoes and realize the pain, anxiety and disappointment they must have felt. My life was rough. Their lives had been worse. Mine was frustrating. Theirs had been overwhelming. I should have been equipped to face my problems. They didn't have a chance.

Neither of them had an education. My father was borderline illiterate. I'm not for sure he could read or write much more than his name. And life had hit them head-on with three children. They were poor. They were struggling, and nothing came easy. No matter how hard they worked, they could not get ahead.

Opportunity had never knocked on their door or stayed awhile. They were fighting for survival and were, I'm sure, feeling as desperate and frustrated and discouraged as I was now. The grudge I had carried against them all of those years began to quietly dissipate as I considered their hopeless plight in life.

A sudden feeling of compassion swept over me. The grudge faded away. For the first time in my life, I felt a sense of empathy for them and the miserable existence they had faced. Two kids trying to escape their predicament. That's all they were.

They had never done anything intentionally to hurt me. They were simply victims of their circumstances. Hard times had simply beaten them down and stolen any dreams they might have had.

I had waited for years for my mother or father to apologize for the way they had driven off and abandoned me. But there was no reason for them to apologize. Not really. My anger toward them began to dissipate. I no longer felt any deep-seated need to keep on punishing either one of them. Time had seared over the wounds, and then healed them.

My mother had moved to Fort Worth several years before Arlene and I did. She was industrious and working hard to make a decent life for herself. She was operating a liquor store near the Will Rogers Coliseum and had begun to buy and sell junk furniture. She bought a house or two, fixed them up, and re-sold them. By now, she was also living with her ninth husband. I guess she had finally gotten it right. She would live with him, and happily, for the rest of her life. I had seen my mother from time to time but had never made a real attempt to restore any kind of a mother and son relationship. I felt differently now.

I began to visit her regularly and tell her that I loved her, even though it was so difficult for her to accept my words and my feelings. I'm sure that, in some ways, she felt as guilty as I did. Maybe we had spent too many years blaming each other when there was really no one to blame but ourselves.

I would sit down in the living room of her home, cup her face in my hands, and say softly, "Mom, I love you." And she would answer,

"We love you, too." No smile. Just the words. For so long, she could not bring herself to say, "I love you."

For so long, it was always "we," never "I." It was, however, a beginning, and I gave her time. Time was all either of us had. And finally, it was "I."

"I love you," she said, and she was talking to me. So few words, and they meant so much. They closed the chasm between us. She no longer felt like a stranger. She was my mother, and I knew that, at long last, I was loved.

On the Importance of "I Love You"

Several years ago, Jim McEachern was telling a few of us at a Tom James gathering that when he was young, he was raised by some relatives. Years later, after he would visit or call them and say goodbye, he would say "I Love You". Their response would be, "We love you, too" as most of us would say in an automatic non-feeling way. He would say, "I love you" and, again, they would say, "we love you, too". He would then emphasize each word to mean that he truly loved them. They caught on and responded with "I love you, too", which is what Jim wanted to hear. He loved being told he was loved, truly loved. He also wanted them to know that he loved them in case he never saw them again.

I took that story and applied it to my family. I began to tell my parents, my wife and my children that I loved them as I was leaving or hanging up. They began to respond that way too. Now, my wife and children tell each other, I love you, whenever they depart and I hope that carries on with their children. I related that story to Jim a week before he passed away and told him I loved him and he told me he loved me too. That was the last time I saw him. He affected the lives of many by just saying "I Love You." When my mother passed in

2007 it was very difficult for our family. My dad had originally wanted her head stone to say "Beloved Wife". She was so much more than that. We eventually decided to put her name, date of birth and date of death on her headstone but we included as her epitaph "I Love You." Now every time we look at her head stone, she reminds us, even in death "I Love You."

Richard Thompson, Tom James Company

My parents never had a chance. I did. I had a college education. I had a diploma on the wall. There was no reason for me to pass through life without finding my own corner of success. But what could I do? Where could I go? And how could I keep from striking out? I already had two strikes against me. I could not bear the thought of a third.

I had hit bottom before, but this was the first time I realized that the bottom had a bottom. I had never felt lower in my life. It appeared that I would be condemned to spend the rest of my days searching through the job wanted ads in the newspaper. I could not find any situation better than the one I had. Every ad, it seemed, was looking for somebody to start on the ground floor and be satisfied with the ground floor. I was at the end of my rope, and it had already begun to unravel.

Little did I know, but God, quietly and methodically, was preparing to send me a lifeline, and I had no idea that the opportunity I had been praying for was already on the way.

Back when I began selling books during the summer, another young man walking the streets of another town was beginning to knock on doors as well. He and I had been together briefly at training sessions through the years, but I did not know him. His name was Spencer Hays. He had been a student at Texas Christian University, and, virtually overnight, he had become the brightest star in Southwestern's galaxy of book sales people.

No one could make more calls than Spencer Hays. No one could sell more books. I read the regular sales reports, and no matter how hard I tried, I could not catch Spencer Hays. I may have finished in the top three from time to time, but Spencer was always number one. For four straight years, he was number one.

When he began knocking on doors for the Southwestern Company, Spencer was like the rest of us: a diamond in the rough. Most of us would remain trapped in the rough. Spencer became a finished diamond.

He had learned early the art of selling from his grandmother. He remembered when he was seven years old, and there was a litter of puppies that needed to be sold. He said, "She put pretty pink ribbons around their necks so they would stand out, and it worked."

Spencer Hays would spend a lifetime developing companies and products that stood out. *Forbes* would call him an "American Original".

While I was laboring for minimum wages with a small, out-of-the-way beauty supply company, Spencer Hays had already been hired full time and promoted to sales manager for Southwestern. By 1963, his personal organization was larger than the entire company had been when he assumed control of the sales department. He knew where he was going and had the ability to get there in a hurry. He was a master recruiter. He was a genius at selling books.

But perhaps more importantly, Spencer Hays understood human nature, knew how to deal with people regardless of the circumstances they encountered, and motivate them to become a success at selling books, too. He had a keen people sense and taught his teams of sales people how to reach out to the customers. His philosophy was and always would be quite simple. "You can't build a business," he said. "You build people. People build a business."

He once told *Forbes*, "People want to be led, not managed." He often traveled on the road for a week with a key salesperson who was experiencing a slump, working to reestablish the young man's morale.

I had left my morale somewhere alongside the highway. It was nonexistent. I was ready to be led. I just needed a leader.

As I searched for answers, I did not name him specifically, but I was aware that I needed a mentor like Spencer Hays to give me the start I needed in a competitive and a crowded marketplace. He had the ability to train people and the compassion to make them believe in themselves.

It was becoming more difficult every day for me to believe in myself. In business, I was only treading water. I had not gone under, but it was becoming increasingly harder to stay afloat. My bills were growing faster than my income. It was difficult to make ends meet with a dead end job.

It stunned me in the spring of 1965 when the telephone rang and I found myself talking to Spencer Hays. I wondered why he had time for me. I knew that Spencer had served as campaign manager for Bill Wills when he ran as a Republican for the U. S. House of Representatives. At the time, a Republican did not stand a chance in Nashville. With Spencer running the show, he almost pulled an upset, gathering forty-eight percent of the vote while Presidential candidate Barry Goldwater only captured thirty-six percent. Spencer had become president of the second largest sales and marketing executives club in the country. And he was still in his twenties.

He was a young man on the move. Always headed in the right direction. Always heading up. Why had he bothered to call me? How did he even know my name?

"I have some ideas," he said rather obliquely, "and I'm looking for some good men to make it happen."

I didn't answer. I might not be the right man, I thought. Old fears worked their way into my psyche. Dread immediately dampened any enthusiasm I might have had.

"I've seen your record at Southwestern," he told me. "You were a fine book sales person. You were dogged and determined, and you sold a lot of books."

Was he going to offer me a job?

"I'm sending one of my sales managers down to talk to you," he said. "He'll fill in the details."

I managed a "thank you."

And Spencer hung up.

A week later, I sat down with Sam Johnson, his sales manager, in a little Fort Worth apartment. We talked awhile. He didn't tell me much about any kind of business Spencer might be contemplating, but he asked a lot of questions about me, my life, and my endeavors in business since leaving college. He smiled. We shook hands. I was still in the dark. I might have remained in the dark if God had not been protecting and watching over me.

Back in Nashville, Sam Johnson met with Spencer to give his report.

"What do you think?" Spencer asked.

"Don't bother with McEachern."

"Why not?"

"He's a loser."

"What makes you say that?"

"He hasn't moved up in the business world," the sales manager said. "He's headed in the wrong direction. I wasn't impressed at all."

Spencer Hays sat in silence for a few moments.

"Don't waste your time on McEachern," Johnson said. "I wouldn't recommend you having anything to do with him."

Spencer nodded. He had the report. He had one man's opinion. He believed in his own gut.

Three weeks later, Spencer Hays showed up at a motel near the TCU campus. He called and asked me to meet him on campus. I did.

And he told me, "I'm thinking about starting a business. I'm thinking about hiring students who worked during the summers for me as soon as they graduate. I believe some of them have what it takes to build the business, and I can offer them a career."

"And you're interested in me?" I asked.

"I am," he said.

My mind reached down, picked up the shattered pieces, and began putting the dream back together again.

My immediate thought was this: *If I can work with Spencer Hays, then maybe I can find out what works for him and allows him to be so successful. It might not work that well for me. But if I only learned a part of what made him successful, I would sure be in a lot better shape professionally and financially than I am now.*

I needed a mentor. I needed someone to help me build the foundation for the rest of my life. I needed someone who believed in me, and he obviously did. Otherwise, Spencer would have listened to his sales manager, shook his head, torn up my phone number and resume', and threw it away.

We all have our opportunities. We just have to know when the right one comes our way. Mine had arrived with Spencer Hays.

Takeaways from the chapter

- *Jim didn't know what he wanted when he was in his twenties and early thirties. He thought he did. He discovered what he was meant to do over time. He failed on numerous occasions and stumbled his way to success. Since success is rarely found on a straight line, am I giving myself the leeway when I fail? Am I continuing to seek what it is that I am meant to do?*

- *Jim liked his first job as a teacher but couldn't adjust to the pay scale and resigned. He was fired from his second job as a management trainee because he lost motivation for the same reason. He was not happy with his third and fourth jobs because he knew he could do so much more. Finding the right job would seem to be the task of discerning who I am and what my gifts, ambitions, and desires entail.*

- *Jim realized that people who had accumulated wealth had one common trait. They succeeded ". . . because they had better ideas and possessed the strength, the vision, the tenacity, and the resolve to give their ideas a chance to become a reality." What are the most powerful ideas in my life? Am I resolved to make those ideas a reality?*

- *Experience teaches us many things. Our parents may have done things we didn't understand as young people but these things may become clearer as we move out into their world. With experience comes empathy and with empathy comes compassion. Have I made peace with my parents' deficiencies?*

- *Jim recognized God's hand in his life at this time. He doesn't attribute it to chance but to the work of God. How aware am I of God's work in my life?*

- *Two perspectives were put forward about Jim in the chapter. The first is an assessment that he was a loser who hadn't accomplished anything and the second was that he was someone full of potential and eager for success. In this case, it is the conclusions that made the difference. Spencer Hays viewed Jim not for what he was but* for what he could be. This would become a major theme in Jim McEachern's life as it related to every person he met.

- Jim realized that in order to be successful he needed to learn from other successful people. He needed a mentor. How teachable am I? Who are my mentors? And how exactly do they contribute to the accomplishment of my life goals?

CHAPTER 8

Choosing to Follow the Right Leader

Spencer Hays was the kind of leader that I had always wanted to follow. I had confidence in him and believed that he possessed the vision and genius necessary to take me to the top. With Spencer Hays in charge and guiding my efforts, I realized that I was not afraid to dream big again. Daydreams were fleeting, little more than a few scattered hopes and wishes that seldom had any chance of succeeding. The opportunity to work with Spencer Hays, however, re-lit the fire in my imagination and ambition. This was the chance I had not expected. This was the opportunity I could not afford to waste.

At the Southwestern Company, he had been able to accomplish more in four years than several generations had achieved in ninety years, and I wanted to learn his secret for success. I knew that he had more than doubled his income during those few years and was earning more than a hundred thousand dollars a year, which would have probably been more than a million dollars in today's economy. There were businessmen in the American marketplace pocketing as much or more than Spencer Hays, but, for the most part, they had been working for decades, were generally old enough to be my grandfather, or had no doubt inherited their wealth.

Spencer was my age. We were contemporaries. All he had inherited was a sixth sense for generating income and building a business. I decided that he must have the right formula or the right philosophy, or he could not have made a significant mark so quickly in his book selling endeavors at Southwestern. Many had succeeded at the company, but he was "head and shoulders" above the rest.

I had obviously taken the wrong fork in the road. The years had tempted me, and then taunted me. I kept trying to dig my way out of a financial hole but only wound up digging a deeper hole. In a relatively short time, I had become worn down, demoralized, and dissatisfied with my own condition, and I was curious to learn more about a man who had traveled to a strange town, just as I had, and began selling books door-to-door the year after I made my first sale. In hardly any time at all, Spencer Hays had risen dramatically to the top of the world.

I had hit bottom and kept right on sliding downward. I had gone just about as low as I could go.

If Spencer Hays had the answer, I wanted to learn what it was. He may have been a good sales person, but that didn't account for his ability to become so much better than the rest of us. For all I knew, it was pure magic.

In an effort to become a better sales person back during the summer of 1964 when I began working with the Southwestern Company, I had diligently read and studied Frank Bettger's book, *How I Raised Myself from Failure to Success in Selling*. It was invaluable and important as a resource for me, but I barely scratched the surface of comprehending the compendium of critical information tucked away between its pages.

In chapter one, I discovered the "power of enthusiasm." That was simple enough, I thought. I could be enthusiastic for eight to ten hours a day. All I had to do was talk a little louder, pump my fists from time to time, jump around a little now and then, smile a lot, laugh a lot, and deliver my sales message with the same fervor used by an evangelist in a brush arbor revival meeting.

But, alas, that was nothing more than artificial excitement. It didn't feel right. I would hit an emotional high when I knocked on my first door every morning, but, by the time I drove back to my room at the end of each day, I was worn out, and my energy had run off and left me. My emotions had run out of steam and were completely depleted. I could run hard for a while, but I couldn't go the distance. I was on an unbelievable pace, running from door-to-door, knowing full well that I was trapped in the middle of a game of numbers. The more presentations I made, the more sales I expected to close. Smile a little more. Talk a little louder. Pump my fist a little harder. It was all good for a time, but I knew there was absolutely no way I could fake enthusiasm for the rest of my life. If I didn't believe in what I was doing with all of my heart, no one else would ever be able to believe it either.

I had only met Spencer Hays one time previously. During a summer training session at the Southwestern Company, he and I, quite by accident, had ridden the same freight elevator to an early morning meeting. It was little more than a brief encounter. He was friendly enough but hardly possessed any charisma that would set him apart. Two things, however, became quite apparent in a hurry. Spencer Hays dressed better and seemed to possess a little more confidence, a lot more self assured than the rest of us.

I smiled to myself and thought: This guy hasn't knocked on any doors yet. After he's been out on the streets for a few weeks, he won't be nearly as confident. He has no idea what he's getting himself in to. The job sounds simple enough; at least it does when the instructor at the front of the class is making his training presentation. It sounds like a good way to make an easy dollar or two for the summer. But this guy called Spencer Hays has no idea what reality really is. He hasn't knocked on twenty doors during a day during the searing heat of summer. No one has told him "no." No one has slammed a door in his face yet.

We shook hands and introduced ourselves then went our separate ways. He may have been young, green, and a raw beginner, but Spencer Hays knew where he was going. I was simply searching for a way to make a little money during the next three months.

He had his eyes set on a career. I just wanted to sell a few books every day. Spencer Hays wanted to get rich. I simply needed to pay my rent, eat a couple of decent meals a day, and have enough money left over to take care of my tuition and board at Howard Payne.

Spencer Hays was moving rapidly toward the summit. By now, I had learned to accept the fact that I was headed in the other direction, the wrong direction, and the ride down was far quicker and much more of a certainty than the long climb back up.

I received a company newsletter on a regular basis and had kept up with Spencer Hays and his meteoric rise within the company. I was surprised and a little flattered that he remembered me or could even recall my name. He had no doubt gone to sales school with hundreds of young men whose names were quickly learned and easily forgotten.

For some reason, he had held on to mine. I had met him only once, and that had been nine years earlier. Now he had come to the TCU campus to recruit a new team of book sales people, and he had taken the time to sit down with me. Our meeting wasn't long. It only lasted fifteen minutes. The impression he made on me would last a lifetime.

Spencer Hays was still employed by the Southwestern Company, and he had no thought of leaving. But he admitted that his goal was to create and establish a business opportunity where his top book sales people could ultimately pursue their own careers after college. He had worked with some good ones. He had recruited some good ones. He had trained some good ones. He did not want to lose them.

Selling books was great. He knew it, and so did I. Selling books was, for a three month period, the most lucrative job I had ever known. But, unfortunately, as soon as the summer ended, so did the work, so did the paychecks, so did the business. Previously, we would always knock on a few final doors, give our last presentations, hope to make one more sale before the season ran out on us, wrap up our collections and head back off to school. Now college was behind us.

The idea incubating in Spencer's brain would, he believed, keep us busy year round. He did not say exactly what kind of business he had in mind. Maybe he did not know at the time. Maybe he was mentally exploring more than one concept and had not yet settled on a single or specific venture.

Only one thing was for certain, he said.

"What's that?"

"It won't have anything to do with books."

I had never thought it might.

"When do you plan to get started?" I wanted to know.

Spencer was honest and up front with me. "It may be a year from now," he said. "It might be a little longer."

I was elated. I was deflated. I wanted and needed a better job. I was searching for a career. I did not want to wait a year.

Spencer had no intention of piquing my interest, then driving off and leaving me to wonder if I would ever hear from him again.

"What I would like for you to do," he said, "is sign up to sell books again this summer while I'm putting everything in place."

I nodded. There were no promises, no guarantees. Spencer Hays had a vague idea for a new business and little else. In my mind, however, the option he was offering me was much better than anything else I could conjure up. It was, in fact, the only option I had.

I sat there thinking quietly to myself: If I am associated with Spencer Hays, then maybe I can figure out why he's successful and I'm not. Maybe his opportunity would give me a chance to experience some success in the business world. I had read about a lot of successful businessmen, but none of them ever told me how they reached the top. As far as I knew, Spencer Hays was the only one who was interested in me and could teach me. Maybe if I followed him around, I could find out what worked for him. And who knows? Even if it didn't work quite as well for me as it did Spencer, I would still be a lot better off than the end-of-the-road, dead-end position where I had presently found myself. If, by working with Spencer, I could attain a reasonable amount of success, then Arlene, the children, and I could afford a nice house with nice furniture and appliances. We could buy a good car, not a luxury car, perhaps, but a good car all the same. We could at last take family vacations and have a nice life. I had long wanted a nice life but no longer had any idea about how I could attain one on my own.

These thoughts all burst through my mind in a fleeting matter of seconds. But they left a lasting impression. So did Spencer Hays.

He wanted to hire me. He thought he could train me. He had seen some potential in me, and I was ready to soak up his ideas and follow him even though, for me, it would be a great leap of faith into a great unknown. I did not know what business he wanted to build. I did not know where I might be living. I did not know what I would be selling, or if I would be selling anything at all. I didn't know what my pay would be. Would I draw a salary or simply earn a commission? Would I be on the streets or sitting in an office? Would I be an executive or simply a hired hand?

I shoved the questions aside and filed them away. None of them really mattered. Not at the moment anyway. Even the great unknown was better than the never-ending carousel of disappointment and disillusion I was riding.

I smiled, shook Spencer's hand, and said, "I'll sell books again."

"I won't have anything concrete to offer you until the summer's over," he said.

"I'll wait."

"You won't regret it," he said.

I didn't think I would.

I returned to the Beauty Supply Company with a whole new attitude and a great load of worry and concern lifted like a heavy burden off of my shoulders. It was a good little business run by good people. I liked them, they treated me right, and I appreciated them. It was the job that had fenced me in. For me, there was absolutely no room for advancement. The owner's sons would take over some day, and I would remain where I sat, taking down inventory off the shelves, packing the supplies into boxes, and filling out orders for the sons to deliver. It was a well-run family business, and I wasn't family.

From the first day, I never really felt as though I was learning anything that would help me in any future endeavors. I did not view the company as any kind of model that I would be able to pursue.

It was built with a lot of inventory, and inventory required a heavy financial investment. I was barely making ends meet and did not have any spare dollars to invest in anything.

Arlene and I were living in a small duplex in the Arlington Heights area of Fort Worth, paying twelve dollars and fifty cents a week for our rent at a time when I was only earning a salary of sixty-four dollars a week. Each time we went to the grocery store, I made a detailed list of our needs, and I calculated the price of every item we placed in the buggy. I had a definite budget, and if we went over, I had to put something back on the shelf. Otherwise, I would not have the bus money I needed to go to work each day. The fare was thirty cents each way. If I didn't keep back at least three dollars a week, I would be taking a six-mile, two hour walk – in summer and winter, hot or cold, wet or dry – to and from the beauty supply company.

Back when I had been teaching school, I bought a Nash Rambler, and the monthly payments were sixty dollars, which were several dollars too much for a man trying to keep his family fed and clothed. The money always ran out too quickly. Too often, when I tried to round up those sixty hard-earned dollars, they were already gone. One morning, I walked into Pacific Finance and gave back my car and the keys. I took the bus home. I had been riding the bus ever since.

Those last few weeks, while I was waiting until the end of May, became a lot more tolerable. I was filled with a measure of relief and excitement. My job behind a desk and out among those endless shelves of inventory was rapidly coming to an end. I was gripped with a sense of anticipation and great expectations. I didn't know what was coming, but I was ready for it. I could not yet see the light at the end of the tunnel, but I had definitely found the tunnel.

It was a long hot summer in Gallatin, Tennessee, although probably no hotter than usual and longer simply because I was anxiously waiting for Spencer Hays to set me on a new career path as soon as September arrived. It was both the best and worst of summers. I was broke as always and still so deep in debt that I had lost sight of ever breaking even again. My mother had co-signed for me to buy a second-hand Desoto, and I learned that Arlene was expecting our third child.

I had my good days and bad days selling books, and I could feel my confidence eroding. On one hand, an old fear had tracked me down, and I was terrified to knock on doors again. On the other hand, I couldn't wait to make my next presentation and the next sale. It was an odd three months. Early on, I had felt lost and unsure of myself. Then the sales began to roll in, and I ended August with the most successful and profitable summer I had spent during my tenure with the Southwestern Company.

Spencer Hays met with me as soon as I drove back to Nashville, and he had both good news and bad news waiting for me. He told me that it would take a little more time before he would be able to launch his new business venture. He just wasn't quite ready yet. He still had some loose ends that needed tying up.

However, Spencer had made arrangements for me to get a job with Cain-Sloan Department Store, which had opened a new facility in the Greenhill's section of Nashville. He told me that I would be working in men's furnishings, primarily selling ties, shirts, and underwear. I could sense that there was "a certain method to his madness." This wasn't just a last ditch, "do-the-best-you-can job." He had a reason for placing me in a department store. He had a reason for me to understand the art of selling fine clothes.

"Learn all you can," he said. "It'll be important to you."

"Now?"

"Soon."

"What are your plans?" I asked.

"Men's clothing," he answered.

"Are you considering opening a department store?"

Spencer's smile widened. "Right now, most men go to a department store or a men's store to buy their clothes," he said. "And those sales people who work in most of those stores are not what I would call professional clothiers. You walk in, you look for your size, you try it on, and if it fits, you buy the clothes. The sales person may make a few suggestions, but mostly he's just there to write up the ticket, ring up the sale, and collect the money. We'll be different."

"How?" I wanted to know.

"I believe that successful men in the business world need a professional clothier they can rely on just as they need a professional banker, a doctor, a financial planner, or an attorney," Spencer said. "He's busy. He's on the go. He doesn't have a lot of time and certainly not enough time to shop for his clothes. All he wants to do is look his best. No. He needs to look his best. In business, so often, it's all about image."

"How will we be different?"

"I want to put together a team of clothiers who have the expertise necessary to help a businessman select the right fabric, color, pattern, and style exclusively for him, and then we will make him a custom suit."

"How can you do that if he is, as you say, too busy to shop?"

"Simple," Spencer replied. "We'll schedule appointments and take an assortment of good, solid ideas about clothes to his office. We'll provide an unlimited selection with hundreds of different fabrics, patterns, and colors. Does he want a suit with one button, two buttons, or three buttons? Whatever he wants, we'll be able to deliver it with a high fashion look. In essence, we will take the store to the man. All professional men love the idea of wearing tailored clothes. In reality, we will be his tailor."

"Have you named your company?"

"Not yet."

"The Spencer Hays Company has a nice ring."

He shrugged. "Not for me, it doesn't," he said.

Spencer Hays would build the spotlight. He never wanted to be in it.

I knew, however, that the mind of Spencer Hays would have the preparation, planning, and strategy in place to make his idea work regardless of the name. He was headed in a new direction but the right direction, and I would be right behind him every step of the way. Whenever we met, I would listen intently to every word he said.

In my business world, his word was gospel. At long last, I was able to dream again, and the dream was no longer a nightmare that kept me awake in cold sweats during the darkness of early morning. It was just a dream, perhaps, but it was beginning to seem real enough for me to reach out and touch.

At the time, Spencer was driving a big new Oldsmobile Toronado. I still had my ten-year-old Desoto. He bought a four-bedroom condo with a nice office and a library. I was still paying rent. He was on top, and he said that there was room enough for me. I believed him.

Spencer Hays had never been an imposing man. He was only about five feet and ten inches tall and weighed just under two hundred pounds. His brown hair was thinning, and he had unusually large eyebrows. He would have never been described as outgoing, but he possessed more confidence than anyone I had ever been around. He was warm and believable, sincere and generous. He wanted to get a job done and done right. He did not want or demand the credit even though his accomplishments in the business world were already extraordinary.

He would build his business on the foundation of one quote. He felt it deeply, and he believed it. It said:

> *There's a destiny that makes us brothers,*
> *None goes his way alone.*
> *All that we send into the lives of others*
> *Comes back into our own.*

The underlying secret possessed by Spencer Hays was his ability to build the people he needed to build a good business. His ambition was to make us successful. He was confident that if he could accomplish that one single goal, we would in time make his company successful as well. He believed in us. I certainly believed in him.

Takeaways from the chapter

- *Jim had a relationship of trust with Mr. Hays. Jim said, "I certainly believed in him." The underlying assumption is that Mr. Hays was someone who was trustworthy. How important is it that my mentors be persons of character and integrity? How important is it for me to be a person of character and integrity? How important is it for the people that I work for be persons of character and integrity? How important is it for a business to have a reputation of character and integrity? Etc.*

- *We all make decisions that at some time or another we begin to regret. At one point, Jim had to give back a car he had purchased to the finance company because he simply couldn't afford it. Are there things that I need to give up that are draining my budget? What are they? If I were to be able to offload these things what would I be liberated to accomplish?* ✳

- *Jim absorbed the truth of Spencer's core philosophy for leadership and life: "If you build the people up, then the people will build your business up." How does this apply to family, ministry, and other areas? Is that really true? How am I doing that with the people around me?*

CHAPTER 9

Choosing Patience

The long wait was getting longer. I had invested a summer of my life selling books in West Virginia, and the company that Spencer Hays had envisioned was still boiling around somewhere in the back recesses of his creative mind. His idea kept on growing and expanding, but it was nowhere close to being a reality. He knew exactly what he wanted to do. As he said, however, the time just wasn't right to do it. Just wait a little longer, he said. You won't regret it, he said. And I had no reason to doubt him. I would talk to him one day, and my excitement neared a fevered pitch. Another week on the floor of a men's department store, selling ties, shirts, and underwear, and I could feel my enthusiasm slowly start to dim and then fade away.

Spencer continued to recruit and direct the ever-changing sales force for the Southwestern Company every summer, and he had more students on the streets and selling books than ever before. As the company's sales director, his every hour was occupied by sales people coming and going, headed to a strange town or on their way home. It was his mission to keep encouraging those who had never knocked on a strange door in their lives, had probably never memorized a sales pitch, and couldn't wait until night overtook them again. For a few spare hours, there would be no more cold calls, no more knocking on somebody else's door, no more presentations to make, no more rejections, and no more books to carry. They ate a little, caught a few hours of sleep, and the cycle began all over again. Sales, however, were nearing record numbers with every passing week, and Spencer did not have the luxury to work intently or exclusively on his own dream. He was helping others, night and day, as they raced to catch a faint glimpse of their own.

For another summer, a sixth summer, I had sold books right along with them.

For one fall and winter, I had practiced the art of selling nice clothes in the Cain-Sloan Department store of Nashville, a town growing so fast that it had already spilled out far beyond its city limits.

I hadn't minded selling books for a summer. The days could be frustrating, but the sales and my commissions made it all worthwhile. I had long ago come to the conclusion that working in a fine men's department store would no doubt give me invaluable training within the industry of men's fashions.

Now I was ready to take the next step. My nerves were tight with anticipation. I looked past the limitations that had always held me inside their own stubborn borders, and had never quite allowed me to attain anything close to a high level of success.

Have patience, Spencer said. I tried. It wasn't easy. He was on the road, devoting every spare hour to meeting with companies that manufactured shirts and shoes, ties and belts, socks and the finest fabrics he could find. He was looking for the nation's top tailors, usually found in the nooks and crannies of large cities, and finalizing deals only with those who produced the finest suits on the market. The quality had to be exquisite. There was no substitute for quality. Spencer's reputation and my future depended on it. There were a lot of moving parts, and he was frantically trying to track them all down and tie up any frayed or loose ends before they could start to unravel.

I had hoped, although there were no promises, that Spencer would be ready to open his business by the advent of summer. When he first approached me that had been his plan. That was the date I had been shooting for. I could endure anything, even a job that bored me, until summer. Sometime during the middle of April in 1966, however, I received the bad news.

"It'll take me a while longer to get the business up and running," he said.

"How much longer?"

"Next fall at the earliest."

I'm sure Spencer saw my face. I'm sure he saw the disappointment in my eyes. Spencer's words kept running through my mind. Have patience, he had said. Have patience, I told myself. "All good things do indeed come to him who waits."

It was an old saying and a wise saying. I had no idea whether or not I should believe it.

I was working at a prestigious Nashville upscale men's department store. I had no quarrel about the money I was being paid. I shouldn't have been concerned. Hardly any good, solid business had ever been built overnight. It takes time. It does indeed take patience. I wondered how much patience I really possessed.

Life was as good as it had ever been for me and my family, but my heart was set on being able to launch a new career. Now that I dared to dream again, the dream was growing larger all the time.

I smiled, tried not to show the dismay and frustration I was feeling, and asked, "What should I do until then? Stay at Cain-Sloan?"

"No."

"You have a better idea?

"I do."

"What's that?"

"I want you to sell books again this summer."

Those were words that I did not want to hear Spencer say. In my mind, selling books had always seemed to be nothing more than a temporary existence. Here I was approaching my thirtieth birthday and searching for permanence. Suddenly, all I had to look forward to were three more months, hustling from neighborhood to neighborhood with a set of books in my case and competing with students several years younger than I happened to be. This was a job for college kids, and I had walked away with my diploma a long time ago. Three months. It might as well have been three lifetimes. I nodded and sighed wearily. I could make them as miserable or as worthwhile as I wanted.

At that moment, it would have been tempting to just give up, say goodbye and good riddance, and head off in another direction. I had chased the brass ring for a long time, and it was always just beyond my grasp.

The difference was, I knew and respected Spencer Hays. He was successful and I wanted to stay close to his success. Some of it just might rub off on me.

It would all work out for the best, I told myself. *There was no reason to quit the race when I could sense that the finish line was growing ever closer.* I couldn't see it yet, but I knew it was there. I prayed that it was there.

"I want you to spend the rest of the spring helping me recruit students," Spencer said.

"I've never done anything like that before," I said.

"You'll do fine," he said. "You'll learn a lot about people."

Thus, my search for a new career took a sudden and unexpected turn. Spencer handed me a list of schools and bought me an airline ticket to Dallas. I spent the next six weeks interviewing prospective student book sales people on the campuses of East Texas State University, Stephen F. Austin University, and junior colleges in Tyler, Kilgore, Corsicana, and Athens. I diligently put my signs out, made sure the interview times were written in large, bold letters, then went back a week later to give any and all who showed up a way to make a goodly amount of money for the summer. I had no trouble answering any of their questions. I probably had as much knowledge as anyone about the rigors, the trials, and the financial opportunities that awaited them behind every closed and unfriendly door. After all, I would be spending my seventh summer selling books. I was an old hand by now. I had become a professional temporary book sales person and was wondering by now if life offered anything better.

Spencer had been right. I did learn a lot about people. I recruited twenty students to sell books that summer. I had their names and their applications in my hand. Only half of them made it to Nashville for the training seminar. Only two, besides myself, stayed for the whole summer.

I spent my three months on the streets of Lexington, Kentucky. It was a beautiful place. Great horse farms. White plank fences, freshly painted, had been built around the legends, those thoroughbreds whose names were synonymous with the Kentucky Derby, the Preakness, and the Belmont Stakes.

It was probably the most relaxed summer of my life. I was under no pressure. I knew by now that I could make at least three sales a day even on a bad day. I spent a lot of time with Arlene and the children, and it was as close to a working vacation as I would ever have.

Mentally, I just kept marking the days off the calendar. August would soon be over. The first of September was on its way. For better or worse, the first of September would change my life forever. I was expecting the *better.*

During that last week, I began clearing up my collections as I had always done. Out of every five sales, I would have to go back to the same houses two or three times before somebody handed over the last few dollars and the account was paid in full.

The excuses were many and always the same.

Some member of the family was ill.

Something bad or unexpected had happened.

Some husband had lost his job.

The utility bills were too high.

So were the medical bills.

The lady of the house thought she could save enough money to buy the books but couldn't.

I'd give you the books back, but I just can't find them. You'll have to wait until I do.

That, too, would be a long wait. I learned early to ask for at least forty to fifty percent of the money when I first left the books behind. It was a simple strategy. When people had made a substantial down payment, they always managed to come up with the money before I left town. There were a few times I had to take the books back. But there weren't many.

Summer ended. My future began.

By the time I reached Nashville again, Spencer Hays was waiting for me, and we drove to his new store. It was located on Hillsboro Road, only two miles from downtown and a mile from Vanderbilt University. On one side was the finest furniture store in town. On the other was a high-end ladies dress shop. And nearby was the number one cleaning and pressing shop in Nashville. What's more, the shopping area was on the way home for most businessmen who lived in the city's preferred residential areas. And in the distance, the crests of timbered mountains rose up on the horizon.

He led me into the store, and it was a portrait of style and class, complete with a red carpet. Even the furnishings were elegant. It was the kind of place where a business executive could feel comfortable and high society would feel right at home.

I stood there. I looked around. I had a sinking feeling. I glanced toward Spencer and said softly, "I don't want to do this."

He looked bewildered and perplexed. "Why not?" Spencer asked.

"I don't want to be in a store," I said. "I didn't know you were planning another men's department store. I've worked in one already, and I can't do it again."

His shoulders relaxed, and he laughed. "Don't worry," he said, "You won't be in the store. You'll be out on the streets just like you were selling books. Only this time, you will be knocking on the doors of Nashville's upper scale businessmen. You won't be selling twenty-dollar books. You'll be selling suits that cost hundreds of dollars apiece. Some of the presidents and CEOs may be willing to spend as much as a thousand dollars or more .

I was feeling better all the time. I did not relish the thought of being forced to spend my workdays cooped up inside, not even inside a beautiful, well-appointed store like the one where we were standing. Who wanted to sit in a store and wait for the next customer to stroll through the door?

I wanted to go out and find them.

I understood the basic concept Spencer Hays had in mind, and I firmly believed that it would work. When I was working for

Cain-Sloan, I didn't just wait on people. I didn't try to sell them anything. I did not pressure customers or twist their arms in an effort to convince them that they should purchase a suit along with an array of quality accessories. I simply introduced them to our brands of fine merchandise and provided customers with the opportunity to buy what they knew they really needed.

If they came to buy a shirt, I helped them select the right color, preferably several colors. Then, of course, I pointed out that a wardrobe would not be complete without the proper ties for each shirt they bought, the right belt, and maybe even the right socks.

A businessman who had worked his way to the top wanted to look like a million dollars, and he was grateful to have a professional clothier around to show him exactly how to capture that million-dollar image.

Our job as sales people was to sit down with Nashville's most successful executives and educate them on the benefits associated with wearing tailored suits. All we had to do was spend a few minutes in their offices, offer our services as their personal tailor, and invite them to come down to the store and examine our line of fabrics, choose a particular style and color, then be properly fitted for a custom look. In addition, these businessmen would also find a line of high fashion accessories from shirts and ties, to belts and socks in the store. A million-dollar look could easily lose its touch of class if a cuff on his shirt happened to be frayed, or if the color in his tie had faded or, even worse, become out of date and no longer in style.

The concept made a lot of sense as long as I didn't feel trapped inside the store. Others could handle the fine accessories. I wanted to sell the fine suits door to door, and it was now apparent that Spencer wanted me on the streets as well. My attitude changed immediately. The sinking feeling that had overwhelmed me when I walked into the store passed as easily and as quickly as a bellyache. I had endured Cain-Sloan as temporary employment. Now I was on the threshold of a bold new beginning. Nothing about my life would ever be considered temporary again.

I started to work the next day for a company founded by a great thinker, a master recruiter and manager of sales people; a man who possessed the uncanny ability to tie all of the viable and critical details into a single big picture. The business had a vision based on a strong, purposeful idea and a distinct difference in the marketplace. But it didn't have a name.

When he was growing up, Spencer Hays had a Sunday School teacher named Tom James. His nickname was "Bronco," and he refereed a lot of high school football and basketball games. Spencer was an outstanding athlete who had earned a scholarship to TCU on a basketball scholarship, and he regarded Tom James as one of his mentors as he grew to manhood. The man had a son, Tom Ed James, who, besides Spencer, was one of the three sales people in place when the store officially opened for business.

On the sales staff were Tom James, Mack Isbell, and myself. All of us had sold books during the summer for the Southwestern Company, and that was obviously the one common thread that held us all together. That, no doubt, was the reason why Spencer had decided to hire us as his vanguard of sales people. He had been privy to our summer sales reports and had witnessed our results first hand. He felt quite comfortable with the fact that we all had experience in making cold calls and knocking on doors hour after hour. He believed that we had the work ethic, the self-motivation, and ability to build a solid foundation in a relatively short time.

But what was the company's name? We had to have something official printed on our business cards. A team of no-name sales people from a no-name company had absolutely no way to make a difference in the Nashville marketplace.

Spencer adamantly refused to name the company after himself. He was far too humble to ever do that. He looked at me. My name was McEachern and much too difficult to spell.

He glanced at Mack Isbell, who had a degree in agriculture and had been on the road, selling agricultural products for several years. He was a man of the earth and looked the part. Mack's name did not possess the sophistication that Spencer wanted to infuse in his business.

Spencer's eyes settled on Tom Ed James. Tom James, he said, had the perfect ring. It was simple. It was easy to spell. It was easy to remember. With the flourish of Spencer's signature on an official document, the company at last had a name.

My life as a sales person for the Tom James Company had begun. Spencer could not yet walk away from the Southwestern Company. His position was too critical. His sales success was too important, and Southwestern could not afford to let him go or lose him. Spencer Hays, quite frankly, was making too much money. And he was plowing virtually all of it into his new business. He kept his focus on books.

He left the fate of the Tom James Company in our hands. We rarely saw Spencer except for breakfast meetings on Saturday morning. His concentration may have been on the books, but he was watching from afar. The business was constantly evolving, and he almost always finished breakfast with a new idea, a new thought, or a new approach to moving the business forward. Spencer Hays listened to us. We were out on the cutting edge of a revolutionary and ever-changing kind of business. We could tell him what worked and didn't work, and he always knew how to re-energize our efforts and make our sales calls work more effectively.

Representatives from a number of tailor shops scattered across the county came to Nashville to train us on trends, fabrics, the art of selecting the right body style for a suit, and the science of taking the correct measurements in order to ensure that we always delivered distinctive custom clothes for a discriminating client.

I learned quickly to immediately check the executive's clothes when I walked into his office. If he was wearing a Brooks Brothers style, I could lose his business forever if I had the audacity to come back with a suit tailored in a Louis Roth style. My goal was not to sell him a one-time suit. It was to keep selling him suits for the rest of his life. He had to like me. He had to trust the Tom James

Company. He would be writing a rather sizable check. There was no room for mistakes.

Spencer decided to keep the store open for six days a week with each sales person staying inside, working behind the counter, and overseeing the operation for two days a week and on every third Saturday.

I did not like the decision. I dreaded those days when it was my turn to remain inside the store. But it was fair, and it was equitable.

We were finally in business and had customers walking through the door as soon as we opened up for business. Ironically, I sold my first suit on the first day I was in the store. It wasn't a real surprise. We had quality, and Nashville respected quality. On my second day in the store, I sold three suits to Billy Bob Robinson, who had risen through the ranks to become sales manager for the Southwestern Company. I was ringing up a few sales, earning a small salary, and pocketing a small commission. But my heart longed to be outside, on the streets, in the parking lot, in the elevators, in somebody else's office.

Tom James was a young attorney who had been named manager of the operation. He was a really good sales person and looked the part, dressing better than any of us, other than Spencer, of course. However, he did not like making sales call after sales call for eight hours a day. His preference was to stay in the store, look cool, calm, and collected, present our fine line of accessories, and work with those businessmen who walked in to be measured for the suits we had sold. He had never practiced law and had always hoped that someday he would be able to open and manage a fast food restaurant.

While we were all still selling books, Tom had even approached Spencer privately and told him about his idea. He thought that maybe Spencer might be inclined to invest in such a project.

"I have a better idea," Spencer said.

"What's that?"

"Instead of opening a fast food restaurant, why don't you go into the clothing business with me?"

"I've never sold suits."

"You've never sold hamburgers either."

So here he was. After a few weeks, Tom and I discreetly agreed on a new arrangement that made life a lot more palatable for both of us. I took his days out of the store, and he took my days inside. Both of us were convinced that we had the better end of the deal.

On my first day as an outside sales person, Spencer Hays went with me, which was exactly the way I had hoped it would be. He was smooth. He was sincere. He knew how to make an effective presentation, and he was, above all things, believable. We called on about ten or twelve customers, most of whom were attorneys and professional people he already counted among his friends. They were easy to know. Easy to impress. Easy to sell. Then I was on my own.

In those days, Nashville was an easy-going, slow-paced town on the threshold of becoming a major city in the South. People living next door, on the sidewalks, and even at work either had time for you or were willing to make time for you. It was not difficult to meet with any of the top-level business professionals in Nashville. They would at least give me ten or fifteen minutes even if that meant they had to work an extra ten to fifteen minutes at the end of the day.

I drove to Life & Casualty Insurance Tower that rose for thirty stories above the Nashville cityscape. I went straight to the top where the executives had their offices. I knew I was free to make my presentation to anyone, and, as I rode the elevator skyward, I thought that it might be advisable to call first on some junior executives where I could practice, polish, and perfect my pitch.

I thought about it. Then I discarded the idea. I walked into the office of the first President and CEO I could find. No sales pitch. No pressure. I simply sat down, and we got to know each other. He liked Tennessee, he said. He loved Walking Horses and happened to own a few. He listened diligently to my presentation without any interruption. He was polite and respectful. It was easy to see why he was the most powerful man in the company.

He nodded at the right times and asked the right questions. He was impressed with the quality of my samples. I was ready to wrap up my first sale. He leaned back and smiled. "No, thanks," he said.

Mister President and CEO hadn't bought anything. Then again, he hadn't walked out from behind his desk and slammed a door in my face either. For whatever reason, I left his office feeling good about the Tom James Company and my ability to help it grow. The formula for success was the same for selling suits as it had been for selling books.

It was still a numbers game. The man who makes the most sales calls, makes the most sales. The only time I didn't make fifteen calls during a day were those times when I made twenty.

I kept knocking on doors and making friends out of strangers. On occasion, I would call ahead for appointments. Mostly I didn't. I would just drive around until I found a nice, high-rise office building, ride the elevator to the top, and work my way back down to the ground floor, walking into offices, shaking hands with each company's top executives, and inviting them down to the store to examine hundreds of fabrics and determine which of them properly and appropriately captured their own individual style.

Clothes did indeed make the man. If he looked good, he felt good. A businessman could be facing a mountain of problems, but if his wardrobe were fashionable, stylish, and up to date, few would ever realize the size of the conflicts that confronted him. We made sure that Mister Executive had a broad array of fabrics and colors from which to choose. Wools. Wool and silk blends. Linen. Hopsack wool for blazers. Stripes. Checks. Plain. Three buttons, two buttons, or maybe even a single button. Broad in the shoulders. Tailored at the waist. Pleated pants. Or straight legged. Double-breasted. It depended on the style of the day.

Most of the businessmen were quite intrigued with our concept. They did not like to shop. They never took time to shop. They preferred for somebody to cater to them and respect their stature in the business world. At least ninety-five percent of them had never owned a custom suit, and they were fascinated with the idea of having their own personal tailor. We took impeccable measurements and filed them away. The first suit, I believed, must be perfect and the next suits even better.

Always, it was the same. Look for the highest executive I could find in the company. He was the man I wanted to see. His was the image that counted most, and he could afford us. A custom tailored Tom James suit was generally two to three times more expensive than the ones found in the South's top men's stores.

When we began, the average suit sold for a hundred to a little more than two hundred dollars. The dollar figure doesn't sound very expensive, but that price in today's market, after fifty year's worth of inflation, would be a thousand to two thousand dollars.

During those early days, I left nothing to chance. So often, a businessman would tell me that he might well drop by the store on his way home and take a closer look at our selection of fabrics before making a final selection. I had no objection. But I didn't leave until we set a firm appointment time. I told him that I would be there, meet him, and take care of his clothing needs myself. I did not want him showing up during lunch, after work, or some Saturday morning when I was out riding elevators up and down buildings. He was my customer. If he bought a suit, and I was convinced that he would, I wanted him buying from me and no one else. That was the creed of a determined sales person. It felt great being one.

At the end of May, we received our summer line of fabrics. We had made sure that a lot of top executives in Nashville were well dressed during a Southern winter. I decided to call on each of them, as quickly as possible, and find out if the Tom James Company could outfit them properly for the warm Southern months as well. My new pitch would be the same as my old one: *Come in to the store when it's convenient. Give me a day and a time, and I will meet you there. You loved your first suit. You'll love your next one just as well.*

I made my first call, and the company chief executive at the other end of the line listened politely, and then said brusquely, "You already have my measurements, don't you?"

"Yes sir."

"Then bring your book of swatches to my office."

"You'll have a better selection at the store."

"You know me."

"Yes sir."

"Then you know what I like."

His message was short. And it was clear. He was busy. He had meetings to attend, a business to run, hundreds of people to manage, and no telling how many short-fused, critical deadlines hanging over his head. He didn't say that. But I knew what he meant.

I did as I was told. I drove to his office, walked in with my portfolio of fabrics, and set it on his desk. He glanced through it and said, "I like this one, and this one."

Within a handful of minutes he had purchased two suits, and I was back out the door. That sales call was my *Eureka* moment. I had listened to what the man said. I understood the urgency in his voice. And it was quickly apparent that every other businessman in town was no doubt facing the same problem. Time. Or lack of it. I began a new tactic.

No longer did I invite any professional businessman to the store. I carried those hundreds of fabric swatches and colors to them. I had their measurements. Whether they realized it or not, they were in the market for a cooler wardrobe because, just around the corner, the blistering sun of summertime was on its way to once again scorch the streets of Nashville. I saved them a step. In reality, it was several steps. And they appreciated it.

By the end of June, I had sold seventy-two suits, which was more than the entire sales team had sold collectively for April and May. That kind of sudden and unexpected success immediately changed the way we thought and looked at our business.

I went out and bought a leather briefcase about eighteen inches long, eighteen inches wide, and four inches deep, then stuffed it with as many fabric swatches as it would hold. When I walked out of my home every morning, I was no longer just a sales person. My patience had paid off. I had become a traveling clothing store.

Takeaways From the Chapter

- *In this chapter, Jim begins to develop patience with his situation. He believed he needed something to happen in a hurry, but that didn't materialize. He was going to have to sacrifice some time in order to attain his goal of Spencer's mentorship. How many "opportunities" are there out there that I have missed because I was simply not willing to "wait for" them? How often am I not willing to make a sacrifice in order to have an opportunity?*

- *Jim states: "The formula for success was the same for selling suits as it had been for selling books. It was still a numbers game. The man who makes the most sales calls, makes the most sales." Is there a deeper truth behind this statement? What is it? How does it apply to me?*

- *Jim had a eureka moment because he listened to his customers. Listening to his customers changed the focus of Tom James sales and catapulted the company to extraordinary heights. What are my customers telling me and how can I use that information to revolutionize my company?*

CHAPTER 10

Choosing to Become the World's Foremost Expert On Building a Custom Clothing Business

As I thought back, the die had actually been cast when I was thirteen years old, drifting from the streets of West Texas towns that no longer had any definition for me. They weren't going any place, and, it seemed at the time, neither was I. On the far edges of the prairies, the world simply came to an end and the roads all came to a stop. When I awoke each morning, nothing had changed. If I went to bed hungry, I was still hungry. If I had not gone to school yesterday, there was little reason for me to go today. I sometimes thought that I was spending more time enrolling in a new school than going to class. But as I wandered from street corner to street corner, from one odd job to another, I had a lot of time to daydream, and it became my favorite pastime.

I made up my mind that someday I would be the best in the world at something. At anything. But what would it be? I had no idea.

The thought struck me that I just might have a chance to become the best baseball player of all time. I had read stories and books about Babe Ruth, and his early life was no better than mine had been. He had grown up above a saloon in Baltimore, and since he was so incorrigible, he was placed in a Catholic orphanage. His circumstances were even worse than mine. But on the playground, no one could hit a baseball as far as Babe Ruth or throw it any harder. As he grew to manhood, the baseballs he hit went farther and usually out of sight, and his pitches were even faster. The Boston Red Sox took notice, signed him as a pitcher, eventually traded him to the New York Yankees, and Ruth would be recognized then, as now, as the greatest to ever play the game.

Babe Ruth hadn't played in a long time. Maybe I would be the one to replace him. At the age of thirteen, it was easy to picture myself as a great hitter like Ruth, as someone who could toss his bat aside, come in, and pitch every fourth day. But then, I always had owned a pretty good imagination.

I concentrated on baseball until I reached the eighth grade, playing during the summers on teams with grown men. We didn't have any baseball diamonds; we just squared off out in somebody's pasture on Sunday afternoons. I may have been too young and too small, but for the most part, I held my own. After all, two teams needed at least eighteen players between them, and one ball club or another could always fit me in. The men liked the way I hit the ball, and I could hit it a long way for my age and size.

The first time I played for an actual team, I was past my fourteenth birthday and stepping on the field for the South Junior High School in Abilene. It didn't take long to make a quick evaluation of the talent around me. I was pretty good. There were a lot of kids better, and I figured there were probably thousands of kids around the country even better than they were. About the best I could do was hold down the job as backup catcher for an eighth grade team. I learned a major lesson in a hurry: I might someday be the best in the world at something. It would not be baseball.

During the next five years, from age fourteen to nineteen, I found myself without any roots, and I never felt as though either my mother or my father loved me. Both were in the midst of multiple marriages, fighting hard to survive with too little food, too much responsibility, too few opportunities, and absolutely no money. For my father, it was one miserable little job after another. My mother was battling to hang on with a husband who gambled away some of his weekly paycheck and drank away the rest of it. For me, those years became null and void.

I didn't think much about being the best in the world at anything anymore. Life became a series of faltering steps. Take one forward and two back and that was on a good day. I don't recall having many good days.

My view of the top was lost in a fog. As I grew older, I again felt those stirrings deep down in my belief that I could do something well if I could only figure out what it was. I was given a break when a kind-hearted registrar offered to let me take my GED in order to enroll in college. That gave me a little hope. On my Army test, I had ranked in the ninety-eighth percentile, and that was encouraging.

But in my mind, and among my ambitions, I wasn't able to pin down any skill or job or potential career that I was actually good at or had a chance to find success. I taught school. That wasn't it. I decided to manage a supermarket. That wasn't it. I peddled snow cones. That certainly wasn't it. I inventoried beauty supplies. That wasn't it. I sold books for the Southwestern Company and thought *this might be it*. I liked the travel. I liked new places. I liked meeting people. After awhile, I didn't even mind cold calls. I sold a lot of books and, for me, made a lot of money. But, alas, the summer came to an end, my case of books was closed, I drove home, and I was right back where I started. My foray into the world of sales would last only until August wound down and the student sales people headed back to college again.

Then along came Spencer Hays. Along came his new idea for a clothing business. He had confidence in me, and my blind ambition was to prove to Spencer that his faith in me had not been misplaced. Here was a foundation on which I could build, and I started building before the door opened on his first store.

I read every book and magazine article I could find about improving my life and my opportunities in business. One passage immediately caught my attention. It had been written about a man who possessed a brilliant mind but a paralyzed body. For years, he had been trapped in an iron lung, lying flat on his back, unable to breathe on his own, and during that time, with nothing else to do, he had become recognized the world over as the foremost expert on guppies. He had become so renowned that he was able to make a nice living financially by providing information to those who owned guppies.

The theory was, the article said, that anyone could become the world's foremost expert at something if he studied the subject thirty minutes a day for ten years. So that was the formula I had been missing. I was running late, I decided. I had a lot of catching up to do.

I thought it over, mulled the idea around in my mind a time or two, and came to the conclusion that I would spend an hour a day, not thirty minutes a day, and become the world's foremost expert and authority on building a custom clothing company within the next five years. Study twice as hard. Cut the time in half. It seemed a lot easier than I had thought. In fact, the formula seemed too easy. The hours would pass. So would the years. The formula worked. It was dead solid perfect.

I was greatly influenced by reading and understanding the Feldman Method, the process used by Ben Feldman as he built an incredible and almost unbelievable lifetime sales volume of $1.5 billion in the insurance business.

As it was written about him: "If you passed Ben Feldman on the street, you wouldn't have any inkling about his sales prowess. He was short, heavyset, and balding. When he spoke, his speech was slow and deliberate … with a distinctive lisp."

He did not look like a superstar. He was. What was different about Ben Feldman?

On Being Quiet, Slow and Unimpressive

When I first met Jim I would have used the following three descriptors: quiet, slow and not particularly dynamic. Over time, however, I would find that I just didn't understand who he was or what he was doing. He was quiet only because he was listening so intently to me and my story. He was simply seeking to understand who I was as a person. Because of this when he did speak, he spoke more loudly into my life than anyone I've ever known. I had the impression that he was a slow moving person because he famously talked slowly and moved slowly but he was, in fact, quite the opposite. He was moving toward accomplishing his goals in a very deliberate manner. This only appeared to be slow to me. The truth is he accomplished more, faster than anyone I've ever known. Finally, I did not think of him as being particularly impressive. When I first met him, I didn't think to myself this guy is going to change my life. Yet, no human being has made a larger impression on my life.

As told by close friend, Frank Sharp

His drive. His dedication. His commitment. Ben would always say that he had worn out twelve thousand pairs of shoes in making his very significant mark in the world of insurance sales. He worked twelve hours a day for seven days a week, then went home and read or studied for another two hours every night. Each week, without fail, he made thirty to forty face-to-face, person-to-person cold calls. He never depended on any warm-up telephone calls before he knocked on a door, no letters introducing himself or asking for an appointment, no warm referrals to give him credibility with his customers. These were, said a newsletter for financial advisors: "Walk-right-in, ask-to-see-the-owner, no-apologies cold calls."

Feldman's drive began early in life. He fell in love with a young lady and asked her to marry him.

"How will you support me?" she asked.

He didn't know. He hadn't thought about it. Ben Feldman sold butter and eggs door-to-door. He would have loved to make a few financial investments to improve his lot in life. He didn't have a lot of capital, mostly just the few bills wadded up in his pocket.

Feldman, with few other options in the workplace, became an insurance sales person with New York Life. It was hard, starting from scratch. He struggled mightily. But each day, each month, each year got a little better.

There may have been better sales people at New York Life. None of them could outwork Ben Feldman. He became the first in the nation to sell five million dollars worth of insurance in a single year. He became the first to sell ten million dollars worth of insurance during the same time frame. He became the first to sell twenty million dollars, then twenty-five million dollars worth of insurance between January and January. Ben Feldman kept working, was never satisfied with his past efforts, and sold fifty million dollars worth of insurance a year for several years.

In the insurance business, he was king. He wrote in his book, *The Feldman Method*, "I rarely use the telephone because he may not want to see me. I have a better chance of seeing the man I want to see if I do go … On calls, I just walk right in … and my first barrier is usually the switchboard operator or the receptionist. On the phone, a switchboard operator can stop me dead. But face-to-face, the odds are I'll get by. And when I go, I may leave something with her. You know what it is? It's a pair of little golden slippers. She doesn't know what they are until I've left and she's opened the box. Then I usually get a thank you note. From that time on, I get in.

"I'm very frank, very open. I just say I want to meet her boss, whatever his name may be. (And you'd better know his name.) The receptionist ordinarily announces me, but it's a cold call, and the odds are he doesn't want to see me. I get thrown out of more places.

"There are many ways of saying, 'No.' He probably won't see me the first time. That isn't so bad. Why? Because I'm coming back, and when I come back, I'm no longer a stranger. I've been here before."

Ben Feldman may have been a stranger to the business executive. The business executive was no stranger to Ben. Before each call, he studied and prepared, using Dun & Bradstreet to determine the executive's name, the names of all of his key employees, the corporate structure, and the approximate sales volume of the company. He had a goal. He was relentless.

An executive might keep saying, "No." That did not bother Ben Feldman. He kept right on coming back, again and again. In time, his biggest supporter was the receptionist herself. He wrote: "If I call once or twice more, and if the answer is still, 'No,' she'll probably begin to feel sorry for me. Now she's on my team. She'll do her best to open the door for me. Particularly if she feels I'd be helping her boss."

That, I had discovered, was really what sales were all about. We take the time and ask the right questions to find out what a person needs, and then we help him acquire it. In fact, I never wanted anyone to buy something from me unless he or she needed it. Many times when I was on the street selling books as an eighteen-year-old college student, someone would have pity on me and say, "Sure, I'll buy a book and help you out."

I always told them, "No, I don't sell the books for people to help me out. I only want you to buy this book if you sincerely want it, need it, and believe it can help you in life. If you think the book can be beneficial to you, I urge you to buy it. If you don't want it or need it, you won't hurt my feelings if you say, 'No.'"

I also recognized the importance of carefully studying the sales situation and learning how to read people. After ten thousand presentations with books under my arm, I got to be fairly good at it. I set a rule for myself that if we were not making some sort of positive connection in the first seven minutes, I would just thank them for their time and be on my way. I did not want to be wasting their time or my time.

Such an attitude, I realized from day one, would be the great lesson I could practice and, in time, pass on to other sales people who were working for Tom James. I didn't want to tell them. I wanted to teach them. I wanted to lead them.

In my own heart, I was developing my own set of values in the business world.

1. I would never have anything to say bad about anybody.

2. I would do my best to see people not as they were but what they could become, and treat them that way.

3. I would encourage people and never degrade them. Time and again, I used these phrases to encourage our sales people: "That's a great idea. I wish I'd thought of that. Tell me more." Such responses can actually inspire them to continue developing new ideas. The ideas may not all work. But some can make a great difference in the building of a great company. On the other hand, I was convinced that the good efforts and vision of a sales person could easily be stifled if the only thing he or she heard was: "We've already tried that, and it doesn't work." Or, "Where did you come up with a stupid idea like that?" Or, "That's a waste of our time." From that moment on, a great idea they may have for the future will be tucked away in their minds, and you'll never hear it. That's a shame because it might be the one idea that can change the direction and streamline the building of a good company.

4. I would never respond to either a sales client or another Tom James sales person before I carefully thought through the response. Too often, statements or decisions made in haste can backfire on you.

5. I would never confuse activity with results.

6. I would never allow myself to become distracted by trivial matters.

7. I wanted to give Tom James sales people hope that our great vision for the future could indeed become a reality.

8. I believed that great leaders did not offer excuses, nor did they accept them.

9. I believed that it would ultimately be my responsibility to keep the Tom James organization growing in people, in sales, in profits.

10. I had a vision, and now it was imperative for me to set specific goals to help our sales force and me better understand and relate to that vision.

11. I wanted to promote a strong self-image among our sales people. If they could actually see themselves as being able to accomplish their goals in business and in life, then I had no doubt they could become as successful as they had always wanted to be.

12. I even had my own definition of *success*. To me, it was the progressive realization of worthwhile and pre-determined goals. The key word was worthwhile. In order for me to define something as worthwhile, it must fit within my value system: my beliefs, the things that were important to me in my relationship with God, my family, my friends, my co-workers, and our customers. If my ultimate objective was not good for them, then I did not believe that it was worthwhile to pursue.

Spencer Hays had been right all along. He had been preaching for years that you didn't build good companies. You built good employees. They were the ones who would build great companies. If I wanted to become the world's foremost expert on building a custom clothing business, then it was essential for me to concentrate on making sure that our sales people had the tools, the skills, the knowledge, the information, the inspiration, the attitude, the personal sales goals, and the commitment they needed to take the Tom James Company to where Spencer and I wanted to see it go.

When Spencer assembled his first sales team, he was paying us a salary of seven hundred and fifty dollars a month. It wasn't a lot but none of us complained. He was the one risking a major out-of-pocket investment, and we all knew that if the company grew as quickly as we all hoped it would, our salaries would continue to grow as well. None of us were worried. We believed in Spencer and trusted him implicitly.

By 1968, early in the year, Spencer walked into our Nashville store, and met with us as a group. He had a new compensation plan, he said, with two options available. We could each make our own decision and take whichever option appealed to us individually.

Spencer wasn't pushing either one. We could remain on salary. It was guaranteed. Or, we could go on straight commission, based on our personal sales, while also being compensated with an override on the sales of any team members we were asked to manage or supervise.

There was potential. There was no guarantee. A salary was money in the bank each month. Those commissions sounded like a good deal only if a sales person had faith in his company, his product, himself, and his ability to sell.

Lindy Watkins and I didn't hesitate. We wanted to go forward and build our financial future on commissions. The other two stayed with their salaries.

The decisions were made with no regrets. Lindy and I might have felt that we were suddenly in a precarious financial situation, but neither of us had any concerns or second thoughts.

Our future was in our own hands, which was the way it should be. The sky was the limit.

At the moment, however, we were still on the ground floor. I carefully mapped out the plans I envisioned for myself and the Tom James Company and continued to read every success-oriented, sales-idea, and motivational book I could find. It was my initial goal to pattern my Tom James endeavors after those who had already gained recognition and riches in the business world.

I had long been infatuated by the impact that Ben Feldman had made on the art of selling. Any man who had the ability, the audacity, and the relentless drive to sell fifty million dollars worth of life insurance in a year was the kind of man I wanted to follow. I read every word and every passage in his book, and then I read them again. Once. Twice. So many times I lost count. If he achieved that kind of success, it was not beyond my reach. But here was the problem.

Ben Feldman sold a million dollars worth of life insurance each week, and I had no idea what his commission might be or the amount of commissions he earned from those sales. I began to talk with every insurance sales person I knew or met in an effort to determine how much clothing I needed to sell in order to create the same kind of earning power that Ben Feldman had achieved. After a few calculations, I finally concluded that, working on the Tom James commission, I would have to personally sell a million dollars worth of clothing in a year to pocket the same amount of money. That meant eighty to ninety thousand dollars in sales every month.

No one at Tom James had ever accomplished that number before. But it was possible. At least, on paper, it was possible.

When I sat down the next Saturday morning to consider the possibilities of my own sales efforts, that was my primary goal, and I wrote it down at the top of the list. *Eighty to ninety thousand dollars in sales a month*. It was set in stone. Whether I could or could not reach the goal depended solely on me.

I had first purchased a copy of Dale Carnegie's book, *How to Win Friends and Influence People*, when I heard him speak at Abilene High School. I was just a young man at the time, had other things on my mind, never thought I had much of a chance to ever get out of West Texas, and believed that my dreams for success were little more than fanciful dreams. I had the book. I stuck it back on a shelf somewhere and forgot it.

Now that I was helping Spencer build a blueprint for the Tom James Company, I discovered the book again. Some of the passages hit me right between the eyes. It threw open the door of possibilities and encouraged me to walk through.

I had spent four days with Spencer in his library, and he was usually on the phone, keeping track of his book sales person at the Southwestern Company. It was a full time job. Students in strange towns. Students homesick. Students having a lot of luck. Students ready to pack up and leave. Students who hadn't sold a book. Students who were selling books all day long. He dealt with the discouraged with the same calm but enthusiastic voice and attitude as he did with the encouraged.

While he was on the phone, I sat across his desk, quietly reading the words of Dale Carnegie. He hung up and, as he turned around, I said, "Let me read this to you." I was excited.

I read the first half of the paragraph, paused a moment, and Spencer quoted the second half of the paragraph from memory. He didn't miss a word. I had only read the book. He had memorized it.

Spencer told me that *How to Win Friends and Influence People* was the first book he had ever read from cover to cover. It had obviously made an impression on him. It was making an impression on me as well.

As I continued to watch Spencer in business situations, meeting with clients, with customers, with his sales people, I realized that he was applying every principle and nugget of advice he had learned from Dale Carnegie every day of his life.

It was working for him. It might as well work for me. I kept the book with me. I carried it everywhere I went in town or out of town. I read the words of Carnegie often and began jotting down specific applications I could use in every day-to-day, face-to-face situation I encountered in business. And I would do so for the next forty-four years.

I had bought a copy of Frank Bettger's book, *How I Raised Myself from Failure to Success in Selling* back in 1955 when I was knocking on doors and carrying a case full of books for the Southwestern Company. It had greatly inspired me then. At Tom James, however, I really began to understand the lessons Bettger was teaching, especially when he wrote of enthusiasm. He said to act enthusiastically on every sales call and, before you realized it, you would become enthusiastic. Bettger said that if I doubled my enthusiasm, I could double my income and my happiness. It was simple. It was effective.

His ideas, along with principles designed by other great books, would change my life and the way I conducted my business at Tom James. My own formula was quite easy to follow. Read books that could make a difference. Make notes. Study hard. Learn the main points.

Write down a specific plan about how I could personally apply them on every sales call I made and whenever I was called upon to train a Tom James sales person.

Then read the books again. Neither they nor their messages would ever grow old or obsolete. My shelves were filled with such books as

The Greatest Sales person in the World by Og Mandino, *Secrets of Closing Sales* by Charles Roth, *The Richest Man in Babylon* by George Clason, *The Common Denominator of Success* by Albert Gray, *As a Man Thinketh* by James Allen, and *Man's Search for Meaning* by Viktor Frankl. These books were absolute classics in the ever-changing world of business but had withstood the test of time.

What worked in 1920 could be just as effective in 1970 or 2020. The world does change. People don't. The way clients and customers should be treated doesn't. For so many, success is the end result of a person's attitude and determination to succeed, the commitment to do more than is necessary, the confidence to take on a new challenge every day, the ability to stay the course no matter how difficult it might be. In reality, a person has no limitations except the ones that he makes for himself. Many stumble along the way, but I was dead set on following the advice of Thomas Edison: "I start where the last man left off."

In my drive to become the world's foremost expert in building a custom clothing business, I understood the importance of connecting with people, with discovering what someone needed, then being able to provide it. My success would be based on turning customers into friends. It was about leadership. I never considered myself to be a leader, but opportunity and circumstances persuaded me to become one.

I am sure that the ultimate success of the Tom James Company wasn't depending solely on me. But I thought it was. I worked as hard as if I owned the company. I kept an eye on the money as though it came from my own pocket. I did what Spencer asked me to do whenever he thought a change would be worthwhile for us all to pursue.

For the next twenty-six years – from 1967 through 1992 – the company's average annual growth rate in sales was twenty-nine percent. There was never a single year when the business did not grow. I should have been pleased. I wasn't. I thought we could do better.

Takeaways From the Chapter

- *Jim was a reader and a student (see appendix 2 for more on this). He was shaped by the books that he both read and studied. What books am I reading right now? How many times have I read them? What notes have I written down to help me succeed? What have I truly taken in from my reading and applied with regularity for success?*
- *Reading, like everything Jim did, was filled with purpose. He wanted to be the foremost person in the world on sales . . . later in leadership. He devoted time to the study of these subjects every day. What am I willing to study for 30 minutes a day for the next ten years in order to achieve excellence?*
- *Jim states: Success is "the progressive realization of worthwhile and pre-determined goals." He emphasizes that the most important aspect for him is the "worthwhile" portion of the definition. On what basis should I determine what is ultimately "worthwhile"?*

CHAPTER 11

Choosing Life's Priorities

Early in my life, I began to establish my priorities even though I probably did not realize at the time what I was doing. My grandfather would sit on the porch and tell me Bible stories, and my grandmother would gather us children together and read the Bible to us. It was more than entertainment. She was instilling deep within my heart and soul the kind of spiritual and ethical priorities that would ultimately guide me for the rest of my life. They were an integral part of me long before I understood their significance or the role they would ultimately play in my business career.

As a boy, it had never been important or necessary for me to set any kind of priorities at all. Through the seventh grade, my time priorities were determined by my class schedules – in the school or out on the playground during recess. During the summer months, I simply did whatever work or jobs around the farm that my grandfather asked me to do. By the eighth grade my circumstances dictated my priorities without me ever having to make any deliberate choices. Go live with my mother and another one of her husbands. Go live with my father and hope he could provide for the two of us. When I looked up one day and realized that two cans of hominy were all the food in the house, my hunger dictated that I find a job washing dishes in a café. It wasn't much money. It was two meals a day. I could not complain.

I had never thought I would be able to go to college. I hadn't even finished high school and no diploma hung on my wall. But a friend at church persuaded me to go see about enrolling at Howard Payne University. The registrar persuaded me to take my GED. Then she saw my score and made the decision that I could start attending classes. Even when I sold books during the summer for the Southwestern Company, somebody would always train me, tell me where to go, how many doors I should knock on each day, what I should say in my presentation, what I needed to charge for the books; when I needed to come home. Someone else hired me. Someone else paid me. Someone else fired me. I had always been a puppet. Someone else was always pulling the strings.

In reality, I reached the age of thirty without ever having to make any choices or establish any priorities in my life. I was simply wandering from one job to another, from one set of circumstances to another, from one dead end to another. I had no control of my existence; my life was just dragging me along behind it.

Somewhere along the way, however, without me ever understanding it, I came to realize that my grandparents, my neighbors, my teachers, my commanding officer in the Army had all influenced those intrinsic values that I had grown to possess.

It was not until I joined Spencer Hays and the Tom James Company that I began to really understand the importance associated with establishing priorities, considering the possibilities that lay before me in a career that would captivate me for the next half-century, and nailing down the series of goals necessary to turn those possibilities into realities.

These were the sixties, a time when the great Coaching Legend Vince Lombardi was leading the Green Bay Packers to five professional football championships during a span of seven years. He was a great teacher, a great motivator, an inspiration to those in business, as well as in football.

Darnell Institute at Northwestern University had produced a film entitled, *Second Effort*, and it focused on Lombardi explaining his underlying theme of achieving success year after year in the NFL. I sat in the darkness of a film room, and over and over, I kept watching him talk to his football players during the beginning of training camp. More than two dozen times I watched and listened to the words of Lombardi. His message was potent. And it had a great impact on me.

Vince Lombardi stood on the field with that chiseled granite face of his, looked every player in the eye, and never wavered. He said in a voice full of grit and gravel, "These are the three most important things in your lives. God. Family. And the Green Bay Packers. In that order."

I never fathomed the thought of achieving the greatness or success of such a well-known and respected coach, but still I began to wonder just how I could apply a modified version of his wisdom to my own career. Then I had the answer. It, too, was simple and potent. From that moment on, I knew that the three most important things in my life were and forever would be:

God. Family. And the Tom James Company. In that order.

For the first time in my life, I had established my own personal priorities. I felt comfortable with them. They did not change or revise my character at all. In reality, they were an extension of the values instilled within me by those who reached out along the way and helped me toward manhood.

I thought: If God is number one, what does it mean? I concluded that I needed to get to know God as well as I possibly could and made the decision to read and study the Bible on a consistent basis. Not when I thought about it. Not when I could find the time. Not when it was convenient for me. But every day without fail. The words of the Bible became more important to me than my sales presentation, and I studied them with great intensity.

My grandparents had first taught me about God and told me that God actually loved me as an individual and believed I was worthy of His love. It made me want to know Him, honor Him, and worship Him. It boiled down to two commandments that I had read in the Bible time and again. I was convinced that it was my duty and responsibility to "love God with all of my heart, mind, and strength," and it was just as vital for me to "love my neighbor as myself."

Since God had risen to and would always remain as number one in my personal list of priorities, I determined to love him and be obedient to him in the same way that I wanted to be responsive in a positive way to other people. Some I knew. Most I didn't. It did not matter. All should be treated with dignity and respect. I took the approach that if I loved other people and acted in their best interests, I would do my best to find out what was important to them. I would then make it my business to help them acquire whatever they needed and feel comfortable that I was doing the right thing for them.

Second on my list of priorities was family.

I remembered the constant struggles of my mother and father as they tried to exist and survive in a world that was so difficult for them. No education. No money. Very little hope of ever finding a good job, much less a career. No opportunities. Theirs was a hard life without any breaks.

I could look back and see their mistakes. I did not want to repeat them. Their marriage had broken up. So had almost all of their other marriages. I vowed that I would never allow such unfortunate circumstances happen to my family.

I made a vow to work hard and ensure that my wife was the happiest woman in the world. It took me ten years to figure it out, but I never quit trying. This was one goal that could not be measured. Why? I had nothing comparable. It struck me that I had no idea how happy other wives might be, or if they were happy at all. I realized that a lot of people, even wives, kept smiling on the outside even when the pain and hurt ran deep on the inside.

I kept asking my wife what would make her happy. She never gave me an answer. I had to learn by trial and error. I noticed that when I wrote her little love notes, she would tape them to the inside of her cabinet doors or on the refrigerator. I noticed that she was much happier when she received them in the mail than when I hand-delivered them. So I wrote a lot of notes, and I bought a lot of stamps. Once I started, I never stopped. And she was happy.

I discovered that Arlene liked receiving flowers, but not just for her birthday or Mother's Day or on our anniversary. She liked having fresh-cut flowers delivered to her on random days of the year. Why? She realized that I hadn't felt obligated to send her flowers simply because it was a special occasion. So on ordinary days, out of the blue, without any reason at all, I would unexpectedly show up at the front door with flowers. And she was happy.

My wife and I and our children – Karen, Mike, Lynda, and Angie – took a lot of vacations, traveled down every long road we could find, and saw great chunks of America the beautiful. Mountains. Beaches. Big cities. Little cities. Historic places. Resorts. And theme parks. But, after awhile, after the children were grown and gone, I began to realize that Arlene liked cruises more than any other way of traveling.

However, I didn't plan the cruises. I simply made it a point to stop by a travel agency, pick up some brochures, and give them to her much like a gift. She had her choice of ships, islands, seashores, itineraries, and dates. Arlene did indeed like cruises. But what made her the happiest was choosing her own cruise.

One night just before bedtime, I would place a piece of candy on her pillow and place a brochure beside it. It would have the page open to the cruise I preferred. It was the one cruise she was delighted to let me select. We started in Copenhagen, Denmark, and, for eleven days, made stops in England, Ireland, Scotland, Iceland, Greenland, and back to New York. For eleven days, she resided in a balcony suite and was treated like royalty. No stress. No hassle. No pressure. No schedule. No packing and unpacking her suitcases. It was just Arlene, the ship, the ocean, and I. As far as she was concerned, the rest of the people didn't count. She was lost in a crowd and preferred it that way. She was happy. And that was important to me.

I never had an interest in or felt any kind of obligation to hang out with the guys at the end of a workday. Too often, it seemed as though a few of my co-workers were looking for any excuse possible to keep from going home. I couldn't wait to get home.

If my children had any activity going on during or after school, I put the event on my calendar at the office and did my best to show up when they expected me to be there and support them: football games, band concerts, wrestling matches, gymnastics, school plays. It didn't matter. I built my schedule around them. On Saturdays, we went to the zoo, had picnics, lay beneath shade trees in a park, paddled boats in the lake beneath Stone Mountain, and fed the ducks. Our excursions on the weekend didn't have to be expensive. We spent our time together. Those days did not have or ever need a price tag. They were priceless.

I did not neglect work. I made my calls and met my sales goals. When needed, I trained our sales people so they could meet their sales objectives as well. I worked to make sure that each year was more successful than the year before. We expanded. We grew. We built our sales and built our company. But I always knew, and Spencer always knew, that family came second to God but always ahead of Tom James.

As a boy and a young man, I had struggled financially. Arlene and I, early in our marriage, spent many weeks wondering if we would have enough money to pay the bills and put food on the table by the end of the week. A man is always on his way to the poor house when the best job he can find is driving a snow cone truck.

Even before we opened the door on our first Tom James store, I had made a firm commitment to myself that I would never allow Arlene or our children suffer financially again. My family was a priority. So was taking care of them.

A stock broker suggested that I buy a copy of "Interest and Annuities Tables." It might not have been interesting reading, but it absolutely fascinated me. Those columns with tables of numbers, printed page after page for over two hundred pages, provided me with a sound game plan I could use to bring a measure of financial freedom to my family.

I had always liked numbers and found the book to be a straight and narrow roadmap to the kind of security I had always dreamed about. These tables opened a door I never knew existed.

I discovered that if I could save ten to fifteen percent of my take-home salary each month, and if the mutual fund that held my money continued at its average growth rate, my net worth, after thirty-five years, would be more than four hundred thousand dollars. It got my attention. I never looked at money the same way again.

It was the first time I ever had a clue about how money could be multiplied in the financial marketplace. The growth formula I created for myself was fool proof, provided the stock market remained stable. It took into account the kind of commissions I expected to earn for myself. Here is the way I looked at my financial future.

1. Build Tom James.
2. Increase my sales.
3. Increase my salary through commissions.
4. Continue to invest ten to fifteen percent of that monthly salary as it continued to increase with the passing years.

And by the time I reached the retirement age of sixty-five, my investment would total four million dollars.

For a young man who had never had a lot of money, such a figure was staggering. I could not believe my eyes. I ran the numbers again and again. It was always the same. The secret was building the company, increasing my sales, and remaining consistent with my monthly investment. That revelation influenced every financial decision I made for the rest of my life.

Arlene and I did have to sacrifice in the beginning. Being able to invest ten percent was a major obstacle when I was only earning six hundred dollars a month. But Arlene and I stayed frugal, lived comfortably but modestly, watched our pennies, and stayed true to ourselves. Money may have been tight, but we were looking ahead with a lot more optimism than ever before.

We had a secure living now. I wanted to guarantee that my family would be comfortable in later years, too.

I made several critical decisions and would recommend them to anyone.

First, I never bought a house that cost more than I earned in a year, even though I might qualify for a house that cost two or three times more money. I did not have any interest in big house payments. I'd rather take that extra money and invest it.

Secondly, I never bought a car that cost more than what I earned in three months. When my yearly salary was seventy-eight hundred dollars, I knew that my limit to spend on a car was two thousand dollars. No more. Other sales people at Tom James, feeling richer than they had in a long time, were going out and buying Cadillacs. I was driving an old brown, second-hand automobile that only cost me nineteen hundred dollars. I was quietly placing the difference in a mutual fund. Others wondered why. I knew. I had my priorities straight.

My car only cost nineteen hundred dollars. My first house was in Powder Springs, twenty-five miles from Atlanta, was purchased for about seven thousand dollars because the price fit my formula. It had three bedrooms, a kitchen, a dining/family room, and a single bathroom. We lived on one side of the home and ate on the other. It sat on an acre of land in the shade of tall pine trees. I could have done better. I could have moved closer to downtown Atlanta and paid a lot more. I didn't want to. Extravagance would never be my style.

By carefully budgeting my money, the family and I were always able to afford to take weekend excursions, nice vacations in the summer, and invest for the future.

In 1970, I was reading in the fourth chapter of Malachi, and God was telling the people that they had been robbing him by not paying their tithes and offerings. For us, money had always threatened to run out before the end of the month, and too often we had difficulty making ends meet.

I came home that afternoon, showed Arlene the passage I had read, and told her, "I believe we should start tithing at church." Her smile faded, replaced by a frown of worry. She was certainly not opposed to tithing, but she realized the size of our budget, and now it was shrinking even farther. "If we do," she said, "I don't know if we can pay our bills."

Jim as a toddler.

*Jim (in the front center) with his parents, grandmother
and two younger siblings, Charles and Peggy.*

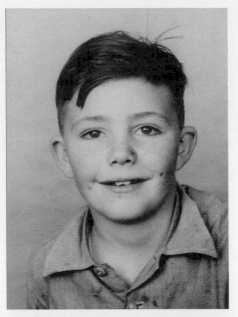

Jim as an elementary student.

**Jim's beloved grandparents, Malcolm and Linnie
McEachern, who raised him from ages 4 to 14.**

Jim's grandparent's homestead, where he grew up (photo taken many years later).

Jim as a high school student.

Jim and Arlene on their wedding day, June 28, 1958.

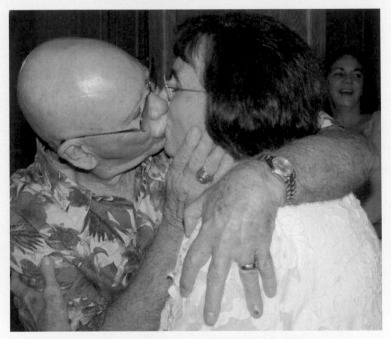

Jim and Arlene still kissing after 50 years of marriage.

Jim with an Army buddy.

Jim in front of the very first Tom James Company
store, Nashville, Tennessee, 1966.

*Jim receiving an award from Spencer Hays, with
his wife, Arlene, standing by his side.*

*Jim with a long-time Tom James Company associate,
Aaron Meyers, on a President's Club trip.*

Jim, his wife, children and their spouses and grandchildren on a cruise celebrating Jim and Arlene's 50th wedding anniversary (not including his son, Mike and his children, who were not able to make the trip).

Jim and Arlene on their last vacation together, May 2011.

Jim and Mike (his son) on a trip together.

But, in the scripture, God had said, "Try me. Test me. And see if I won't pour out a blessing on you." My mind was made up. We would overnight be forced to take our commitment of frugal and modest living to a whole new level. I was now earning sixteen thousand dollars a year.

That meant we would be tithing one hundred and thirty-three dollars a month. We tightened our belt. We had to with two children in school. We paid ten percent of my income to the church. We invested ten percent of my income in our mutual fund. We paid our taxes. We lived on whatever amount was left. But not once was I ever tempted to compromise on either tithing or investing. Both became integral parts of my life.

That year, I increased my sales and earned twenty-three thousand dollars. The next year, it grew to thirty-one thousand dollars. The third year saw a rise to thirty-seven thousand dollars. "You must be doing something right," people told me. I smiled and nodded. I was. God had promised to pour out his blessing on me. And that's exactly what he was doing.

My third priority had been Tom James. As we grew the company, as we expanded our stores across the country, as we hired new sales personnel and trained them, as we worked diligently to build Tom James into one of the nation's most successful businesses, these were my primary priorities:

When dealing with customers, I always tried to find ways that I could best serve them. I didn't need to be creative. I didn't need to be clever. I didn't need to be loud and flamboyant. I didn't need to strut into their office as though I knew it all and had the answers to all of their basic clothing needs tucked away in my case.

Instead, I listened. I asked questions, and, sooner or later, they provided their own answers. Sooner or later, they told me what they wanted and why they wanted it. Only then was I able to help them find the right clothes.

If a man had a small wardrobe, I knew he needed clothes that he could wear a lot and still not wear out. The durability of the fabric was important to him.

If a businessman traveled a lot, he might only carry a couple of suits with him on the road and switch them out every day. Each new day was a new town. The suit he wore the day before should look brand new to brand new customers today. It was vital that Tom James customize clothes for him that would not wrinkle no matter how long the sales trip might be.

I was always diligent about asking each customer: "What's the best way for me to help you dress properly in your business?"

Some wanted casual, some formal. Some wanted to look like a New York banker; others preferred the sports attire of contrasting jackets and trousers. Each dressed the way his clients expected him to dress. He wore one suit in the financial district and another to call on a boat manufacturing company on the lake. It was my job to make sure he had the right uniform for the right occasion.

I realized that often in business, a man's time was his most valuable asset, and his lack of time my greatest detriment. At first, I thought that when I was being hurried along by a harried executive it was because he wanted to get rid of me. I learned that might not be the case at all.

I had an appointment with a prominent attorney who happened to be president of the Atlanta Bar Association. He was pleasant but brusque. He had money. He did not want to run out of time.

I gave him my best five-minute sales presentation. At that point, he had endured enough. He said, "I'll try you out, young man. Go back, pick out two suits you think I'd like, and customize them for me, if I like what you've done, I'll buy new suits every time the seasons change." I was in and out of his office in six minutes.

The attorney had a very successful law practice and made his living with billable hours. All of his hours had price tags attached, and he did not want to waste any of them listening to me. In his line of work, even the minutes were critical. He was depending on me to size him up, check the style of suit he was wearing, then go back and select the clothes I thought he would be proud to wear either in meetings or the courtroom.

To him, his image may have been important, but not nearly as vital to his success as maintaining every billable hour he could provide his array of clients during a sun-up to sun-down day.

Another customer did not care as much about time as simplicity. Every season, it was always the same. He picked out four suits exactly alike: same color, same pattern, and same style. He looked the same every day. But then, that's the way he wanted to look, and he did not want me or anyone else trying to modify, alter, or create a new style for him. He was satisfied with his appearance and had no intention of ever changing.

An insurance sales person told me he wanted to wear the kind of quality clothing that Tom James marketed, but unfortunately, he had absolutely no sense of color. He became one of my best customers for one basic reason: I would take the time to stitch numbers into the suits, shirts, and ties I sold him. He had no idea which colors went together. He thought I did and depended on me to correctly match his clothes.

When he dressed for work, he faithfully wore the suit, shirt, and tie that all had a *number one* placed inside. Or a *number two*. Or a *number three*. If he ever walked out of the house with a *number one* suit, *number two* shirt, and *number three* tie, his image was in deep trouble and on the threshold of being ruined.

Businessmen all had their own eccentricities. It was my job to know what those eccentricities were. Some wanted me to get in and out of their office without wasting their time. Some needed clothes that looked fresh and unwrinkled even after a week's worth of traveling. Some had small wardrobes and demanded clothes that didn't wear out quickly. Some were only interested in me selling them clothes that were color coordinated.

And some preferred convenience. One client owned an auto parts store in Noonan, Georgia, about thirty miles out of Atlanta. When prime-time traffic was thick and crawling along the network of interstate highways strangling the city, the journey to Noonan could easily take an hour or more.

My customer, however, loved shopping. He would drive down to our downtown store, browse at will through just about every style, color, pattern, and fabric we had, and then make his final selection and head back home.

I wouldn't see him back in the store again until he wanted or needed a different or new wardrobe. He expected me to manufacture the suits, and then deliver them all to Noonan. Since that's what it took to keep a satisfied customer, that's exactly what I did.

Some men, at least at home and in the workplace, led two lives. I dealt with the dealer of an air-conditioning place who dutifully wore his work clothes during the week but made it a point to dress formally, if not elegantly, when he went to his country club parties at night.

By day, he looked like a hard-working man on the inside pages of *Popular Mechanics Magazine.* A little wrinkled. A little dirty. A little stained. Casual at best. At night, when he swaggered through the front door of the country club, it was as though he had just walked off the cover of *Gentleman's Quarterly.*

He selected three or four outfits from Tom James before the winter season, always ordering topcoats to match. A black or gray suit. A black topcoat. A Navy or blue suit. A Navy topcoat. He dressed sharply. He dressed conservatively. He dressed with style, class, and sophistication. He had a genuine, basic belief that underscored our whole business. Clothes did indeed make the man.

I realized early on that I could best support my third priority – the Tom James Company – by always connecting it with the basic principle of my first priority – doing what God had taught me to do.

Love people.
Always act in their best interest.
Listen.
Listen closely.
Take the time to find out what was important to them.
Take the time to help them identify their dreams.

> *Then help them acquire what was important to them.*
> *Help them achieve their goals in both life and clothing.*

That's what I would have wanted someone to do for me. Then, and only then, would I be doing the right thing for them, not just as my customers, but also as my friends. Customers could come and go. Friends were for a lifetime.

Takeaways From the Chapter

- *Jim makes a point of not just identifying priorities in the abstract but defining precisely what fulfilling these priorities would look like. What are my priorities? If I know what they are, how am I fulfilling those priorities in life?*
- *Can I honestly say that my priority is to make my spouse the happiest person on earth?*
- *Jim made his family a priority in life. What does my calendar look like? If my priority is family, it should be packed with family life events.*
- *I can know my priorities by looking at my calendar and my checkbook. Jim realized that to be successful meant realizing people matter and that listening to what they wanted and providing it was critical. What can I learn from this?*
- *How am I planning to make the people that I interact with in business better off than when they met me?*

CHAPTER 12

Choosing to Develop Your Character

Nothing defines us the way our character does. Not our name. Not our job. Not our position in the community. Certainly not our looks. Dwight Eisenhower once said, "The qualities of a great man are vision, integrity, courage, understanding, the power of articulation, and profundity of character." I have always believed that power is what a man or woman does, but character is who they are. As the nineteenth century newspaper editor Horace Greeley wrote: "Fame is a vapor, popularity an accident, riches take wings, and only character endures." And no one ever explained it any better than Revolutionary War statesman Thomas Paine. He said, "Reputation is what men and women think of us; character is what God and the angels know of us."

I had not been working long for Spencer Hays and Tom James when I began to seriously think about developing a list of character traits that I believed every sales person in our organization should know, understand, and adapt in their own lives and profession. We all have different personalities. We all have different styles. None of us ever quite make the same sales presentations the same way. We all have different ambitions and goals in life. But every man and woman can be the architect of his or own character.

My life had been impacted by the thirteen virtues that helped Benjamin Franklin improve himself as a person and as a leader. He wrote them when he was twenty years old and dutifully followed each of them until his dying day.

1. *The Personal Virtue of Order*: Your priorities in both life and business should be well managed and always kept in their proper place. When it's time to work, concentrate on your business. When it's time for family activities, never let business interfere. Keep a balance and a harmony in all of the things you do.

2. *The Personal Virtue of Temperance*: Keep your mind sharp. Avoid the extremes in life. As Franklin indicated, a person should never drink to elevation or eat to dullness. In your business practice, he said, never be afraid to compromise or look for common ground in your negotiations.

3. *The Personal Virtue of Frugality*: The whole basis of Franklin's personal and business philosophy was "waste not." Make it a point to live within your means. Save your money. Invest your money. That was, he believed, the only way to build a lasting wealth while being smart with your finances and resources.

4. *The Personal Virtue of Resolution*: Resolve to do what you should do, then go ahead and do it. There is never any reason to procrastinate and let a good idea go to waste. Remember the promises you choose to make to your family, friends, bosses, and customers in business, and keep them without fail. In order to build wealth, your business, or a friendship, it is necessary for you to stay true to the goals and promises you made to yourself. If you happen to fall short, as we sometimes do, resolve to do better the next time.

5. *The Personal Virtue of Moderation*: Franklin believed that it was vital for anyone to avoid extremes and strike a happy balance in business and in life. For example, people who work so hard to achieve wealth and lose their family pay a terrible price.

6. *The Personal Virtue of Industry*: For example, don't confuse being busy with accomplishing anything. It's alright to be busy but only as long as you are doing something useful or

worthwhile. Any actions that are wasteful or unnecessary should be eliminated as quickly as possible. Your goal in business should be to achieve as much as you can. A person who is only killing time is killing his future.

7. *The Personal Virtue of Tranquility*: Don't let the little things in life prevent you from accomplishing the big things. Problems at home or in business occur frequently and are many times unavoidable. Don't ever let them distract you. Take a few minutes, solve them, and then move on. Too often we become so mired down with minor obstacles that we let real opportunities escape us.

8. *The Personal Virtue of Cleanliness*: Franklin's dictate means more than simply taking a bath each morning and scraping the dirt from beneath your fingernails. In today's business climate, the successful man or woman is the one who takes the time to both look and act in a professional manner. Clothes do make the man or woman. We can dress for success. We can go to work today with a successful image. That's why Tom James was even in business.

9. *The Social Virtue of Sincerity*: As Franklin believed, never lie, trick, or deceive someone in your business endeavors. Be truthful. Be sincere. Be forthright. As he always said, "honesty is indeed the best policy."

10. *The Social virtue of Silence*: An age-old proverb probably says it best: "Even a fool is considered wise when he keeps silent." A friend of mine often breathes a short prayer when she talks with someone. Before she utters a word, she asks the Lord to "bless it or block it." Don't let harsh words or criticism ever become an enemy. It will be your worst enemy. Besides, an idle conversation that has no meaning will never get you anywhere in life or in business. As J. Petit Senn wrote, "It requires less character to discover the faults of others than to tolerate them."

11. *The Social Virtue of Justice*: Take care of people around you. Never treat anyone unfairly regardless of the situation or

circumstance. If you do build up your wealth, treat your money responsibly. Ten percent goes to God. At least ten percent should be saved or invested. And no investment is more appreciated than when you use your money to help lift up someone who may not be nearly as fortunate as you.

12. *The Social Virtue of Humility*: Refrain from talking about yourself, which is usually a subject no one else cares about. Work hard to achieve what is important in life, but don't ever be guilty of bragging about what you have achieved. *Pride always goeth before the fall.*

13. *The Social Virtue of Chastity*: At home or in business, people always have a deeper appreciation and respect for those who work diligently to live a clean, pure, and admirable life. What others think, really does count. As one of my favorite proverbs says: "A good name will shine forever."

The more I thought about it, the more I came to realize that life and business is all about character. We may try to be a lot of different things. We may try to put on a lot of new fronts. We may live in the largest house and drive the fastest car and travel the world over on the largest cruise lines. We may run in elite social circles, have celebrities as our best friends, spend most of our waking hours at the country club, play golf on the finest courses in America, fly first class, speak to massive crowds in the country's largest venues, sell the best brand names, and wear the most fashionable clothes. But that is not who we are.

When it is all said and done, character is who and what we are. Abraham Lincoln believed that "character is like a tree and reputation like its shadow. The shadow is what we think of it; the tree is the real thing." Or, as one pundit said, "Character is what you do when nobody is looking."

Many times I sat in the office with Spencer Hays while he was on the telephone, talking with another of the young student sales people on the road and selling books for the Southwestern Company. He would tell them: "What you are someday going to be, you are now becoming," or "what you are speaks so loudly that I cannot hear what you are saying." His were the kind of insights that could make a positive difference in a young man's outlook as he developed the important links in his own character.

My character was formed, shaped and molded when I was just a small boy and my grandparents took the Bible and made its words come alive. The Ten Commandments were absolute. They were not flexible. I was taught to trust them, believe them, obey and follow them. I could not pick and choose which ones I liked best or discard any that I felt like breaking. Each one had been chiseled in stone just as those words were chiseled in my own mind and heart.

I grew up thinking that lying was as bad as stealing, but neither was as bad as refusing or forgetting to love my God with all of my heart, soul, and mind. We should walk a straight and narrow path in our lives and in our business endeavors. There were no exceptions, no shortcuts, and no excuses. As a boy, I was taught to understand the value of character long before I learned the importance of my A, B, C's.

When my grandmother died in a Houston hospital, I deeply regretted not being able to reach her bedside before she lost consciousness. I regretted not having written her more letters telling her how much I loved her, how much I appreciated her caring for me all of those years on the farm, how much I missed her, how much I missed seeing her every day. No matter how hard life became, I could look up, see her soft, gentle smile, and know everything would be all right. But I never told her. The grief and regret was almost unbearable.

I sat there in the darkness of her hospital room, held her hand, and vowed I would never let that happen again. I have been told there are five things a person cannot recover in life: a stone after it's thrown, a word after it's said, an occasion after it's missed, the time after it's gone, and a person after they die. By morning, I understood.

However, I was also fortunate. My grandfather lived another few years. I rode with him to California once and reminded him every day of how much he meant to me. He smiled. I told him I loved him every chance I got. He smiled.

When he came to live with my father, I saw him often and was always thanking him for taking me into his home, for letting me work with him on the farm, for telling me Bible stories, for letting me know the difference between right and wrong, for helping make the man I was to become.

The last time I saw him, I hugged his neck. He didn't say much. But I knew he was proud of me. I saw it in his eyes. The love was there among the tears. I had never seen him cry before.

At his funeral, I missed him greatly. The one giant force that had shaped my life was gone, and I was so sorry to see him leave. The world was suddenly empty. My heart was empty. A void now swallowed the fields where he had walked. But I had no regrets.

I would never be just like him, but a part of him and my grandmother would forever live within me. They gave me the greatest gifts of all. They gave me the character traits that would make a difference in the way I treated those around me. I would falter from time to time, but they had left with me a bridge that would always carry me back from wrong to right, that would lead me to where I needed to go. By 1967, in fact, I was well on my way to becoming the person I was to be.

I sat down in the cool of an early morning and began working on my own list of character traits. It shouldn't take long, I thought. I'll jot a few ideas down and let them serve as my guide. What works in business should work the same at home or even in my neighborhood. Who knew? I might even finish before I got to work.

Compiling the list took me five years. I worked on them a few hours every week. I wrote down a few, added a few, discarded a few, combined a few, and then thought up a few new ones. I took the time and the care necessary to get them right, at least in my own mind, because my life, my business, my future, my reputation, my relationships with others, my success, and my friendships depended on them. I could not make a mistake.

Choosing to accept both responsibility and accountability:

I always believed that it was important to accept responsibility on the front end of any endeavor, especially in business, and be wholly accountable for whatever happened on the back end. A man who is willing to take the credit for any successes must sometimes be willing to stand up and accept the blame when a deal or an opportunity falls apart. It might be his fault. It might not. Sometimes, as the poet said, "the best laid plans of mice and men do go astray." But when the shooting stops and the field is silent once more, it is the leader who is the last man standing. Win or lose, it was his responsibility. Win, and he moves on. Lose, and he tries again. But never does he quit.

I recognized quickly the importance of standing up and admitting it when I had messed up, and in business, sooner or later, we all make mistakes. We may try to be and wish we were, but no one is perfect.

I have always found it extremely frustrating when I see employees do something that's not quite right, and then multiply the problem by frantically trying to cover up the error with deceit and lies. One lie always requires another. A pack of lies pulls you down as quickly as if you were in quicksand, and sometimes there's no way back out.

This has always been my philosophy: Admit it. Correct it. Learn from it.

During the hectic and often frantic pace of building a business and dealing with people, it was so easy to find myself facing a new array of problems on a daily basis. I know there were times when I allowed my temper to flare up, and I'm sure that I made someone feel uncomfortable.

I had not solved the original problem. More than likely, I had probably created a new one. I could forget it and go on. I could let a split in our relationship fester and become much larger than it should have been. It would have been easy for me to ignore. After all, I wasn't upset at the person. I was upset at the situation. But my employee walked away believing that I was angry with him. As soon as I realized it, I admitted my error. I corrected it. I apologized. And I learned from it.

I made the decision to never let it happen to me again. As soon as I could feel the frustration rising up within me, I would walk away or leave the room until I was able to get my temper under control. Only then would I return so we could continue to look for a solution. I realized early on that it was much easier to solve a problem than restore a friendship.

On Being Responsible:

The following is a letter that Jim sent out to Tom James employees in April 2008 specifically dealing with responsibility.

Some Things I've Been Learning
A. I believe in a double standard . . . for example:

1. Always hold yourself to a standard of integrity that gives other people a basis for trusting you, while at the same time making allowance for the imperfections of others.
2. Always freely give respect to others, while expecting to have to earn respect from other people.
3. Give honest and sincere appreciation even if you don't feel appreciated.

B. Hold yourself to a higher standard than anyone else would ever expect of you in attitude, in effort, and in results.

C. Treat "today" as the most important day of your life. Treat "now" as the most important moment in your life.

D. Be thankful for everything. Show appreciation for your leaders, your peers, those you lead, those in support roles, your family members, your customers, etc.

E. John Wooden said, "Things turn out best for people who make the best of the way things turn out." So make the best of your current circumstances.

F. It is great to be alive and healthy, and to have a limitless opportunity, to be able to give yourself a pay raise any time you choose to do so.

G. Be the most inspiring person you can be by being your best and doing your best.

By Jim McEachern

Choosing to be Grateful:

I'm sure that it was the result of the regrets I felt when my grandmother died, but over the years I have written thousands of letters and cards and emails, expressing my gratitude to both employees and customers. At Tom James, I might have a secretary type the letter, but when I signed it, I always included a hand-written personal note at the bottom of the page, letting them know just how much I appreciated what they had done or accomplished. It only took a few minutes, but genuine gratitude can last a lifetime. When I wrote notes to customers who had purchased clothes from me, I would say, "Thank you for allowing me to serve you." When I didn't sell a suit, I still wrote a note, saying, "Thank you for allowing me to have some of your valuable time to tell my story."

On Letter Writing:

One of the things that Jim was known for was his letters of encouragement and affirmation. As I have interacted with many people who knew him they would often report having received letters from him that inspired them. I understand this well because he wrote me many letters affirming the man that he knew that I could be and encouraging me to be the leader of my family and to pursue my goals professionally. I also know that he, with consistency and regularity, had written many letters to family members expressing his love, gratefulness, appreciation and hopes for each individual. In these letters he was encouraging and affirming us to be the people he knew that we could become. He wrote these letters to his children, to his son-in-laws and daughter-in-law. He wrote these to his grandchildren and I'm sure anyone else in the extended family who he could speak affirmation and encouragement to. His letters are still treasured heirlooms for many members of our family.

This is not where the letter writing stopped though. Jim wrote many letters to Tom James employees. Dave Shepard of Tom James in Memphis sent me a group of letters that Jim sent to the TJ sales people over the years. These letters were so inspiring that many people would hold on to them as encouragement. The letters that Dave sent me were from one period during 1997-1998. These are letters that he had personally kept for over 15 years. Wow!

One of Jim's many loves was the Ovilla Christian School at his home church the Ovilla Road Baptist Church. He gave generously to the school financially and he also was a mentor to the head administrator of the school, Julie Weyand. He wasn't just helping develop leadership within Tom James but within the school as well. In a discussion with Ms. Weyand she reported to me that she had many letters from Jim and that she had kept every one because they were so meaningful. It also seems that Jim's letter writing extended beyond family, church, and Tom James.

Jonathan Snow, Jim's oldest grandchild, who is now a salesperson for Tom James made this report to me in an interview in 2012. "I went to visit a customer who had been a Tom James customer from the past. In our conversation this customer, who didn't know who I

was, told me why he had become a Tom James customer.
He opened a drawer and pulled out a letter that Jim
McEachern had written him 30 years ago, thanking
him for being a customer and encouraging him in his
business." Stories compiled by Michael McDowell

At the checkout lines in restaurants, grocery stores, or even toll booths, hardly anyone ever bothers to say *thank you* to me. I'm the one who says *thank you* to them. With my wife, my children, and my friends, I make sure that I express my appreciation and gratitude every time I am given the opportunity. At home or at work, I never simply say, "thank you," "I am grateful to you," or "I appreciate you" without giving a specific reason. I don't want those words ever to sound empty or routine. A reason gives the recipient positive reinforcement. A reason puts a smile on someone's face.

Choosing Selflessness:

Too often, we go through life so busy that we never slow down along the way to really express the way we feel to someone. As I think back, I can remember all sorts of people who passed my way, made a real impression on me, and still I didn't take the time to tell them *thank you*. A first grade teacher. A pastor. A coach. A Sunday School teacher. A college registrar. The man who hired me. The man who fired me. Someone I worked with or worked for or even let me drive a snow cone truck. I would not be here without the help or motivation from so many people. But seldom if ever did I get around to letting them know how much I really appreciated them. And now I don't even remember all of their names. That is my constant regret.

Too many times, we all have the same fault. We are too busy and tend to be too self-centered or believe that we are too important to treat others as we would like for them to treat us. I've heard people say, "This is my secretary," or "This is my employee." I'm sure they mean nothing by it, but it sounds as though they suddenly have ownership of the person standing or sitting beside them. I make it a practice to never introduce "my sales person" to anyone. Instead, I say, "I would like for you to meet my friend who's a top sales person for Tom James." I don't want anyone to ever feel awkward or embarrassed.

Traditionally, in an office, a person who might have a lower position in the company is always expected to get coffee for the others. I decided when I began working at Tom James that I would be the one serving coffee even if I happened to be the highest-ranking or longest-tenured employee in the room. I worked with one man in the early days of Tom James, and I didn't like some things about him. He irritated me. He was loud and boisterous and liked to make a big deal of himself. If there happened to be a spotlight shining, he wanted it to shine on his face. But I realized that we had to work together, and I did not want his traits to become a factor in the way I treated him.

I would awaken an hour early each morning and race to beat him to the office. I brewed the coffee, listened for his car to pull into the garage, and then had the back door open for him when he walked inside. I poured his coffee and handed it to him. None of my actions made any difference to him. He rather expected to be treated like royalty. But my actions made a big difference for me. I made myself accountable for my thoughts and deeds.

On Kindness:

I wanted to share a small story that is still impacting my life to this day. Many years ago I had the privilege of teaching for a couple of days in the Sales Training Program for Tom James with Mr. McEachern. Since the training was held in Mr. McEachern's home office in Mansfield, Texas, I'd often get the opportunity to spend some one-on-one time with him, and he would join the students and myself for lunch at a nearby Luby's Cafeteria. The small yet powerful example that Mr. McEachern modeled for myself and others was his humility, manners, and gratitude. When going through the cafeteria line each of us going before him would order our entree asking, " I'd like that entree, give me that vegetable, I'll take that roll etc." When Mr. McEachern ordered he first would greet the server warmly, then order by saying " may I please have _____," then he'd thank them kindly, ask for his next item the very same way, "may I please have _____," and again he'd thank them kindly and politely. I know it seems like such a small thing especially for such a magnanimous human being who had such Christ–like qualities, and who accomplished and contributed so much to so many. But this small example had such a profound impact on me. While seemingly small, I think in many ways it exemplified the kind of man and leader he was to me and many others. This small example continues to impact the way I treat others, and the way that I've taught my own children to behave and treat others. Steve N., Tom James Company

While working with sales people, I never wanted to criticize anyone in such a way that might humiliate or embarrass them. A steady dose of harsh criticisms can often be extremely damaging to a person's self-confidence, self-esteem, and drive to succeed.

More than once, I would ask, "If you ever saw me do something that you thought would be detrimental to me and my ability to sell, would you be willing to tell me?"

The sales person would pause a moment, then say, "Certainly."

And I would ask, "Do you know of anything that you could tell me that would be beneficial in the way I make a sales presentation?"

Sometimes, the sales person would nod.

And almost every time, he or she would ask me, "Do you see me doing anything that I might do differently in order to sell more clothes or close more sales?"

I would frown. Scratch my chin. Look toward the ceiling in the hallway. Think seriously about their questions, then say, "Let me think about it. If I come up with anything, I'll certainly tell you what it is."

The door was now open for me. I could wait awhile, but, sooner or later, I would be able to point out something that could benefit their sales efforts. I hadn't made a snap judgment or delivered an opinion off the top of my head. I had taken my time and thought it over.

And to a person, our sales personnel appreciated any suggestion I had to offer. No one took it personally. After all, they had asked for my thoughts and were expecting me to help or advise them. They would have been disappointed if I ignored them.

Choosing Integrity:

The lessons I learned while walking the streets and selling books for the Southwestern Company were hard ones, but they were invaluable to me. I had always taken pride in being known as an ethical sales person. I didn't twist any arms. I never resorted to deception or played tricks with my potential customers. But, during one summer in Point Pleasant, West Virginia, I was doing well and, as always, wanted to do better. I let my ego rear its ugly head and outtalk my common sense.

A Church of Christ minister loved the Naves Topical Bible I happened to have in my portfolio. The verses had been arranged according to subject matter, and he believed that every member of his congregation should have one. He gave me a list of members, smiled with encouragement, and said. "Go see every one of them, and tell them I sent you."

He was a godsend. His name opened every door. I sat down with one lady and, early in the presentation, she interrupted me and asked, "Are you a member of the church?"

In my heart, I knew what she was asking. She wanted to know if I were a member of the Church of Christ. In my mind, I quietly and surreptitiously told myself that certainly I was a member of the church. I was a God-fearing member of the Baptist Church. It was a church all right. It just wasn't "The Church."

I tried to soothe my conscience by telling myself that the lady just hadn't been specific enough. I thought over her words: "Are you a member of the church?"

I smiled and said, 'Yes, I am."

I knew immediately I was lying to her. I knew immediately I was trying to deceive her. I knew immediately that my answer was a grave mistake. But I was trying desperately to make a sale.

She bought just like her minister had suggested she do, but, for weeks, I dreaded the thought of returning to her home and delivering the Bible. I knocked on her door. Her eyes cut into me when she opened it. She said without any hesitation or small talk, "You lied to me."

I took a deep breath and tried to cover up my deception. "What did I say?" I asked. My throat tightened. So did the nerves in my stomach. I knew exactly what I had said, and I wasn't proud of saying it.

"You told me you were a member of the church," she said.

"Well, I am."

I hadn't solved anything. I had only compounded my mistake. She stared at me. I stared back. She won. I admitted I was a Baptist.

When I walked away from her front porch, I felt so badly that I quietly promised myself that I would never again tell a lie or be deceitful in order to make a sale, no matter how desperate I might be. I would choose to be truthful. I would choose integrity. Both were more important to me than a sale.

For a few dollars, I had tainted my reputation and saw the values my grandparents had taught me unravel and come apart at the seams. The few dollars I gained would never be worth what I lost that day.

Choosing to be Loyal:

If nothing else, I knew that I would remain true and steadfast to my God, my family, my friends, my employees, Spencer Hays, and our business. I would never abandon or desert them. If any of the Tom James sales people I managed made a mistake or an error in their judgment, I would forgive them. Even lying, cheating, and stealing were not considered unforgivable sins. Intolerable, perhaps, but not unforgivable.

I would do my best to help them if they wanted to change and did not try to con me, but I would not condone those serious flaws in their character. It was bad for them. It hurt my reputation as their manager. It tainted Tom James as a company. If they changed their ways, I kept them, and they appreciated knowing that I was ready to stand behind them and support them by offering them another chance.

Loyalty has always been a two-way street. I never believed in giving up too easily on an employee unless his or her behavior was undermining his company or his team.

The Tom James Company had a sales person in Nashville who was caught smoking pot in his office. I was not his direct supervisor, but his boss thought that I should be told of the incident. The sales person valiantly tried to talk his boss out of informing me, fearing that I would fire him on the spot for unacceptable behavior. In our organization, it was certainly an offense worthy of termination.

I had never before been confronted with any kind of business situation where marijuana was concerned. Inwardly, I was angry and frustrated because I felt as though our sales person had let us down. If he had genuinely cared about the business or the success of the company, he would have never been guilty of such a reprehensible deed.

I sat with him alone in a private office and said, "Do you have any idea of the potential damage you're doing to yourself? What if you had had an accident while you were still under the influence? What if someone had died because you were selfish enough to want to sneak a few minutes of personal pleasure? Do you realize how any information about this incident can cause your customers and co-workers to lose their trust and confidence in you?"

He didn't say a word. He just nodded. And his gaze never left the floor.

"I cannot force you to quit using pot," I said. "Outside the office, your business is your business. But if you ever use pot while you are at work or on the way to call on your customers, it won't be tolerated."

I talked. He listened. He talked. I listened. After two hours, I asked him, "What can we expect from you going forward?"

At first, he had been sheepish and embarrassed about getting caught. He was apologetic, and he never denied the allegation. After awhile, the embarrassment he felt turned to regret. It was as though a knife had touched his heart. At last, he told me, "I realize that I let you down. I messed up. Big time, I messed up. But you can count on me not ever doing anything like that again."

If he did, I never knew about it. All I know is that we were loyal to him, gave him a second chance, held nothing against him, and watched him become a top sales person at Tom James, building a large organization of people who followed his loyalty, dedication, and determination during their time in the company workplace.

Choosing to Think Big:

I never allowed myself to be intimidated by a belief that something was impossible. I was never afraid to think big. I tried to influence others to think big when they set their goals and considered the possibilities for their careers.

I recently met with a young man at Tom James who was earning a nice salary of a hundred and twenty thousand dollars a year. But he was discouraged. I could see him losing sight and grasp of his goals. In the course of our conversation, I asked him, "How can I be helpful to you?"

"I make a lot of money," he said, "but it's never enough." That was the biggest issue facing him. It is the biggest issue facing a lot of sales people. For them, it's almost a game. The good ones don't have any trouble making a lot of money. For so many, however, the problem arises when they find themselves having trouble holding on to it. Easy come. Easy go. It's always the same.

I said, "If I help you see a way to earn more money without spending more hours at work, would that be helpful?"

"It would." He was smiling now.

"How would you like to grow your income to three hundred thousand dollars a year?" I said. If no one at Tom James was earning that kind of salary, he would have tuned me out and quit listening to anything I had to say. But by 2011, we had several sales people pocketing that much. The barrier had been broken. Such a top-drawer salary was no longer outside the realm of his possibility.

Over the years, I had developed the "Essential Success Habits for Sales People" at Tom James. I handed them to the young man.

"Follow these," I said. "Follow them faithfully. Don't look for a shortcut. It's not there. These are the steps. If you let them guide you, then you won't have any trouble making three hundred thousand dollars a year."

He silently read them over. He nodded. "I can do this," he said.

"Then do it," I said.

He did. He thought bigger than he had ever thought before. The mountain was just as high as it had always been. He was no longer afraid to climb it. Think big. Think big often enough, and the idea or the challenge never seems nearly as big as it once did.

Now, as he walked away, my only concern for him was: "Can he hold on to three hundred thousand dollars a year?"

Choosing to Be a Self-Motivator and Self-Starter:

When I first began working closely with Spencer Hays at the Southwestern Company, I realized that he spent a lot of time on the phone and in meetings, motivating his sales people. He was always trying to encourage them, guide them, lead them, educate them, and build up their self-confidence. And I began to wonder: "Who is motivating Spencer Hays?" No one.

During one of our conversations, I said, "You're always energized every time I see you. You are always on the run, full of ideas and enthusiasm, constantly working with others and developing new plans for the company. What motivates you each morning?"

Spencer thought for a moment, shrugged, and answered, "It just seems like the right thing to do."

So it was. He did not need anyone else to get him started in the morning, rekindle a new fire of energy and ambition and the overwhelming desire to succeed. Spencer Hays was motivating himself.

If he could do it, then so could I, and I made an immediate decision that I would become a self-motivator and a self-starter in every assignment I had at Tom James. No one would ever have to tell me what should be done in business, how to do it, or when the task should be completed. I would never give anyone a reason to check up on me to determine if I was doing what I had been assigned to do. Besides, I never wanted to be in a position where I had to respond to something I should have already done.

If my boss or supervisor ever asked, "Did you do it?" I wanted to be able to say without hesitation, "I have." Leaders lead. Followers follow. Self-motivators don't wait for assignments. Self-motivators find something important to do. And they do it well.

Business is that simple. Those with vision and ambition and a willingness to lead others always complete their journey to the top. I knew that as long as the company had a top waiting for me, I was determined to reach it.

In reality, I had always been a self-starter. During my first two years of marriage, while I was in the Army, I, as all soldiers, had a very limited income. However, I noticed that the Fitzsimmons Army Hospital had a golf course and driving range. I chose not to sit at home and lament the few dollars in my pocket. As soon as I left my job every day, I walked out to the golf course and went to work again. I picked up golf balls for a dollar here and a dollar there. I washed windows on the buildings of the base. As soon as the officers realized that I was eager to work, they began hiring me to clean their apartments.

I never got rich. I lived a very modest lifestyle. But I never had to feel insecure. I could find a job. Even during the lowest and most frustrating times of my life – when I struggled financially to finish college, left teaching, was fired from my supermarket position, drove a snow cone truck, and loaded delivery trucks for a beauty supply company – I still had faith in myself and my ability to find a better way of life. I kept working. I kept looking. I stayed motivated.

Spencer Hays found me. He always hit the ground running early in the morning. So did I. He would get to work at six o'clock. I made it by five-forty-five. I knew that in the dark hours of morning, before the rest of the business world woke up and opened their doors, he would have time to see me. Spencer was by far the most successful businessman I had ever known, and I realized that I could learn a great deal from him.

More and more, he began to depend on me. When I moved away from Nashville and opened the store in Atlanta, Spencer called me at odd times – maybe six o'clock in the morning or nine o'clock at night – and I didn't know why. I finally concluded that he was calling me on a break or between his appointments and probably checking up on his investment. He was financing the building of Tom James out of his own pocket, had an enormous overhead pay out each month, and wanted to make sure the company was headed in the right direction. I could have just waited for his phone calls. I didn't. He deserved better than that. I began sending him a copy of my plan of action each week, letting him know what goals I had established for our sales people and me, and at the end of every month, I prepared a sales report and mailed it to him. He no longer had to be concerned. Spencer needed a self-starter in Atlanta. I wanted to reassure him that he had one. Some of my self-motivation just happened to be a part of my natural tendencies. The rest had been learned from successful people like Spencer Hays.

Choosing to Be a Good Finder Rather than a Fault Finder:

During my career as sales manager at Tom James, I spent a great deal of my time going with sales people on their appointments to determine if I might find some way to help them improve their presentations and increase their sales.

After we left the office, I never told them, "You could have done better than that." It would discourage them. As a result, they might well become so worried about their last appointment that their self-confidence would erode and ruin their next presentation.

I may have seen them make a lot of mistakes, but I didn't mention any of them, not at first anyway, and never unless they asked me.

I would smile broadly and say, "That was a nice job. I think you have developed a good relationship with your customer, and I was quite pleased with your presentation. In fact, let me tell you the really good points that I saw this morning."

I would then point out at least four or five things I thought they did right.

Sales people now knew that I was proud of them and approved of the professional way they had conducted the appointment.

They were relaxed.

They were no longer fearful.

And most of the time they asked, "Was there anything you saw that would help me improve my presentation?"

"Let me think about it."

I would later give them my thoughts. But they weren't worried, and they would be open and receptive to any ideas I might offer them because I had magnified the positive instead of dwelling immediately on the negative.

They walked away encouraged.

I had not criticized them.

I made them feel good about themselves and their ability to become a success in the Tom James Company.

I never pointed out a mistake. I simply offered a little advice. I might say, "In your presentation, I heard you say *this*. Instead, what if you had said *that*?

Again, there was no criticism.

I gave them an option, and they could choose the best way to make their presentations without thinking I had tried to burden them with my own opinion. He or she had the last say. The smart ones realized immediately the changes they needed to make when dealing with a customer.

In business, if people face enough discouragement, they tend to give up.

They may try.

But, often, someone is always criticizing them.

No one ever finds anything good to say about them.

They become discouraged.

They are disheartened.

They feel rejected and dejected.

They quit.

They lose.

And the company loses a potentially good employee.

At Tom James, we worked hard to be a *good finder* instead of a *fault finder*. We established a lot of rewards for our employees, and we created a lot of categories. We were looking for new and different ways to provide recognition for a job well done. We even published a magazine with photographs of all of the award winners.

We rewarded some.

We gave others a target to shoot for. Their feeling was: *I might not have won this year, but with a little more work and a few more sales I have a solid chance to win next year.*

Employees, sales people in particular, thrive on recognition.

Most have two goals:

More money.

And more awards.

Being a *good finder* also works at home. When my daughter, Karen, was in the fourth grade, she wanted to play the piano, so we went down to the music store to buy one.

"Don't buy it," the sales person said. "Lease it. If your daughter sticks with the piano, then you can buy it."

It was good advice.

We found a good teacher, and Karen practiced faithfully every afternoon. When I got home, I would sit on the bench beside her or in a chair nearby and applaud every time she finished playing a song. "That's really good, Karen," I said.

"I messed up," she confessed.

"I thought it sounded very good. I am so proud of the way you are playing."

She knew her efforts were appreciated, and she kept on playing. Day after day, she kept on playing, and she kept on getting better.

During the final concert of the year, Karen was chosen to play the first and the last song.

She was named Student of the year.

Karen obviously had talent, but I do believe that the encouragement she received at home motivated her to practice.

She hoped she could do well.

Now she knew she could do well.

When my son, Mike, was born, his right foot turned severely out to the side. The doctor told me, "Lay him on his back, take the foot in your hand and push it. He will naturally push back and strengthen the muscle. There's a chance that exercise will straighten it out on its own."

Every night, even when he was a baby, I pushed that foot, telling him, "Mike, you're the strongest little boy in the world."

He giggled.

He had no idea what I was saying.

He was just playing our little game.

Week after week, year after year, I kept working with his foot and telling him, "Mike, you're the strongest little boy in the world."

When he was a sophomore in high school, we had moved to Midlothian, Texas, and he was working on the leg press machine in the football field house. The maximum weight any football player could press with both legs was six hundred pounds.

Mike could press six hundred pounds with each leg.

He had grown up believing that he was the strongest little boy in the world, which didn't hurt when he twice won the Texas High School State Wrestling Championship.

As Henry Ford always said, "Whether you believe you can or believe you can't, you're right."

I prefer to find the good in people.

Be loyal to them.

Motivate them.

Teach them to be both responsible and accountable for their decisions.

Allow them to think big.

Ensure that they face life and business with honesty and integrity.

Help them build character.

Because when it's all said and done, life at home, at work, and in the community will always be about character. As Thomas Edison once said, "What a man's mind can create, man's character can control."

Takeaways from the chapter

- *Abraham Lincoln said "Character is like a tree and reputation like its shadow." How do I know if I have good character? If I really want to know, all I have to do is look at my reputation. What does my shadow look like?*

- *Spencer Hays repeatedly said to Jim, "what you are someday going to be, you are now becoming." What would it take for that truth to penetrate my being today?*

- *Jim reminds us that it's one thing to say "thank you" and it's another to say "thank you for this action, attitude, personal consideration, etc. How am I specific in my gratitude to others?*

- *Speaking words of affirmation about someone in introductions. What we speak about someone frames them as someone of significance. How do I introduce the people that I know to others?*

- *Jim had a style that first and foremost was careful to avoid embarrassing the people he was relating with? Am I as cautious in how I handle my business and personal relationships?*

- *Jim emphasizes the value of truthfulness as it relates to his business practices. A little old lady who caught him in a lie brought him to an important decision. Am I known as someone who tells the truth, even when it hurts?*

- *The decision to extend grace generously. Jim was willing to forgive mistakes and sought to redeem people who truly wanted to change. Am I someone who extends grace to people at every opportunity?*

- *Jim realized that he could help people "think big" through goal setting but he also gave them a plan for accomplishing their goals. He wasn't just their cheerleader, although he was that, he was also their coach. Who am I cheering on and what kind of coaching am I providing?*

- *Jim anticipated Spencer's concerns as his superior and primary investor and then began without being asked to provide the information that he believed that he was looking for. In what ways am I anticipating my superior/leader's concerns and addressing them?*

- *Jim promotes the value of learning to highlight the good aspects in others and only later (if asked) about areas to improve. Do I approach relationships with people in this manner? How does this approach affect my family life? My relationship with my wife? Children? Parents? Siblings?*

CHAPTER 13

Choosing to Consider Possibilities

Even before the day I entered the world of selling, I knew the importance and the value of goal setting. Back during my brief career stocking and collecting inventory at the beauty supply company, I read all of the business magazines in the office, especially the stories highlighting the successes of America's top businessmen. All of them, without exception, credited their strong commitment to goal setting for helping them build and grow their companies.

It all made sense to me, but the real necessity for setting goals did not really sink in until I immersed myself in Paul J. Meyer's *Million Dollar Personal Success Plan*. It was one of the most beneficial things I ever did because his ideas and concepts helped me further develop my creativity, energy, fulfillment, happiness, and the level of motivation I have enjoyed. It often makes me shudder to think what would have happened if I had not studied and applied Meyer's course to my own life and to those responsible for building Tom James.

By now, I knew where I wanted to go in life. I had witnessed first-hand those who made it, and they had left big footprints for me to follow.

At a fairly young age, I had known about Carson Echols who lived just down the road from my grandfather's place. He was a neighbor. I knew he was rich but had no idea how rich. I didn't even realize how much money a man needed to be rich. I did, however, learn that during the severe drought of the 1950s, the time it never rained, the years when good land lost its crops, the grasses grew brittle, and the hard winds blew away the soil in great sandstorms, most of the farmers went broke. They were ready to sell cheap, or the banks stepped in and foreclosed on loans that were long due and might never be paid. Carson Echols stepped in and persuaded the bankers to give him long-term contracts for the empty and barren land. He was pretty much the only one around with any money in his account, so the bankers were glad to oblige. When the drought ended, Echols made big crops, paid the banks, and owned it all. He built the nicest house in Lamesa and even sent his son to Texas Tech driving a new pickup truck, hauling a horse trailer, and bringing along his horse with him. Even as a small boy, I was impressed with the Echols family and their elite status in Dawson County. I would lie there in my bed at night and think, *If I could be anybody in the world right now, it would be Mr. Carson Echols.*

I had long ago been inspired by sitting in the audience and listening to the words of R. G. LeTourneau. He had built big, powerful earth-moving machines, and then used his substantial fortune to support missionaries in South America and Africa. He was larger-than-life, and his heart was even larger. He ultimately sold his firm for thirty-five million dollars, didn't get around to cashing the check for two days and lost thousands of dollars in interest. Today, that sum would equate to more than three hundred and fifty million dollars. I decided as a young boy that someday I wanted to be like R. G. LeTourneau. I wanted to rise to the top, gain the respect of everyone I met in my business endeavors, and give away as much money as possible to a variety of charitable causes. Hoarding the money I earned had never appealed to me. I did not view a person's financial account as a scoreboard to keep track of his success. As long as my family was comfortable, my single most important goal was to use every spare dollar I possibly could to help someone else. I believed that a stack of money piled back in a bank vault, only counted and never used, was surely a waste. I walked out of the Baptist church auditorium that night with a great admiration for R. G. LeTourneau, his accomplishments and his values. Back in my mind, I was thinking, *If he can do it, maybe I can, too*. I had set my first goal and didn't even realize it. He was a man I never forgot.

I had read a library full of success books and heard a lot of tapes from a lot of motivational speakers. All of them believed that, without goals, we would wind up lost somewhere on a highway that led us nowhere, and I never doubted it for a moment. Gene Donohue once said that a man devoid of goals will never reach his destination. He wrote: "We dream about where we want to go, but we don't have a map to get there." A dream is something we think about and keep shoved back in our minds. A goal, like a map, is written down. It's not ethereal. It's real. We can see it. We can read it. We won't ever forget it. The goal gives us direction. It adds clarity to our journey.

H. L. Hunt had been one of the early swashbucklers of the oilfield. He had found millions of dollars worth of oil, maybe billions. He had so much money going out and coming in that it was difficult to ever establish his financial worth.

Someone once asked him, "What's the secret of your success?"

His answer was direct, to the point, and memorable.

"Success requires two things and two things only," Hunt said. "First, you must know exactly what you want. Most people never make that decision. Second, you must determine the price that you will have to pay to achieve it, and then get busy paying the price."

As Brian Tracy wrote in his book, *Goals: How to Get Everything You Want Faster Than You Ever Thought Possible*, "Your inborn potential is extraordinary. You have within you, right now, the ability to achieve almost any goal that you can set for yourself. Your greatest responsibility to yourself is to invest whatever time is required to become absolutely clear about exactly what you want and how you can best achieve it. The greater clarity you have regarding your true goals, the more of your potential you will unleash for good in your life."

So, as the years passed, I diligently followed all the rules and filled out all of the workbooks and made sure my goals were solidly in place. Of course, as I changed my course in business, as I moved from selling books to selling clothes, I realized that my goals needed revising from time to time. Some people make the mistake of starting over with new goals every year. In reality, our substantive goals never change. We revise them from time to time. We even add new goals. But the heart and soul of our basic goals remain the same.

It had long been my opinion that nothing ever happened in a vacuum. There has to be a plan. There has to be a strategy. In order to achieve the success that we want for our life and our family, we do need that map to follow. It keeps us moving in a straight line. It directs us in case an obstacle ever blocks our path, in case something quite unexpected ever stands in the way of our journey to the top. It keeps us from straying off course. It keeps us from getting lost.

For so much of my life, I had been a devout goal-setter. I put them on paper. I read them daily. I knew where I wanted to go and what I wanted to do. I was always looking for better ways to get there. I had long-term goals. They were my destination. Then I had a lot of short-term goals. They were the stepping stones I used on my journey. The goals, both large and small, kept me focused. Achieving the small goals along the way kept me from ever becoming discouraged as I strove to reach the large ones.

1. I wrote my goals down. I never left them floating around in my mind, easily misplaced, easily forgotten. *I will become the top sales person at Tom James.*
2. I was very specific. *I will sell a hundred thousand dollars worth of clothes a year.*
3. I knew that I must have goals I could actually measure. Otherwise, I'd never be able to manage either them or my expectations. *I must sell more than eight thousand dollars worth of clothes a month or two thousand dollars worth of clothes each week.*
4. I set goals that I believed I could actually achieve. Some were larger than others, some, in my mind, were even grandiose, but they were always within my reach. *I will become a manager at Tom James instead of a sales person.*

5. My goals were realistic. They weren't dreams. It was easy for me to devise a plan to achieve them. Straight line. Straight course. Easy steps along the way. *I can sell fifty thousand dollars worth of clothes this year, seventy-five thousand dollars worth of clothes next year, and reach my goal of a hundred thousand dollars a year by 1970.*

6. I put my goals within a certain time frame and believed that I could attain them in a week or a month or maybe even a year. But I had a definite deadline. I knew there was a finish line, and it was waiting for me. That, more than anything, kept me focused. *I will reach my goal of selling a hundred thousand dollars worth of clothes a year in three years.*

I didn't just limit my goals to my business and my profession. In life, it was important to establish my priorities:

God.

Family.

The Tom James Company.

Health.

In the same manner, I began to develop my goals, using practical guidelines to better understand what I needed in business in order to afford a better life for my family. Both were intertwined. My profession would provide for my family, but in the process, I realized that I should never devote so much time to my business that I neglected or turned away from my family. For today's businessman, that bridge forms a delicate balance. The tragedy is: so many good businessmen and businesswomen work so hard, work such long hours, devote so much of their time to succeeding in the workplace that they come home someday, and their family is gone. They may have earned a great position in the company and an important title on their door. But they have lost the most important thing in life when they lose their family.

I had never been afraid to think big. In fact, I always believed that it was as easy to think big as think small. The battle to achieve success for me was exactly what the struggle up Mount Everest had become for mountain climbers. It was there. Others had stood on top. It was time for them to make room for me.

I remembered the story I had read about Ben Feldman who had become the number one life insurance sales person in the world.

Ben had his own agency.

He worked alone.

And he sold fifty million dollars worth of life insurance a year. For three consecutive years, Ben averaged selling a million dollars a week.

The amount stunned and amazed me.

I did a quick calculation, based on two hundred and forty work days, and Ben Feldman, at the top of his game, was selling a little more than four thousand dollars worth of insurance a day.

At the time, there were fifteen hundred insurance companies in the United States, and Ben Feldman, all by himself, with revenue based on annual sales, would have ranked in the top third.

My mind was made up.

Ben Feldman had achieved a monumental amount of success.

In fact, it had been done dozens of times.

Who was to say I couldn't do it as well?

Others had indeed achieved greatness, and my goal was to pattern my life in the business world after their lives. After all, I was hungry to accomplish something that wasn't ordinary. I don't ever remember a time when I didn't feel that way.

My life had always been something of an enigma.

I had been poor.

I never felt poor.

My circumstances were poor.

I wasn't.

I always dressed the best I could, sometimes sacrificing food money, even at the age of fourteen, so that I could wear nice suits to church.

I probably had less money than anyone else attending classes at Howard Payne University, seldom ever having as many as five or maybe ten dollars in my pocket, which would usually have to last the entire month.

But no one walking across campus ever knew that I was always on the verge of being broke.

At the time, I had my dream. It burst a time or two. But I never lost sight of it, not even when the only job I could find was driving a snow cone truck.

There was no disgrace in falling down the mountain.

Failure would have been not climbing back up.

For most of my life, I had followed the lessons of those who told me to set goals that were realistic.

That was good advice for me.

That, I believed, was an important thing to do.

I knew exactly what kind of specific goals I was establishing for my faith, for my family, for my job, and for my health.

They were all within reach.

If my goal had been to climb three steps and I made it, then I was a success. But if my goal was to climb ten steps, and I only made it up three steps, I felt like a failure. The theory made a lot of sense to me, but somehow only striving to reach the top of those first three steps never left me fulfilled. You never know how high you can really go until you make the effort.

I had set several significant goals and had achieved them, but when I studied Paul J. Meyer's *Million Dollar Personal Success Plan*, I began to fear that, perhaps, my goals may have been realistic all right but were set far too low.

His suggestion was to establish goals as high as I could possibly imagine. It did not make any difference whether or not they seemed realistic at the time.

Aim high.

Then shoot higher.

It was, a wise man had once written, better to shoot for the stars and miss than aim down a hole and hit it.

Achievement was the challenge, and I wanted to see if I could meet that challenge head on and win. Just sitting around and thinking about, just wishing for it, just hoping for it were all losing propositions. I had to go for it.

So many believe that goal setting deals almost exclusively with business and a person's accomplishments. When I began making my first lists, I dwelled on the little things that brought day-to-day and month-to-month satisfaction.

Rather than merely setting those kinds of goals, however, I began to look ahead and start considering the real possibilities that lay before me.

It freed my mind.

It broadened my parameters of thought.

Goals were still critical and important in my life and business. But when I dared to reach out and *consider the possibilities* for my life and for Tom James, I discovered that my ideas had no limitations.

I was outside the box.

So many people in business believe they can sit down, spend a couple of hours jotting down hopes and dreams and plans, and completely develop the goals they will follow for the rest of their lives.

It's a start.

And it's never too early or too late to start.

Goals, however, keep changing – just as your business or your family life keeps changing. For example, one of my first goals for my wife and three children was having a home with four bedrooms and two baths. When my fourth child was born, however, I immediately had to take a pencil and erase that earlier goal. Now I needed a home with five bedrooms and at least three bathrooms.

Life is filled with sudden and unexpected revisions.

Be ready for them.

Make sure your goals are, too.

During a five-year period, from 1967 through 1972, I stole away every Saturday morning, while the rest of my family was still sleeping, and spent a couple of hours alone on the back porch, *considering the possibilities* I could achieve.

Think big, I told myself.

Then I tried to think even bigger.

And I began writing down ideas that would allow me to fulfill those possibilities.

They weren't necessarily for me.

They weren't all about Tom James either.

A lot of the possibilities dealt with my family. Regularly on my way to work in downtown Atlanta, I stopped at a travel agency and picked up brochures. On Saturday morning, I began listing places in all fifty states and Washington, D. C. where we could take the kinds of vacations we had never experienced before.

Beginning in 1971, we had moved to Dallas, and we took our first big trip, flying to Miami, renting a room on the beach, and driving down to the Keys. It was such a good trip that we decided to drive home in a rent car, skirting the Gulf coastlines of Alabama, Mississippi, and Louisiana, easing into Houston and heading north toward home. From then on, it was New Jersey and New York, Annapolis and Gettysburg, then six weeks in Santa Monica and Hollywood California, and eventually on to Hawaii.

None of these trips had been on my original list of goals. I had merely written down: *take a family vacation*. Now I was *considering actual possibilities* and putting the money aside to make them happen.

These vacations came out of those Saturday mornings when I looked past my list of goals and began *considering all of the possibilities* that my family and I had never experienced together before. So many of those possibilities I wrote down made life more meaningful and valuable to us.

Most people don't *consider the possibilities* available to them. They keep letting the difficulties of life prevent them from pursuing big dreams. And so often, their self-image is the primary problem. They don't see themselves as capable of achieving any significant goals. Too many times, they view goal setting as nothing more than an exercise in fantasy and futility. It takes too much time, they say. It'll never happen, they say. I'm wasting my time, they say.

Don't fall into that trap.

Don't settle for mediocrity. Don't let disappointment or fear overwhelm you.

We all want to enjoy the satisfaction and benefits that are derived from our achievements. However, many people never take the time to think through their possibilities, so it is difficult for them to ever make any specific decisions.

Developing goals and possibilities boils down to four factors:

1. Know what you want to do.
2. Know why you want to do it.
3. Know how you can do it.
4. Know when to do it and how long it will take to do it.

I love taking the time I need to *consider the possibilities* for all aspects of my life and my career. It enables me to make better choices. It is stimulating. It is motivating. It is one of the real pleasures I find in my existence.

By taking time to *consider possibilities*, I am not trying to pull goals out of the air. I'm focusing on the direction and the distance I want to travel. I was never on a short road. I am now on the long one with no end in sight.

When simply setting goals, I wanted to be a good sales person, help Spencer Hays build a successful business at Tom James, live in a nice house with a nice yard, buy a new washer and dryer for my wife, drive a nice car, attend a nice church, donate to a number of charities, and take meaningful vacations with my family.

Those goals were important.

They were all worthwhile.

On Goals

"During the summer of 2009 I lived with Poppa and Grammy while I was earning money to go back to college in the fall. It was during that time that we were able to talk for many hours together. I absolutely loved it. He mentored me during this time and gave me a definition of success that I will never forget. He helped

> *me memorize this definition: 'Success is the progressive*
> *achievement of previously determined and worthwhile*
> *goals.' During this time he encouraged me to work on*
> *my goals. All the things I wanted and hoped for. He*
> *had this incredible ability to affirm and encourage*
> *in such a way as to call for 'greatness' out of me. He*
> *saw something in me that others did not. Like a great*
> *coach or mentor he knew exactly how to encourage me*
> *to pursue my goals. I had observed this in other cases*
> *as he interacted with our family. I now realize he was*
> *calling for 'greatness' from virtually everyone he had*
> *influence over." Daniel McDowell (Grandson)*

But when I sat back on a Saturday morning, took my workbook in hand and began *considering the possibilities*, I wrote down the idea, and then developed the strategy and game plan, for turning Tom James into a hundred-million-dollar-a-year company.

It was daring.

It was specific.

I knew, however, that there was no reason to establish a goal unless I was willing to work hard enough and long enough to make it a reality.

Most people in business are impatient.

They want it now or by next Monday.

They are not willing to go the distance.

I was.

I was determined to build Tom James into a hundred-million-dollar-a-year company. I set the goal, and gave myself the time I thought I needed to accomplish it.

I wrote down twenty years.

Takeaways from the chapter

- *Jim said of RG LeTourneau: "He was a man I never forgot." Who are the people that I will never forget and why?*

- *Jim's desire to not only accumulate wealth but to give it away is an important part of his identity. He has mentioned giving on a number of occasions in this book. His goals seem to have been to earn enough money to provide for his family into the future and then give as much away as he could. Am I someone who wants to give to others? Am I someone who hoards money? Wastes money? Am I responsible with the money that I earn?*

- *Jim spent many years of his life emphasizing the importance of written goals that are regularly rehearsed and updated. What are my goals? What is my plan to achieve those goals?*

- *Jim seemed to find a balance between family and work? Do I have that balance? What can I do to achieve that balance?*

- *Jim states "I love taking time to consider the possibilities for all aspects of my life and career. It enables me to make better choices. It is stimulating. It is motivating. It is one of the real pleasures I find in my existence." How often am I sitting down to 'consider the possibilities' of my goals?*

CHAPTER 14

Choosing to Embrace New Responsibilities

We may not have conquered or even controlled the Nashville clothing market, but, within a year, the Tom James Company had made a definite impact. It did not take Spencer Hays long to realize or determine that his well-crafted idea did indeed have wings, had taken flight just as he had hoped, and could be transferred with success to any major city in the country.

Spencer sat down with me in July of 1968 and told me that he had decided not to wait. Sales were good. Tom James, as a clothier, had gained acceptance by some of the most prestigious and influential businessmen in Nashville. We were learning on the fly and making changes that affected the bottom line in a positive manner. As a result, he was going ahead and opening three new locations.

"Where?" I wanted to know.

"Atlanta, Memphis, and Dallas," he said, and I've already committed to sending Lindy Watkins to Dallas."

I had my choice of the remaining two cities.

Instantly, without giving it any thought at all, I said, "I'll take Atlanta."

Spencer Hays had found the location he wanted at 91 Peachtree Street. For me, responsibility and opportunity both seemed to be changing directions every time I turned around. In the back of my mind, I remembered the hard economic times of the past and was convinced that, with Tom James, I would never have to worry about them or deal with them again.

Arlene and I immediately made preparations to pack up our belongings, gather up our three children (at the time), and move south. Those hard days of desperation and despair from my past were quickly fading, and I strongly believed that divine providence had at last allowed me to find and grasp the brass ring I had dreamed about as a young man in the fields of West Texas. I had always seen myself someday reaching the top of the business world. I wasn't there yet, but I had the top within my sights.

Spencer Hays and the Tom James Company were going places. And they were taking me with them.

As I drove into downtown Atlanta, I was suddenly stricken by curious pangs of regret. Maybe I had looked so far into the future that I had ruined my present. The street was lined on both sides by the steel and glass of tall, regal, and contemporary buildings. Atlanta was the New South. And I was a part of it. Yet, as the traffic crept along from red light to red light, slipping from sunlight to shadow, it was like making my way tenuously down a dark, cavernous avenue where I wasn't quite sure I belonged.

I kept thinking: *I don't know anyone in this town. I don't know anyone in these buildings. And more importantly, they don't know me. Maybe they don't even want to know me. I had a lot of good customers back in Nashville. I kept them dressed well. I could keep right on making sure they were dressed well. When I walked into their offices, they were glad to see me. But what about here? What about Atlanta? No one here even knows or cares I'm coming to town or even in town. I would be making sales calls today if I were home in Nashville. I would be making money today if I were home in Nashville. Instead, I'm driving on a street that's brand new to me in a city that's brand new to me. Why did I leave Nashville? What am I doing here?*

I took a deep breath, did my best to shove the negative thoughts out of my head, parked my car, and walked toward the Tom James store. It was waiting for me to open the doors for business. It was waiting for me to fill it up with customers, or at least the sales from customers. I was starting all over again. I was starting from scratch. I glanced around at the sculptured wall of buildings that surrounded and towered over me. Beyond those dark windows were offices. Inside so many of those offices sat my next customers.

Those businessmen did not know it now.

They would know it soon.

The momentary anguish of regret had come and gone. Life was a series of starts and stops and starts again. Sure I missed Nashville. I always would. Nashville was the city where I had begun the rest of my life. But I would not be going back again. Not for good anyway. I suddenly wasn't worried anymore. Business is a daily and a constant struggle with confidence. Some days you have it. Some days you have more of it. You can never begin a good day without it. I smiled. I knew what I was doing in Atlanta.

I opened the doors to Atlanta's new edition of a Tom James store, walked inside, turned on the lights, and found a telephone. The city around me might be different. The businesses might be different. Awaiting me however, were new executives with new faces and new names. Whether they knew it or not, they all needed new, tailored suits.

They had probably never heard the name Tom James before.

But that was all about to change.

Style and fashion had come to Atlanta.

I began dialing numbers.

Someone, I knew, would see me before the morning ended.

He happened to be Ben Hyman, a wholesale jeweler whose office was located about four blocks farther north.

When I walked out of the store about ten o'clock, I had a firm appointment, and I always equated any kind of appointment with a sale. Of course, it might not necessarily be on the first call or even during the next month or so. But if a businessman did indeed care enough about his clothes and his image to see me, I believed that he would, sooner or later, be interested in everything we had to offer at Tom James.

He would learn before he realized it that we simply provided him with the best custom tailored clothes in town.

I was convinced of it when I walked into his office.

He believed it by the time I walked out.

As I entered the executive office to keep my appointment with Ben Hyman, I noticed that he had the cover of *Look Magazine* bronzed and hanging inside the front door. I pointed to the cover. After all, I had never seen one bronzed before. And I said, "This must really be important to you."

I smiled.

He smiled back.

"It is," he said.

"What's the story?"

Ben Hyman could not wait to tell me. Maybe the magazine cover had hung there for years, ignored or overlooked. Maybe no one else had ever asked him about it. Maybe no one else had ever been interested.

I was.

He appreciated the fact that I was.

"It's a regional edition of *Look*," he said proudly. "In this particular issue, I had more pages of advertising than any other company has ever had."

"How many pages?"

"Eighteen."

"That's a lot."

His smile softened and grew even larger. He felt as important that morning as he had ever felt. I made sure of it.

Perched on Ben Hyman's desk was the model replica of a C54 transport plane. I touched it with my fingertips and said casually, "I guess this one has a pretty good story behind it, too."

"It does." He nodded. "I had a friend who worked for the company that built the C54," Ben said. "My friend helped develop it. When the plane was ready to fly, I was the first civilian to ever ride in it."

"That's quite an honor."

I knew by looking at him that Ben Hyman thought so as well. We talked for ten or fifteen minutes, then he leaned forward and said, "You didn't come here just to talk to me, but I'm glad you came. It's a fortuitous time. I need some new clothes. Go ahead and show me what you have."

I did.

There was no sales presentation, no discussion, and no negotiations, no *let me think about it and I'll call you maybe next week.*

Ben Hyman gingerly felt the rich fabrics in my portfolio case and glanced over our selection of colors, patterns, and styles. He carefully studied them. I could tell that he was weighing the pros and cons of owning a tailored suit.

I was wrong.

"I can have you a new suit in about six weeks," I said.

"I don't want a suit," he said.

"No?"

"I want five of them."

Tom James was on the ground and running in Atlanta, Georgia.

Our meeting that morning forever instituted a monumental change in the way I approached my sales presentations. Ben Hyman had known one thing for certain. I had taken the time to show my interest in him and in the important parts of his life. As a result, he immediately became interested in me and in the merchandise I represented.

He didn't know me.

But he accepted me.

I had given him a reason to feel good about himself.

He had given me a reason to feel good about selling Tom James suits.

From that moment on, I would walk into an executive's office and quickly glance around to find what might be important to him. It might be a college diploma, a picture of him in his fishing or hunting gear, a family portrait, an autographed football, an award for some achievement in business, or perhaps a certificate of appreciation from some civic club, little league baseball team, local or national charitable organization, or a university's sports program.

It didn't take long for me to realize that the important treasures of a man's life always hung on the walls of his office.

Behind each of them was always a story dear to his heart.

I always asked to hear the story.

With four short words – *tell me about it* – I ceased to become a sales person, and I became his friend, even if he had to look on my business card to remember my name. As a rule, we all like to do business with our friends.

He never thought I was in a hurry – even if I was – because I surely didn't try to limit the time I was in his office. I encouraged him to talk at length about those vital memories of his life, framed on his office wall. For me, it was a simple principle, easy to understand, and one I never forgot.

It wasn't a sales trick.

There was nothing phony about it.

My reasoning was simple: *the more I knew about the man, the better I could help him choose the clothes important to him, his image, and his work.*

If I listened intently to him, then my customers were more likely to be anxious to listen to me. If I gave him the opportunity to tell me what he considered important in his personal and his business life, then he would sit back and hear every word I spoke about the importance of image, tailored clothes, and Tom James.

I came to better comprehend just how valuable it was to learn as much as I could about the customers with whom I met. They all had stories and hardly ever a reason to talk about them. Most sales people waltzed in, and all they cared about was the order. If I cared enough about the man sitting on the other side of the desk, then sooner or later, the orders would come.

They always did.

In a career that spanned more than fifty years, only a handful of times did I ever hear an executive say, "I'm sorry. I don't have time to talk about that."

This realization greatly influenced me even when I began calling to schedule an appointment. I always took the time necessary to cross-reference a customer and find out as much as I could about him: where he lived, who his neighbors were, and the names of those who shared the same office with him. I recognized the value of him as a friend long before he knew who I was or anything about me.

For example, on more than one occasion, I called the receptionist and asked, out of the blue, "What has Joe been up to lately?"

My tone was nice and casual, and she immediately made the assumption that I was a good friend, or at least a pretty good acquaintance, and trying to catch up with Joe. In a bustling, fast-paced city like Atlanta, we all knew how difficult it was to keep up with each other. The demands of business kept us running through too many airports in too many directions.

She would laugh and might say, "Joe and his son have just gotten back from their annual fishing trip off the coast of Mexico."

I immediately gathered that information and packed it away. It was invaluable. When I did walk into Joe's office, I would make my approach personal and personable. I guarantee you that we spent a lot of time talking about a man going fishing with his son – whether it was in Mexico or along the banks of Atlanta's Lake Lanier – before we ever got around to discussing fabrics and colors, then making a decision on the clothes he would need to fill out his winter wardrobe.

I might not be able to recognize a customer before I walked into his office, but I had taken the time to learn as much as possible about him. If he were a fisherman, I was ready to talk fishing. If he preferred hunting, then I could discuss the intricacies of deer, duck, goose, squirrel, bear, fox, or raccoon hunting as though I had just packed away my rifle or shotgun before knocking on his door. If he were an Atlanta Braves baseball fan, I knew who had homered, pitched a shutout, or given up the winning run in the ninth. If he had come to Atlanta from St. Louis, I would track down information on the Cardinals as though I had warmed up Steve Carlton before his last start in Chicago. If he happened to be planning a vacation to New York, I had a list of don't-miss restaurants and the new musicals on

Broadway. If he were building a backyard jungle gym for his child, chances were I had built one or knew enough about jungle gyms to help him build one on a piece of scratch paper. Whatever was important to my customers was important to me. It took a little extra time and effort, but the dividends it paid were too numerous to calculate. Some businessmen groaned when they saw a sales person standing in the door. I wanted them to be glad when I walked in. After all, regardless of the subject, we had a lot to talk about.

I had settled down in Atlanta and was determined to build a legacy for the Tom James Company in the one city that harbored the heart and soul of the Deep South. By the end of 1969, I could sense the winds of change stirring again. We had developed a growing business that was bursting at the seams throughout Nashville, Memphis, Dallas, and Atlanta, and Spencer Hays was making a critical decision to move our concept and our business farther west. Fort Worth, Houston, and Tulsa had survived without the benefits of Tom James long enough. Virtually overnight, the center of the company had dramatically changed.

Within the South, I had regarded Atlanta as the storied region's cornerstone city. In the broadening scope of the Tom James Company, however, it was only the eastern corner. It became apparent that Spencer Hays would keep expanding the business until it touched as many borders within the nation from east to west as he could reach. That left Dallas placed firmly in the center.

During those early, unpredictable years, there was only one constant at the Tom James Company. Nothing was ever constant. Building an innovative new idea into an innovative new business, we were always in the flux of never-ending change.

By the time the decade of the seventies arrived, I felt as though I had bought a ticket, climbed on the next plane, and was flying off in all directions at once. Spencer Hays had assigned me to Atlanta, and I immediately began hiring and training as many new sales people as I could possibly unleash on the city and its burgeoning suburbs. When Spencer flew in to meet with me that night, I was in charge of an operation that had eight other sales people riding the elevators of Atlanta.

Our aim was simple. Collectively, we wanted Atlanta to be the best-dressed city in the South, and we were well on our way, developing new clients and new sales with every day that passed.

I even stayed awake at night, trying to figure out creative new ways to expand the Tom James presence in the city, add a cadre of new sales people, and double our prestigious client list of Atlanta's top businessmen.

With a single meeting, my life changed and took another unexpected turn.

It began with a simple statement. "I want you to give up your clientele here in Atlanta," Spencer Hays said.

I stared at him in disbelief.

He waited for a response.

"I'm sure you have your reasons," I said, carefully choosing my words.

He did.

I waited for an explanation.

"You understand the culture and the sales philosophy of the Tom James Company better than anyone," Spencer said. "I want you to give up your clientele here so you will be free to travel to Dallas, Fort Worth, Houston, Tulsa, Memphis, and even Nashville, going with members of our sales force on their daily calls and teaching them all to sell exactly the same way you do."

"That's quite an assignment," I said.

"You have a lot to offer."

Maybe I did. Maybe not. I would soon find out.

The confidence Spencer had in my ability and sales record triggered a new and bold excitement within me. My mind was already racing by the time he boarded a plane and flew out of Atlanta.

For the next few days, it kept racing day and night.

How could I repay him? I wondered.

Then it dawned on me.

The formula, even on a grand scale, seemed so simple on paper.

In my mind, I was developing the fragmented edges of a concept that would grow Tom James to a hundred million dollar company.

How many years would it take?

I didn't know for sure.

But I knew that the goal was something we could achieve.

Some in the clothing business would no doubt ridicule me, and others, probably behind my back, might even label me a little unbalanced.

Maybe so.

But I was undaunted.

I knew how it could be done.

And I was determined to do it.

Takeaways from the chapter

- *"Life is a series of starts and stops and starts again." Jim says in so many words "change unavoidably happens." With that change comes opportunity. Am I ready to embrace change so that I can find the opportunities?*
- *Jim realized that when one understands what's important to another that this opens the opportunity for relationship. What am I doing to find out what is important to other people? Am I observant enough? Do I really care about what is near and dear to the people I interact with? How much research have I done regarding the people I interact with?*
- *The BHAG (big, hairy, audacious goal): It is during this time that Jim begins to develop what would become his vision for his career and the company. Am I looking to that goal that is so big that some might suggest that by the very mention of it that I'm "a little imbalanced"?*

CHAPTER 15

Choosing to Think Big

I had never been afraid to think big or dare to dream big dreams. Even as a young boy, working on a farm in West Texas, struggling to understand why my brother, sister, and I had been left behind by our parents, I could look far down the road in my mind and visualize myself as a success in business. I did not know if I would someday own a farm or ranch or chain of grocery stores, but I never believed that the top was out of my reach. Of course, my journey took a few wrong turns and an occasional detour, but, thanks to the values my grandparents had instilled in me, I kept forging ahead. "The poor house" was full of people who gave up along the way. I may have resided just outside "the poor house" from time to time, but I never wanted to think it had a room for me. I certainly didn't plan on checking in.

Throughout my years, I had been greatly influenced by those who achieved a measure of success in the business world. While I was still in high school in Abilene, occupying the same little house where my mother lived with her hard-drinking, hard-gambling husband number three and trying without any luck to figure out what I could possibly do with the rest of my life, I made it a point one Sunday night to slip into the First Baptist Church and hear the words and wisdom of R. G. LeTourneau. Here was a man whose existence had no doubt been as difficult as mine, a man who knew all about the hard climb from rags to riches. He had been hauling in dirt to level out a section of farmland near Stockton, California. The days were long and sometimes longer, the sun unbearable, and the work backbreaking; difficult enough to bend a strong man's back forever. He was a common laborer. That was all. But while he was working with his hands, his mind was free to develop a better, more efficient way to move dirt. Within a decade, he had built the country's first all-welded scraper that was lighter, stronger, and less expensive than other machines. By the time World War II stormed across Europe and threatened the safety and sanity of the world, LeTourneau was producing seventy percent of the army's earth-moving machinery. In time, he would become known as a mover of both mountains and men.

In business, he believed that "the only difference between can and can't is a little extra effort." It was said that LeTourneau never backed down from any monumental task. If he happened to be confronted with a problem that seemed to be insurmountable, he did not worry or fret or let the obstacle frustrate him. He simply prayed about it, studied it, and worked at it until he was able to solve it. As a result, he designed and built machines far beyond the imagination of ordinary men. What impressed me most, however, was that LeTourneau never let his desire and his ability to earn great sums of wealth ever stand in the way of his firm allegiance to Christ and Christianity.

He earned millions, no telling how many, and it was always said that LeTourneau gave ninety percent of his profits to God's work and kept only ten percent for himself. He would always smile and say that, as far as he could tell, the money came in much faster than he could give it away. He believed that he could not out-give God. "I shovel it out," he explained, "and God shovels it back. God has a bigger shovel."

I had heard about R. G. LeTourneau. I had read about R. G. LeTourneau. On that Sunday night, I was able to actually be in his presence and see him up close and personal. I never did get the chance to meet him, but I never forgot that I had the rare privilege of sitting in the same room with a great man.

He spoke to a large gathering, but he might as well have been talking only to me. His words made me aware of two distinct challenges that lay ahead of me. I could rise above any barriers, real or imagined, lying in my path and become the person I believed I could be. But regardless of whatever success I might accomplish in life, I knew that I had an unwavering financial responsibility to my God and to those around me.

I was still in college at Howard Payne when I sat down in chapel one morning and immersed myself in the deep-seated and heartfelt wisdom of Howard E. Butt, who, much like LeTourneau, started virtually from scratch and managed to build the multi-billion dollar H-E-B supermarket chain. It all began with a small store in the Texas Hill Country. His father had long suffered from tuberculosis, and the family moved from Tennessee to Kerrville in hopes that a dry climate might improve his condition. With an investment of sixty dollars, Florence Butt opened the C. C. Butt Grocery Store in 1905.

The three brothers dutifully hit the narrow little road each day and delivered food from one home to another in an old baby carriage until they saved enough money to buy a little red wagon. Within three years, they had moved up in the business world and were handling their delivery chores with a horse and wagon, advertising that their mother's store was a dealer in "staples, fancy groceries, and fresh meat."

Three times, the company tried to expand its little homegrown country enterprise to another town. Three times, the Butt Cash and Carry grocery store failed. Finally, after years of frustration, it began to take root among the mesquite brush of South Texas, and under the untiring leadership of Howard E. Butt and his son Charles, the supermarket continued growing until it gained recognition as the nation's fifteenth largest grocery store chain based on annual revenues.

Both LeTourneau and Butt fired my imagination. I could see myself following their footsteps in business. Neither company began with a lot of money. I was broke as well. But both men had a big dream and never let go of it. I could feel my dream building and growing bigger when I walked out of chapel after Butt's closing words that morning. It lost air every now and then. There were occasions when my dream seemed to simply burrow down in the recesses of my mind and lie dormant for a spell. But sooner or later, it would always awaken and drive me onward. My dream was an unforgiving taskmaster.

It caused me to think beyond the ordinary.

I might be little more than a small speck upon the earth.

My ambition was somewhat larger, and my mind would never let me forget it.

Back on my grandfather's farm, the elevation was two thousand feet, the nearest town was fourteen miles away, and there were very few if any artificial lights at night to spoil our view of the sky. The illumination above the downtown streets of Lamesa was only a distant and dim glow. The stars seemed to sit down upon our shoulders as we lay on the ground and watched them stretch from one flat horizon to the other. A black sky. Bright stars. They were endless.

My grandfather told me about the constellations and pointed out the Alpha Centuri. "Do you know what's important about it?" he asked.

I didn't.

"It's the star that's closest to us," he said.

"How close?" I wanted to know.

"It's four a half light years away."

I grabbed a pencil and paper and began the calculations. That was 186,000 miles per second times sixty seconds times sixty minutes times twenty-four hours times three hundred and sixty five days times four and a half years.

I whistled softly.

"That's a long way," I said.

He nodded.

"And it's the closest star?'

"It is."

"And we can see it with our naked eyes?"

"We can."

"How many stars can we see?"

"About three thousand."

"With our naked eyes?"

"That's all we need."

"And they're all farther away than Alpha Centuri?"

"They are."

It boggled the mind. But the big numbers, the larger the better, did not scare me. I loved working with big numbers. They were easy for me. Back in elementary school, as soon as I learned how to multiply one multi-digit number by another, I realized that I had a propensity for dealing with big numbers.

When I taught school at Post, I was given sixth-grade science. The textbook was so simple; the students were able to run through it in a month, so I decided not to limit my lessons strictly to the book. I began trying to create totally new materials that would both interest my students and expand their thinking.

I had them calculate the distance earth had to travel in order for our planet to work its way completely around the sun in three hundred and sixty-five days.

That was ninety-three million miles times 3.1416, or Pi, which came to more than three hundred million miles, which was only slightly less than one million miles a day. Earth – and we upon it – had to be moving along at a pretty good speed. Maybe that was the reason why we usually felt the West Texas wind blowing in our faces. Probably not.

Big numbers were intriguing to me. I occupied a lot of my spare time working with them, and I do believe they greatly influenced my thoughts about which direction I would finally take my in life.

Near the end of 1967, Spencer Hays gave me a copy of Paul J. Meyer's *Million Dollar Personal Success Plan*. Paul J. Meyer, who founded Success Motivation Institute, had devoted his life to helping others better understand their potential for leadership, for personal development, and for professional excellence. I diligently listened to the tapes and began filling out the workbooks. If this was what Spencer expected me to do, I did not hesitate to do it.

Meyer once said, "The farther out you can think in terms of goal setting, the better off you are."

It made sense to me. When I looked toward the future as I planned my career, I began to stretch my mind, and I had no idea how far it was capable of stretching. The impossible might take a while longer, but it was definitely possible. Paul Meyer taught it. Spencer believed it. And so did I.

Meyer had five key points that every successful man or woman needed to know and implement in their own lives and business. He wrote:

1. *Crystallize Your Thinking. Determine what specific goal you want to achieve and dedicate yourself to its attainment ... with unswerving singleness of purpose, the trenchant zeal of a crusader.*

2. *Develop a Plan for Achieving Your Goal, and a Deadline for its Attainment. Plan your progress carefully: hour-by-hour, day-by-day, month-by-month. Organized activity and maintained enthusiasm are the wellsprings of your power.*

3. *Develop a Sincere Desire for the Things You Want in Life. A burning desire is the greatest motivator of every human action. The desire for success implants success consciousness, which, in turn, creates a vigorous and ever-increasing habit of success.*

4. *Develop Supreme Confidence in Yourself and Your Own Abilities. Enter every activity without giving mental recognition to the possibility of defeat. Concentrate on your strengths, instead of your weaknesses, on your powers, instead of your problems.*

5. *Develop a Dogged Determination to Follow Through on Your Plan, Regardless of Obstacles, Criticism, or Circumstances ... or What Other People Say, Think, or Do. Construct your determination with sustained effort, controlled attention, and concentrated energy. Opportunities never come to those who wait ... they are captured by those who dare to attack.*

I believed everything that Paul J. Meyer said. After all, he was one of the world's most enterprising and profound success gurus. He had been an insurance sales person and built a huge organization of sales people during the 1920s. He wasn't just giving me a list of what I should do. He had already achieved it. If he had climbed the ladder, I was looking for the bottom rung. Whatever Paul J. Meyer had to teach, I was ready to learn. Although I didn't realize it at the time, he was providing me with the necessary tools I needed to one day turn Tom James into a hundred million dollars a year company.

As I interpreted his words, Paul J. Meyer wanted me to write down what I really wanted to achieve in my professional, financial, spiritual, personal, and family life. He did not want me to think about it from time to time. He expected me to sit down, decide what exactly my primary goals should be, then put a pen to paper and write them down. His belief was that I – like any other man or woman – should set their goals as high as we could imagine. I might not think they were realistic at the time, but that didn't matter. He thought I should decide exactly what I really wanted in life, and then go for it.

I did.

Every time I jotted down my goals, and I did so regularly to make sure I did not forget them, these were the first words I wrote at the top of the page: *Grow Tom James to a hundred million dollar company.*

It made me extremely nervous to write down those words. I would lay my pen down on the desk and feel a wave of nausea and anxiety. That single thought put me far outside my comfort zone. My muscles knotted up, and I found it suddenly difficult to breathe. I had never thought in terms of being able to do something so big. That goal was so simple to say. It was so hard to write down. I often had to force myself to do it, and several times I merely wadded up the piece of paper and threw it away. No one knew about those words but me. No one might ever know if I looked in the mirror, glimpsed the face of a fool looking back, and realized just how ridiculous that goal might be. But I could not forget the promise I was making to myself, to Spencer Hays, and to Tom James.

When I said it, the idea was no more than a passing thought. When I wrote on paper *Grow Tom James to a hundred million dollar company,* it was a commitment in both principle and deed. Once it was on paper, it was an indelible and undeniable fact. Once it was on paper, I had no choice but to do it.

I kept writing the goal down. Over and over, I kept writing it down. And the more I wrote about growing Tom James to a one hundred million dollar company, the more comfortable I began to feel about the idea. After awhile, it did not seem out of my reach at all.

During my life, I had been influenced by great men who had accomplished the impossible on a shoestring, so I knew it could be done.

I had an affinity for big numbers, but until now, big numbers had always been more of a game than anything else.

Now the success of my future in business was riding on them.

As Paul J. Meyer suggested I do, I had set a goal for the Tom James Company as far out as I could possibly imagine. But there was a definite method to my madness.

While I was still selling books each summer for the Southwestern Company, my sales manager, Fred Landers, taught me a lot about sales. He taught me even more about business. One morning after I had returned to Nashville, Landers took me to see a Merrill Lynch stockbroker in the Third National Bank Building. He had them give me all of the promotional and financial information they had so I could figure out the strategies behind investing in a stock, a mutual fund, or a group of stocks.

It piqued my interest in just who the major companies in America might be.

Who were the biggest?

Who were the best?

What management strategies had made them grow so large?

I learned that out of the top one thousand publicly traded companies in the United States, all but three of them had sales of more than a hundred million dollars a year.

That had given me my perspective.

My vision was for the Tom James Company to one day be recognized as one of America's biggest and best corporations. The benchmark had already been set and pretty much chiseled in stone.

All we needed were annual sales of a hundred million dollars.

I kept reading, studying, and trying to determine just how those top one thousand companies happened to grow that large, and how many years did it take. I discovered that most of them had attained the necessary level of sales within a single generation.

That gave me hope.

Others had done it.

We could, too.

And it would not necessarily have to take two or three lifetimes.

A hundred million dollars in sales was well within reach. The formula I developed was tried and true. It had worked for J. C. Penney. It struck me that the concept would work for Tom James as well.

His middle name, appropriately enough, was Cash, and James Cash Penney was a man after my own heart. As he once said, "I am grateful for all of my problems. After each one was overcome, I became stronger and more able to meet those that were still to come. I grew in all of my difficulties."

Penney's father had been a poverty-stricken farmer, always fighting the weather, and a Baptist minister, waging his personal war against sin. The family, even if it had nothing else, clung to the teachings of the Golden rule and a code of self-reliance, self-discipline, honor, and education. J. C., as a boy worked for neighbors, and by the time he was eight years old, he was buying his own clothes. Money was scarce. It was thought, perhaps hopefully, that J. C. would become a lawyer, but his father died, and the young man took a job in a dry goods store. His life would never be the same.

J. C. Penney bought a butcher shop in Denver, Colorado. It failed. He traveled on farther north to Wyoming, went to work at a dry goods store, and eventually owned it all. The sign above the door said *The Golden Rule Store*. In reality, those four words said everything there was to know about Penney's honesty and work ethic. His first store in 1902 was packed in a one-room building. He and his wife lived in the attic. Penney sold quality products for mining and farm operations for fair prices, and that would always be the theme of his business. His slogan was: *Honor, Confidence, Service, and Cooperation.*

J. C. Penney, whether he realized it not, created the perfect formula for expansion. He never had employees, he said. He had associates and believed that men who ran their businesses should never hire anyone who wasn't viewed as a potential partner. He did not look at his associates as merely hired hands. They became his manager-partners when he opened new stores, and they shared in his profits. They had a stake in the business. They had every reason to make sure that the stores were a success.

Besides running a good, profitable operation, a manager was given one mission. Hire another honest, hardworking associate and train him to become a manager. Every time a new associate was ready to take charge of his own operation, J. C. Penney was ready to open a new store.

J. C. Penney's goal was not to have a chain of stores.

He wanted a chain of good men.

The dry goods stores began to grow and expand all over the country. By 1909, he had thirty-four Golden Rule Stores with more than two million dollars in sales. Six years later, Penney was operating eighty-three stores and moving east of the Mississippi River. After twenty-five years, Penney announced that the business had a decent chance to be recording a billion dollars in sales by the time it reached its fiftieth anniversary,

His model had worked to perfection.

By consistently hiring good people and training new managers, Penney was able to keep doubling the size of his company until it had ultimately nailed twelve hundred stores into place, all doing business with honor, confidence, service, and cooperation.

What J. C. Penney had managed to do seemed so simple to duplicate. In my mind, I could envision the Tom James Company going nationwide with stores and a force of quality sales people knocking on corporate doors from one end of the country to the other.

My goal was not complicated. At the moment, the average sales person was selling around forty thousand dollars a year, although a scattered few had managed to touch as many as ninety thousand dollars in annual sales.

With the proper training (I would be on the road and responsible for the training), I was convinced that our sales people could each average selling a hundred thousand dollars a year.

All I needed was one thousand sales people. In reality, all I needed was one thousand sales people each making enough calls to sell a hundred thousand dollars worth of Tom James clothing and accessories each year. Then I could reach my magic mark. Then we could achieve a hundred million dollars in sales. I wrote the number down again and stared at it for a long time. I chuckled. A hundred million dollars didn't seem nearly as impossible and ridiculous to me as it once had. I wondered who in the company and behind my back would call me mad first. It didn't matter. I had the map, I knew where we were going, and I had an idea of how long it would take to get there even with the obstacles that would no doubt show up along the way.

Spencer Hays came to town, and he and I were walking down the sidewalks of Atlanta together on our way to meet a man who had opened an answering service with Spencer's financing. It took all of the nerve I could muster up, and I dug into my mind searching for the right words to say, and then finally blurted out, "Spence, I think we can grow Tom James to a hundred million dollar company."

He looked at me. He didn't say a word.

"All we need," I continued, "are locations all over the country with enough sales people to man them. Spence, we can reach that mark. I have no doubt about it."

I held my breath. This much I knew. If Spencer had anything negative at all to say about the idea, I would drop it, forget it, and never mention it again. It was important for me to know whether or not Spencer thought the goal was possible and reachable. After all, he had grown the direct selling force at the Southwestern Company to more than a thousand sales people. He had always been a thinker and never afraid to think big. I knew he would weigh the facts, carefully decide whether the idea had more pros than cons, try to determine the level of my commitment to make it happen, and then make a decision.

The question Spencer asked that morning, the one everyone would ask later on, was simply: "How do we attain that number?"

"It's not difficult."

"How do you plan to get there?"

"We ultimately open three hundred stores with three to four sales people in each location." I smiled. "Of course," I said, "we could probably make it work with fewer stores and more sales people at each location."

Spencer frowned.

Everyone who heard my idea would initially frown.

"How do we get there?" he asked again.

I didn't flinch.

"I'll explain when we get back to the office."

Spencer grinned. "I can't wait to see what you've come up with," he said.

Back behind my desk that afternoon, I stayed true to J. C. Penney's formula and began putting the numbers on paper. My early projections called for a minimum of four sales people for every new store in the Tom James expansion program.

Here's what I told Spencer.

I would keep one store with four sales people and train a new manager for a new store that would hire four new sales people.

That gave Tom James two stores and eight sales people.

The new manager and I both would each train a new manager at our stores, giving us the executive manpower we needed to open two new stores.

That gave us four stores and sixteen sales people.

The four managers would each train new managers to take over four new stores.

That would give us eight stores and thirty-two sales people.

I explained that we would only have to double our number of stores and managers and sales people eight times in order for Tom James to have more than two hundred and fifty stores and slightly more than a thousand sales people.

Sure, I knew there would be attrition along the way.

Not all potential managers worked out.

Sales people, because they are sales people, would no doubt come and go.

Still, we had a shot, and my plan was to move forward as quickly as possible.

"How long do you think it will take?" Spencer asked.

I shrugged. No one could accurately predict such an ambitious venture.

"Twenty years," I said.

"Good," he said.

"Why?" I wondered.

Spencer laughed. "I know you," he said.

"I think it's possible," I said.

"Maybe it is," Spencer said. "But I was afraid you wanted to do it overnight."

Reaching such a lofty goal as a hundred million dollars in sales did not and could not happen overnight.

It did not happen in twenty years.

It took twenty-five.

True to form, it took only one generation, and we were there. It was a long journey and a difficult climb, but we made it. If Spencer Hays ever doubted we would achieve a hundred million dollars in sales, he never told me about it.

He was behind me and by my side every step of the way.

Takeaways from the chapter

- *Jim highlights in this chapter the power of people and their biographies. How many stories of other people's lives provide me with inspiration for the pursuit of my own personal vision?*

- *Jim has argued consistently in this book that I can achieve that which I can imagine and make as my goal. If I can reasonably believe it is possible, then I can achieve it. All that is required is a focus and willingness to work for that end. What is that I want to accomplish with my life? What is it that I must get done?*

- *Jim decided what he wanted out of life and then began the task of actively seeking it. What do I want out of life and what's keeping me from actively seeking it?*

- *Jim's goal became real, when he wrote it down. Have I written down my big impossible goals? Have I written down any goals?*

- *Jim first shared his BHAG with the person he most trusted and the person he thought was most likely to tell him whether it was possible. At this point, Jim needed someone he trusted to affirm the possibility and give him psychological permission to go after it. Who would that person be for me?*

CHAPTER 16

Choosing to Become a Good Listener

For a new company, less than five years old, venturing to new cities and having to rely on the abilities, the professionalism, and the determination of new sales people involved in building the foundation for a brand new kind of business, I realized that I was facing a monumental task. It would never be easy. There would be as many stops as starts along the way. The formula was sound, but I realized that it would never be perfect, not as long as we dealt with the unpredictable whims and foibles of human nature.

As we marched along, Spencer and I, at any time, would always be dealing with three sales forces. One group would be working hard and meeting their sales goals week after week. Unfortunately, another group would knock on a few doors, make a few calls, sell a few suits, then walk away to pursue another career. And I had been in the business long enough to realize that Spencer Hays and I would constantly be hiring and training those new sales people who made up the third group. Any business understands that the winds of change are continually blowing in its face. The strong companies learn to bend against a strong wind, but never break.

I was personally convinced beyond any doubt that the Tom James Company could really become the business I envisioned it to be. I believed that with the right strategy and the right amount of energy,

I would be able to wake up one day and see the firm wedged solidly among the nation's top *Fortune* 500 companies, bringing home a hundred million dollars a year in sales, maybe more.

That's what I had promised Spencer.

He had given me the chance I needed when he asked me to give up my clientele in Atlanta and begin working with sales people in our other stores: Nashville, Memphis, Dallas, Fort Worth, Houston, and Tulsa.

My focus had to abruptly change.

I no longer sold clothes.

I had suddenly been placed in a leadership position, and it was my duty and my responsibility to train men, to turn average sales people into good ones and good sales people into great ones.

Within every man or woman, there was a spark of genius.

It was my mission to find it and ignite it.

In the past, I had worked long hours and spent many nights and weekends reading every sales book and success manual I could find, trying to learn, then master, every trick and technique I could about the successful art of selling.

My goal was to have a competitive edge in the marketplace.

Every Saturday morning, I would sit for one to two hours with my workbook in an effort to develop new ideas for hitting that hundred-million-dollar mark. Some of the ideas I kept. The others were quickly discarded and thrown away. The key was to keep thinking, to keep challenging my mind, to keep acquiring more knowledge, to know that for every ten bad ideas I wrote down, I might actually come up with a good one. It was like being a prospector. Dig through enough mud, and, every now and then, I might find a nugget worth keeping.

It dawned on me one morning that, in reality, there was little difference between selling clothes and training sales people.

The technique was certainly the same.

When I called on a businessman or senior executive with my sample case full of fabrics and colors, patterns and styles, it was my job to ask him enough key questions to discover what he really wanted and needed, and then show him how I could deliver it for him.

When working with a sales person, I could easily show him the fine points of making a sale. After all, I had read Charles B. Roth's book, *Secrets of Closing Sales*, and packed away all seven kinds of his closes in my sales portfolio of winning ideas. I wrote down two ways to use each one of them and memorized them. Now I knew how to ask a client to buy fourteen different ways. I sat in my home at night and practiced them like John Wayne must have practiced his lines for a movie. I could recite each one of the closes as easily as I could tell you the names of my children.

However, those seven critical closes, even if I believed so strongly in them, did not guarantee the success of a sales person unless he was motivated to hit the streets each morning, eagerly knock on every door he could find, and sell. Most everyone had his or her own distractions. A sales person was no different. It was vital for me to ask him enough questions to learn what he really wanted in life, what he wanted to buy, what he would like to do for his family, what kind of home he dreamed about, what kind of car he would like to drive, what kind of vacations did he wish for himself, his wife, and his children. Then it was imperative for me to show him a way to accomplish his goals.

Early on, I falsely assumed that everyone was as excited about working for Tom James as I was. To me, the company, the quality of its merchandise, its commitment to employees and customers alike, its financial plan, its commission structure, the integrity of the man at the top all convinced me that if I could properly train a sales person, then we would all do well.

No two sales people, I knew, were the same. One single, catch-all motivational message would never resonate with everyone, at least not at the same time. We were dealing with individuals who all had their own dreams, their own plans, their own hopes, their own concerns, their own fears, and their own set of problems that they almost always kept to themselves.

On Following the Golden Rule

I was 29 years old and I had been with Tom James Company for only 2 weeks when I attended the July 1994 national sales meeting in Tampa, Florida. It was the very first day of the meeting and I was a little nervous since I didn't know many people yet. I was sitting at the pool with my leader when Jim approached us. We were introduced and of course he hugged me! I'll never forget it. At that time, the TJ training program was set up so that I would be out selling on my own in the month of August and if I were able to sell 50 units, I would qualify to attend sales school in Texas in September. The only problem was, when I looked on the calendar, the dates of the September sales school were during the holy day of Yom Kippur. The next day at the meeting, Jim approached me and asked me about my goals. When I told him that I didn't have a doubt in my mind that I would qualify for September sales school, but that I was disappointed about the Yom Kippur conflict, he said, "Well we'll just change the dates of sales school Heidi." I couldn't believe it. What CEO of a company would change the dates of an important meeting to accommodate one person? It was at that very moment that I was sold on my future at Tom James, and of course sold on Jim McEachern. What Jim did for me that day was show me that I mattered. That my religion mattered, that my sales contribution mattered, and that Tom James was where I belonged. He has since influenced me to be a better leader, salesperson, and human being. Heidi G, Tom James Company

It was my decision to work with our sales personnel one at a time. Frank Bettger's book on how to raise yourself from failure to success in selling told me that if a person knew exactly what he wanted, and if I could show him how to achieve it, then he would move heaven and earth to get it.

I might not know a lot about human motivation, but psychologist Andrew Maslow did. I began studying his Hierarchy of Needs, a concept suggesting that people must be able to fulfill their basic needs before they are ready to move on and satisfy other needs, particularly those found in the workplace. It was vital for me to learn and understand all five of them:

1. *Physiological Needs, which had to do with survival, such as the need for water, air, food, and sleep.*
2. *Security Needs, which included a desire for steady employment, health insurance, safe neighborhoods, and shelter from the environment.*
3. *Social Needs, which were linked to a sense of belonging, love, and affection from family and friends.*
4. *Esteem Needs, which were based on a person's feeling of self-esteem, personal worth, social recognition, and accomplishments.*
5. *Self-actualizing Needs, which were underscored by a person's concern with personal growth and his or her ability to fulfill their potential in life or at work.*

Maslow's words became my basic guide to help identify the real needs that were standing as an obstacle in a sales person's way as he marched methodically on toward either success or failure. As in dealing with objections on a sales call, I knew I had to look past the obvious and concentrate on the underlying needs of a sales person.

The challenge was to find them.

While I was still working with Spencer Hays in Atlanta, my family and I became members of the Calvary Baptist Church in Cobb County. Behind the sanctuary was a small library where I could always find some book that was new and inspirational to read. While browsing among the bookshelves one afternoon, I discovered *The Awesome Power of the Listening Ear* by John Drakeford, a professor at Southwestern Seminary in Fort Worth.

The title alone intrigued me. As I read what Drakeford had to say, I remembered that my old sales manager at the Southwestern Company, Fred Landers, had indeed been a really good listener and therefore an effective motivator and leader. His strength was being able to ask the kind of questions that gently persuaded his sales people to open up and give him a basic idea of whatever problems might be troubling them. If someone paused in the middle of making a point, Fred never believed that the sales person had necessarily come to the end of his statement. He sat there and patiently waited for us to continue. Fred Landers was genuinely interested in what we had to say. He never felt the necessity to jump in with a phrase or two just to fill silence or occupy dead air.

He believed – and I soon learned to believe after reading Drakeford's book – that most people were desperate for someone to listen to them, not just hear their words, but actually listen intently enough to really understand the conflicts or obstacles that were standing in their way to making more sales or achieving a greater degree of success.

Months earlier, I remembered, I had been discussing our sales goals at Tom James with one of my colleagues.

He made a statement.

I cut him off before he finished.

My mind quickly and impulsively thought it understood what my colleague was talking about, but, in reality, I hadn't taken the time to hear him out and fully understand his point of view.

Our argument lasted at least thirty minutes. It wasn't heated, but at times it was intense. Suddenly, when I took the time to let him finish his opinion, I realized that we didn't really have a disagreement after all. We were both saying the same thing, just in different ways.

It wasn't his fault.

It was mine.

I had just failed to be a good listener.

If I wanted to be a help to our sales force, instead of being a hindrance, I needed to revise my way of thinking and particularly change my listening skills. Conversations that were one sided – with only my side being heard – were a deadly way to lose a good sales person, lose business, and diminish the strength of the company that relied exclusively on direct sales. I studied Drakeford's book as thoroughly as if it were the Bible and began to work hard in a sincere effort to develop *the power of the listening ear*.

When I began managing sales people and asking one to meet with me or spend the day with me, I recognized that he or she might well show up tense, maybe stressed out or perhaps on the defensive. Too many of them probably walked into my office wondering if they were in trouble, had made a mistake or had done something wrong.

Was I there to help them, criticize them, and maybe even fire them?

My immediate job was to make the sales person feel comfortable.

I might say: "I do have some things I would like to cover this morning, but if we never get to them, that's all right. What I really want to do is hear everything you have on your mind."

The door to anything bothering them had now been flung wide open.

At that, I sat back in my chair and listened.

On other occasions, I might say, "I envision my role as helping you get what you want and overcome any difficulties that you are facing."

That put the discussion in an entirely different light.

I was concerned with him or her, so they didn't need to be concerned with me. I could see them visibly relax, and a faint smile might crease their face.

Any signs of stress or fear had flown.

I wasn't there to judge them. I was there to listen to them, and learning to listen enables anyone to ask the right questions in order to pull those troubling answers out of the darkness of their minds. If people believe you care about them and the unfortunate situations they are confronting, then you are generally able to persuade them to begin talking and, sooner or later, reveal the problems that are affecting their lives at home and in the workplace. So often, the wall they hit at work has absolutely nothing to do with work or with the company. Some other issue, usually dealing with their finances, has dragged them down, and, as a result, their job performance begins to seriously suffer. They lose focus. They lose sight of their goals. They become a victim, a prisoner, of their own troubles.

On Peacemaking

I had the joy of being Jim's pastor for more than twenty years. During that time he served as a deacon and an elder with me. One of the many contributions he made was that of a wise peacemaker. A few times we had to deal with some rather tense and inflammatory situations. Jim always knew how to keep everyone calm and speak words of wisdom and conciliation. He could use appropriate humor, biblical examples, and personal experiences to bring a sense of peace and reconciliation. I remember tense moments when it appeared that anger would control the meeting. Without 'taking sides', Jim would ask the right question or simply pause for a moment of prayer and the atmosphere would change. His calm demeanor, joyful smile, and genuine heart of concern for everyone involved would conquer the anger. This is true leadership. (Rev. Nick Harris)

I received a phone call from one of our managers in Chicago. He had been with the Tom James Company for sixteen years and was training a young lady who was new to the organization. In his mind, she had the potential to one day become one of his top sales persons, but she wasn't growing her sales nearly as quickly as he thought she could. Something was bothering her, and he was at a loss.

He could not figure out what the problem might be. He just knew that one problem, maybe more, existed, and it was ruining her chances to advance and achieve the kind of success he had envisioned for her.

She wouldn't say what it was or even admit that an obstacle, real or imagined, was blocking her path. She would just smile and say, "Oh, it's nothing. I'm just having a bad day."

Or week.

Or month.

Her manager knew better. He asked me to talk with the young lady by telephone.

After we spoke a few minutes to become better acquainted, I said, "I would like for you to tell me exactly what you are feeling and experiencing in your work."

She only gave me a few assorted tidbits.

She left out all of the crucial details.

I replied, "It sounds to me like you no doubt feel as though you are in a rut and just can't get out."

"I do," she said.

That was progress. I kept listening to her every word – what she said and, just as importantly, what she didn't say – and she kept giving me a few scattered clues, enough so I could detect that she might be struggling with her inability to deal with a debt.

Her situation wasn't new.

So many were afflicted by the same kind of burden.

The door had been cracked. I opened it even wider. I knew her approximate age and guessed that she had recently received her degree. So it wasn't much a gamble. I asked, "Do you have any college loans?"

"Yes sir."

"Are they weighing you down?"

"At times, they certainly feel that way."

"May I ask what the total amount of the loans might be?"

There was a long silence at the other end of the phone. Finally she said, "Thirty thousand dollars."

"And your payments?"

"Six hundred dollars a month."

I quickly figured what her sales total had to be each month just to make her loan payment. As a new sales person, she probably thought that the amount was probably beyond her reach. For her, it was a heavy burden to carry.

However, as soon as I discovered the reason behind her struggles, it was easier for me to help her find a solution. In business, so often, good, loyal, hard-working people fail because a major distraction becomes so overwhelming that it prevents them from paying full attention to their job. The more they worry, the worse they handle their duties. In the young lady's case, the worse job she did, the fewer sales she made, the more difficult it became for her to earn the money necessary to pay off her debt. Worry was robbing her of her ambition and confidence to succeed.

In business, if management doesn't take the time to understand the problem, the company has a chance of losing someone who could become and remain a very valuable employee. And, chances are, no manager will ever really understand the problem unless he or she becomes a good listener.

Not a better than average listener.

A good listener.

I've known company executives who become aware of someone not quite doing the job as effectively as he or she has done it in the past, walk in an office, and bark out an answer when they haven't yet heard the question. They have one solution for every occasion, and yet no two people, no two employees, no two personalities are the same. The issue may certainly be similar, but it affects everyone in a different manner.

The executive hasn't solved the problem.

He has simply become a new problem.

He has added to an employee's stress level, which may already be at or near the breaking point.

He has suddenly become the employee's major distraction in the workplace.

Everyone must be treated on an individual basis.

One of our managers in Rochester realized that one of his good sales people had become quite discouraged. He called me. "I know something's wrong," he said, "but I don't know how to deal with it."

"Would you like for me to call the man?"

"Please."

I did.

He and I had never talked before. I may have seen him from time to time at one of our sales meetings or conferences, but he and I were not acquainted at all. Our phone call began simply with one strange voice talking to another.

I opened the conversation by getting straight to the point, "Your manager told me that you have begun to struggle a little in your work," I said. "Would you like to tell me what the problem might be?"

"Well," he answered, "my basement flooded, and I found out my deductible was a thousand dollars on my home insurance. That's a pretty big hit I wasn't expecting. Then my boy had an injury, and we were facing a pretty big doctor bill."

"So you felt distracted at work."

"I did."

"You were worrying more about paying off the deductible and doctor's bill than making sales presentations."

"I'm afraid I was."

I knew those were minor problems and easily solved. But if I had stopped there, it would have been like putting a band-aid on open-heart surgery. Somewhere down deep, I felt as though he had been confronted with a much more serious issue, and, to help him, I needed to know what it was. I also believed it was important for him to realize that I was not just some distant and unfamiliar voice on the other end of the line, asking a lot of questions. I was trying to find the heart of the issue.

Whatever his troubles might be, I had probably experienced something similar to them. I believed he would be more upfront and honest with me if he understood that I had walked in his shoes. I was no stranger to troubles myself. The road in my life probably had as many twists and turns as his did.

I paused a moment for effect, then asked, "If those monetary problems were resolved today, is there anything else that might be an issue?"

A pained silence hung between us on the phone.

I knew the answer.

"Let me tell you a brief story about myself," I said. "Its purpose is to let you know that I can relate to any issues you're now facing, whatever they happen to be."

If he didn't think I could relate to him, then I knew he would discount anything that I had to say. I told him about trying to make ends meet as a schoolteacher, being fired at the supermarket for having a bad attitude, selling snow cones with a wife and children at home to feed and clothe, my dead-end job at a beauty supply company, the desperate financial troubles that had begun to bury me before I was thirty years old.

He might be down.

I had been on bottom.

"Let me ask you a question," I said. "Do you, by chance, still have outstanding college loans that haven't been paid?"

He did.

"Is it a substantial amount?"

It was.

In fact, the money he owed was so monumental in his mind that it had completely destroyed his ability to realize there might be any near-term resolution. He was drowning in debt and couldn't free himself from deep water.

He had a hard road ahead of him. But by carefully listening to him, by asking the right questions, I was able to comprehend the "illness" before I was asked to offer a "cure." If you don't learn the problem before trying to provide a solid solution, it is little different from prescribing penicillin for a broken leg. Now penicillin is a miraculous wonder drug and has been saving lives for a long time, but I don't think it can mend a cracked bone.

Problem solving in the business world isn't all that difficult.

Get people to talk.

By careful listening, you'll know the right questions to ask.

In so many cases, the right questions allow people to frequently come up with their own solutions. During the struggle, the problems all seem jumbled up. They are difficult to sort out. People view them in a confused state of mind. However, the process of thinking as the person is gently persuaded to talk about the problem often helps erase the fog and makes the issue much clearer to comprehend and much easier to understand.

The man at the top, in a lot of companies, cares only about an employee's productivity. If someone is not producing, then the boss replaces him, and it's not unusual for the replacement to come to work with just as many problems.

If the man at the top cares enough, he will sit down with his employee, listen well and recognize the mental, emotional, or financial distraction that has triggered the sudden lack of productivity.

It's far better in the long run to resolve the issue, rescue the employee, and set his feet in the right direction. It prevents you from having to start over with someone new. It eliminates the high cost in money and time of training someone new. And if you help one of your employees get through the maze of issues standing in the way of their success, you will most certainly see a huge payback in profitability. Instead of continual turnover, you will have a workforce that is grateful for the chances you gave them.

Believe in them.

And they will believe in you.

Support them.

And they will remain loyal.

Work for them.

And you will be surprised at how they work for you.

Direct sales is a pressure-packed job. No one can ever succeed by being passive. You have to get up every morning and walk into the office as a self-motivated sales person. You have to initiate everything: the phone calls, the appointments, the presentations, the sales, the deliveries, the follow-ups, the referrals. It's a never-ending cycle.

And worst of all, the direct sales person is always forced to deal with rejection and the constant possibility of rejection. It's never personal, but it feels that way, and it happens just about every day.

I knew a sales person who maintained a great attitude after his sales presentation. If the potential customer said, "Yes," he was elated. However, if the prospect said, "No," the sales person simply walked out of the office, shaking his head and thinking to himself, "It's a shame that fellow wasn't smart enough to see what a great deal I had for him."

Jim McEachern's Daily Affirmations

Jim used positive self talk as a tool to keep himself motivated. The following are affirmations accumulated over the years and taken from his last goal notebook. He would read these aloud and repeat them daily:

"I choose to be ambitious, bold, creative, disciplined, enthusiastic, and fearless."

"I am as bold as a lion and as a tough as an elephant."

"My goals are big and worthwhile. I refuse to set small goals and I respect but refuse to be influenced by those who do not believe I can accomplish big and worthwhile goals.

"I may have limits, but they are so high that I'm certain I can multiply my value a hundred-fold without reaching my limits."

"Today is my favorite day and right now is my favorite time. I choose to act now."

"Everyday offers challenges but I'm able and willing to attack and overcome them."

"It's like me to do well."

"As a leader it is my job to help people set goals and write them in affirmation form."

"One of my greatest joys is the joy of achievement. I work to achieve. I love my work. I radiate joy as I do my work."

"I set high goals. I write down my goals. I clearly define them. I figure out why my goals are important to me."

"I am committed to achieving my goals. I try, and try, and keep on trying. I never give up. I constantly renew my commitment."

"I believe that integrity and trust are foundational elements in business. I choose to be 100% honest in all of my business dealings."

"I am enthusiastic. I radiate enthusiasm. I think enthusiastically. I feel enthusiastic. I act enthusiastic. I am enthusiastic."

"I recognize that one characteristic of professionalism is thorough preparation. I am a professional. I prepare myself thoroughly to do my job as a professional."

"I am consistent in my efforts. I am a diligent and tenacious worker. I am firm about quality and quantity of efforts."

"I, Jim McEachern, am a self starter. I take great pride in my personal initiative and my ability to motivate myself. While others procrastinate, I get on with the achievement of my objectives."

"I, Jim McEachern, am as courageous as a lion, I cannot be intimidated. I find a way to achieve my goals. I go over, under, around, or right through any obstacle that stands in my way."

"So long as there is breath in me, Jim McEachern, that long will I persist. For I know one of the greatest principles of success, I will persist. I will win."

Sales people, in particular, are continually confronted by major and disconcerting distractions at work and at home.

They may be well trained.

They may know their job.

They may know their product.

245

They may have all of the personality in the world.

They may be driven by a great ambition to succeed in life.

But if they are worried more about something, large or small, and it is interfering with their sales performance, then they are traveling in a fast lane toward failure.

The troubles may come from inside the job.

They may be triggered somewhere outside the job.

It really doesn't matter.

A problem is still a problem of major proportions, and sales people need someone who cares enough to help them unlock the secret bothering them and interfering with their success, who has a genuine interest in them, who makes a sincere effort to resolve the issue or allow them to resolve it, and whose goal is to put their feet back on the right track and headed in the right direction.

The first step is to stop talking and learn to properly listen.

Maybe that's why God made us with two ears and only one mouth.

Takeaways from the chapter

- *Jim states: "Within every man or woman, there . . . [is] a spark of genius." Is this true? If I believed this, how would it change the way I relate to people?*
- *Bettger's book says that "if a person knew exactly what he wanted, and if I could show him how to achieve it, then he would move heaven and earth to get it." What do I want? How can I achieve it? How can I help other people figure out what they want?*
- *How often do I assume people are incompetent when in fact they are dealing with issues that distract from their work? Am I willing to help redeem/rescue a person at their point of need? Do I understand how to find out what that is?*
- *Jim states: "If he didn't think I could relate to him, then I knew he would discount anything that I had to say." Whenever I discuss struggles with people, do they know that I have struggled too?*
- *Debt is a recurring problem in this book. It seems to become a noose around many people's necks. Is there any such thing as good debt? Can I avoid it altogether?*

CHAPTER 17

Choosing to Schedule My Time

As the decade of the sixties came to an end, I felt as though I had made substantial progress in the development of a new career in sales for the Tom James Company. Of course, the only measuring stick I really had was the amount of money I brought home each year. During those first twelve months after our Nashville store opened, I earned a grand total of seven thousand, eight hundred dollars. It doesn't sound like much. Based on the value of today's dollars, however, my salary and commission equaled forty-seven thousand dollars. I had built a solid foundation, I was working hard, I continued to read as many books on selling as I could find, and I listened to every piece of advice that Spencer Hays could give me. My days began early and ended late. I made sure I had at least five appointments a day. I told my story with sincerity and conviction. I always asked for referrals to lead me to my next client. I made sure that I understood what each customer really needed and delivered him the clothes he needed to dress for success. And I learned the art of maximizing each sale, always striving to add shirts, ties, socks, and underwear to every order.

My sales climbed each month. My list of regular clients grew. And, consequently, my earnings continued to increase as well. By the end of the second year – again based on the value of the dollar in today's market – I reached sixty thousand dollars, almost hit ninety-five thousand dollars my third year, and by the time I had been selling for Tom James for seven years, my commission had topped two hundred thousand dollars.

I had a good product to sell.

And that was extremely important to me.

But at the close of 1970, I made a dramatic change in the way I worked, and that single decision would make a significant and meaningful difference in my approach to life as well as business. We are given only so many hours, minutes, and seconds in a day, and our successes and failures often hinge on the way we utilize the time God gives us.

We can spend it wisely.

We can carelessly and foolishly throw it away.

We can control it.

Or time can strangle us.

It almost killed me.

Although it was totally unexpected for me, Spencer Hays asked me to give up my clientele at the end of 1970 and begin working closely with our sales people as we grew and expanded across the country's heartland. We needed a close-knit and cohesive band of sales people all working in unison, telling the same story to customers, and providing the same kind of service that was rapidly becoming a Tom James trademark.

It was important for someone to direct the sales teams and keep them all headed in the same direction, the right direction, and Spencer Hays named me vice president and director of sales, placing the burden and the responsibility squarely on my shoulders.

I had perhaps auditioned for the job without ever realizing it. I'm not sure that, at the time, the necessity to create the new position had even crossed Spencer's mind either.

Spencer and I were in Dallas one morning, and I had just finished conducting an early sales meeting. He turned to one of his new sales people and asked, "What do you have scheduled for today?"

The young man took a deep breath, nervously rubbed his hands together, and answered, "I'm afraid I don't have any appointments set for today."

Spencer did not reprimand or criticize him.

Instead, he turned to me and said, "Jim, why don't you go out and show this young man how to make successful cold calls."

The pressure was removed from our salesman.

It was thrust on me.

Here I was a stranger in a strange town.

I didn't know anyone.

I had never called on anybody in Dallas.

I did not have a pocket full of referrals or miracles.

I may not have been in a state of panic, but I certainly felt a little more anxious and uncertain than I had a few minutes earlier.

I smiled and nodded for the young man to follow me. We rode the elevator to the ground floor, walked a block through downtown Dallas, and, without any reason, stepped into the lobby of the Republic National Bank Building. It was, I decided, as good a place to start as any. Tall building. Full of offices. Take a deep breath and select one. I glanced quickly up and down a row of names on the wall directory out front and chose the office of an attorney.

There was absolutely no logic behind my decision.

I just picked the name at random and out of the blue.

We rode up the elevator to his floor. I straightened my shoulders, put on the best smile I could muster, and strode purposely into his office. The salesman lagged behind a few steps.

I told the attorney's receptionist: "My name is Jim McEachern, and I came to see Mr. Caldwell."

Her eyes narrowed. "Do you have an appointment?" she asked.

"Not yet," I replied, "but I feel certain that Mr. Caldwell will like to hear what I have to say."

She was not impressed.

The door to Caldwell's office was open. He had heard me. He may not have been impressed either. But the lawyer was definitely intrigued.

He walked out and introduced himself.

"I know you don't know me," I said politely, almost apologetically, "but if you allow me five minutes of your time, I don't think you will be disappointed, and I will be out of your way."

"I've got five minutes," he said.

"Thank you," I said.

"But no more than five minutes."

"I won't need any more I said."

I gave my abridged five-minute presentation and opened my case. Caldwell looked down at the samples I had placed before him.

"I'll take one," he said.

"Which fabric?" I asked.

"This one," he said.

"What color?"

"I'd prefer the gray with pin stripes."

"What style?"

"Similar to the one I'm wearing."

"I'll need a deposit," I said.

"How much?"

I told him.

As he wrote the check, I said, "We'll expect you to come to the store to be fitted."

"How late are you open?"

I told him.

"I'll be there this evening if I don't get tied up."

"If you know you may be late," I said, 'just call me, and I'll wait for you."

He nodded.

Inside of ten minutes, we were gone, and a young man who had no appointments scheduled and who had not said a word beyond, *Good morning*, had just made a sale.

He was elated.

Spencer must have been carefully watching. I had begun my career making cold calls. Now, I preferred appointments and referrals, but making a presentation to someone I had just met face-to-face had never worried me. I knew how to listen to my customers. I knew how to detect what they wanted or needed in a suit of clothes. I knew how to make a sale.

Being a sales manager, however, was a whole new game. I was no longer merely responsible for myself and the results I could personally bring to Tom James. Suddenly, I was accountable for the success of every other salesperson in the organization.

It started out as a challenge.

The challenge became a nightmare.

As I traveled from city to city, worked with one sales person and then another, tried to resolve one problem while another crisis in another office in another city was veering wildly out of control, I found myself having to react to a lot of sudden and unexpected issues. I was acting more like a firefighter.

Find the fires.

Put them out.

Smell the smoke.

Find the next fire.

Charge with a bucket of water. Sometimes I didn't even have the bucket.

I was so busy fighting fires that I was not able to do anything to prevent them, and the job was on the verge of suffocating me. For the first time since becoming a part of the Tom James Company, I dreaded crawling out of bed each morning, almost always in a different and unfamiliar town to face another day. It was one problem after another. If there were no issues, then I wouldn't be there.

By 1970, we had operations in seven locations – Nashville, Atlanta, Memphis, Tulsa, Dallas, Fort Worth, and Houston – with twenty-five sales people all striving to find success with Tom James. With the exception of Aaron Meyers, Lindy Watkins, Mack Isbell, and myself, all of them had less than two years of experience. We were a new company with a new concept, selling a new product, in an expanding array of new cities, and depending solely on the commitment and the ability of new sales people.

A glitch here, a series of complications there, and the business, even while on the threshold of busting loose and booming, could unravel at any moment. I always believed that the key to the success of any business was sales – after all, nothing ever happened until a sale was made – and I was driven to help our sales personnel make as many of them as possible. Spencer, I knew, was depending on me. My days became a maze of cities and airports and hotels, of meetings and presentations and training, of hiring new sales people and working long hours to keep the older ones motivated and on the right track. The pace was grueling and unforgiving.

Spencer may have owned the company, but mine was the face they saw.

Mine was the voice on the other end of the telephone.

And the phone never stopped ringing.

Got a problem?

Call Jim.

Got a crisis?

Call Jim.

Having difficulty making appointments?

Call Jim.

Something wrong with your presentation?

Call Jim.

Can't close a sale?

Call Jim.

Have a problem with your customer?

Call Jim.

Each store had its own leader, but the leaders, as a whole, had not stepped up and taken the responsibility of solving any of the problems. They were waiting for me to do it for them. After awhile, the sales personnel no longer bothered to go to their leaders with a question or when they faced some obstacle they were not able to overcome on their own.

The answers were seldom complicated. Mostly, the solutions were quite simple. I knew. I had already experienced a great deal of them in my own business endeavors. But the constant work of resolving a myriad of issues in the expanded Tom James workplace was taking a great deal of my time. My life was no longer my own. It belonged to them. I had a home, but I hardly ever slept in my own bed. I felt like a stranger when I returned, usually late at night, at the end of each week. My job was as exciting and as stimulating as it had always been, but the miles were piling up, and my next week was little different from the last one. My position had turned into a mental chess game, and I never had the last move.

In each of the seven locations, I was in charge of recruiting new employees and conducting classroom training for all of the sales people, usually one-on-one. I worked with them in the field. I went along with them on sales calls and listened, day after day, to their presentations. As Vince Lombardi had once said, "Practice doesn't make perfect. Perfect practice makes perfect." Sales people were expecting me to make a suggestion on scheduling appointments, a recommendation on better connecting with their customers (a change in the presentation, no matter how small) to give them an edge in closing sales. Monday in Nashville. Tuesday in Atlanta; Wednesday in Memphis. Thursday maybe in Dallas and Fort Worth both. Thank God, they were close. Friday in Houston. And, with any luck, I could catch Tulsa on my way to Dallas next week. The only reading I had time for was airline flight schedules, and, after awhile, I had them memorized. I tried to sleep on planes. I would have preferred reading more success-oriented books to provide me with the clues, ideas, and techniques I needed to excel in the world of business and the art of selling.

The duties and obligations of business had become all consuming.

I would tell the sales people who were having difficulties: "You know when I'm coming next, so go ahead and arrange appointments with your customers. I'll go with you and see if we can straighten out the issues you are encountering."

Maybe the measurement had been wrong.

Maybe the pants did not fit quite right.

Maybe the color of the shirt didn't match the suit exactly the way a customer had wanted.

An unhappy customer was a customer we might lose forever. Happy customers were money in the bank. My job was to teach our sales people how to replace a frown with a smile. Some solutions could be easily identified and explained by phone. But when some mistake or misunderstanding had created within the customer a lack of confidence in Tom James, then it was time for me to meet him face to face. After working so hard to build a strong and growing customer base, we could not afford to start seeing it erode one client at a time.

Spencer was occupied with running the business end of Tom James. He expected me to find the wrinkles and iron them out.

I had chosen to work with a new salesman in Dallas one morning. He had a lot of potential, and I envisioned great things from him. But, for whatever reason, there seemed to be a hitch in his presentation. He always had a full slate of appointments each day. He made his calls just like clockwork. But he wasn't making sales.

"Would it be all right if I went with you this morning?" I asked.

"Sure," he said, "I'd be glad for you to come along."

"He's your client," I said.

Craig nodded.

"You have the relationship with him."

Craig nodded again.

"But would you have any objections if I made the presentation this morning?"

He shrugged. "I guess it'll be all right," he said.

I had learned long ago that a good sales person, if he or she listens carefully and diligently, can detect whether or not a client is willing to buy within seven minutes, so that was the length of my presentation. If the signs were right, I would show a customer my clothing samples. If I realized that the executive had no interest in owning a custom tailored suit and felt I was wasting his time, I would simply smile, shake his hand, thank him for his time, and be on my way out the door. Prospects had all kinds of legitimate reasons for not buying a suit. He didn't want one. He couldn't afford one. He had his own business problems on his mind. He didn't have time to hear a presentation. He had a deal just about ready to close or crumble.

Another time, and he might welcome us through his door. It would generally take me seven minutes to find out.

As always, I finished my story in the time I had allotted for myself. The executive thought it over, finally leaned forward and said it would be all right for me to show him the samples I had packed in my case.

He knew what he wanted.

So did I.

He liked what I placed on his desk before him.

I knew he would.

"I'll take five," he said.

"Suits?"

"Five suits."

"What about new shirts to match them."

"Make me up some shirts, too."

"And ties?"

"Might as well. My old ties might not work as well with the new suits."

I nodded. "I'll need a deposit," I said.

He reached in a desk drawer for his checkbook. It had already been a good day, and the morning was still young. My salesman had watched my presentation. I hoped he was mentally taking notes. There was nothing else I could tell him. Within those seven minutes, I expected our sales people to be on the same page with the client. Each minute was important. No. Each minute was critical. The presentation might go extremely well for six minutes, but if a sales person lost a prospect during that seventh minute, it was all over. Each minute was a single stair step to the top and we could not afford to stumble over any of them.

When working with our individual sales personnel, I was making a sale about fifty percent of the time on the first call, even on cold calls. But I was slowly wearing down. How in the world could a man so young feel so old, I wondered. I looked in the mirror of my hotel room one night and realized that the young man was looking old as well.

When depending on an airplane to carry me to my next destination, I was always at the mercy of the weather, and nobody could predict the weather. Time and again, my evening nine o'clock flight wouldn't leave until closer to midnight, and I felt imprisoned by the cold, sterile walls of another airport. Not even the colorful neon signs pulsating up and down the concourse could brighten my dreary existence. I sat alone, too tired to read and too weary to think, surrounded by stranded and frustrated passengers who were no different from me. After awhile, I lost interest in them as well.

By the time the flight arrived in my next city, it would be two in the morning, and sometimes later. By the time I picked up my luggage, grabbed a taxi, and found my way to my hotel, daylight was only a few short hours away.

Up at five, breakfast at six, and meetings with sales people began at seven. I did not want to interfere with the valuable time they needed for their appointments.

Each sales person had his or her own individual problems.

Each operation had its own set of problems.

I was burdened with all of them.

The cycle never ended. It never even slowed down.

By the end of 1970, I was physically and mentally exhausted. A tired individual is not nearly as efficient or as proficient as someone well rested and energized. Those all-night, never-ending, and unpredictable travel schedules had taken their toll. The thought of quitting or walking away never entered my mind, but I knew the time had come to make some drastic changes in business and at home. It would begin with me. I would no longer be at the mercy of a hectic schedule. I vowed to take charge and control the time I had to devote to Tom James and my family.

After all, what good was life when I didn't have one? A year was gone, and I had totally missed out on having any kind of relationship with my children and my wife. They had gone their own way, and I had, unfortunately, gone another. Even when I came home on Friday nights, I was never really at home. I spent most of Saturday catching up on my sleep and Sunday afternoon, after church, thinking about all of the things I had to do the following week. My wife and children lived in their world. It seemed as though I no longer had time to be a part of it.

As January of 1971 dawned, I sat down with Spencer Hays and told him that I never wanted to repeat the previous year again. The growth of the Tom James Company had been dramatic. Sales had shot through the roof. But I was little more than a skeleton of the man I had been.

I said, "Spencer, I'll be happy to work in Atlanta, build a strong sales team, and re-build my old clientele. Or I will be happy to keep traveling for you and Tom James, working with our leaders and sales personnel. However, if you want me on the road, I need to move to Dallas. It is more centrally located, and by working out of Dallas, I can be home an extra hundred nights each year. That's a hundred fewer hotel rooms and three hundred fewer meals that won't come out of your travel budget."

Spencer didn't hesitate.

"Move to Dallas," he said. "Work out the schedule you think is best, and we'll see what happens."

I had managed a sales organization.

I had managed the sales people.

I had managed to survive hotels and airports.

Now it was time for me to manage my schedule and perhaps even rejoin the human race. I had been away for a long time.

I took out my calendar and began to schedule each month carefully. Knowing in advance what I planned to do next week, next month, the next quarter, and finally even the next year allowed me to become much more effective in my work.

No longer would I simply react to one crisis after another. Instead, I worked to prevent problems instead of merely trying to solve them after they had already erupted.

I had devoted a year, training sales people one-on-one.

I decided to take a different tact.

My new game plan was built around training leaders and then giving them the authority and a chance to train their own sales teams.

The store managers no longer had to depend on me. They became the leaders they were always meant to be.

I was there for support. But their individual burdens no longer fell heavily on my shoulders, and no longer did they keep me worried and lying awake at night. I learned an important and invaluable lesson. Provide someone with the opportunity to take the reins and become a leader, and those who possess real leadership qualities will rise to the top. *So often, all they need to succeed is a manager to believe in them, support them, and give them a chance to fulfill their roles in business.*

We found a lot of dedicated and resourceful managers.

We replaced a few.

We grew stronger as a team and an organization.

I decided that time or the lack of it was no longer an enemy as long as I chose to control it. It was vital for me to take charge, so I sat down and began to seriously identify my priorities on both sides of my front door. Those priorities would ultimately become the map that I would follow from that moment on.

1. My children's school events: Whatever was important to Karen, Mike, Lynda, and Angie was important to me. If they were involved in a school program or an athletic event, I promised myself that I would be there. I had been out of their lives long enough. Before I planned anything else, including sales or recruiting trips, I wrote down those events on my calendar. I would build everything else around them. I would be in business a long time. My children would one day leave home before I ever realized they were grown. I did not want to miss anything important in their lives.

2. I made the decision not to work on Saturdays. I would give the company my total commitment during the week, traveling where I needed to go, working late if necessary. But Saturdays were reserved for my family.

3. I would spend two days a month recruiting new sales people. They would form the backbone and become the lifeblood of Tom James.

4. I specified the days and the times for each of those days that I would devote to writing letters to sales people. My goal was to motivate, encourage, assist, and support them as they grew their sales. After all, in my heart, I knew that if I did my part, then the sales people would do their part, and one day Tom James would indeed become a major company, perhaps even attaining a place in the *Fortune 500* list.

5. I set aside certain times each day to make my phone calls and talk regularly with those leaders and sales team members with whom I was working. I made it a point to allow at least thirty to forty-five minutes for each call. For those who were facing the most difficulties, I scheduled an hour. I never wanted any of them to feel rushed or pressured or hurried. Each would have the time they needed to fully discuss each of their issues in detail. After all, their successes meant the ultimate success of Tom James.

6. I scheduled fifteen minutes each week to talk by phone to the entire sales team in each individual office. I began early, calling Atlanta on Eastern Standard Time and working my way west to Fort Worth.

7. I arranged my travel schedule far in advance, spending only two days and possibly two nights each week on the road. Each office knew when I would be arriving, and it allowed those team leaders and sales people with problems to set aside the time necessary for us to discuss the obstacles and figure out ways to overcome them. I had planned in advance. Now they could do the same. It really streamlined our endeavors at problem solving and problem preventing and making problems go away.

8. I knew how much time to devote each week to reading sales reports, and that gave me time to recognize who was meeting their sales goals and who might be falling short. Those reports were invaluable. It was easy to determine who were maximizing their sales efforts and who still had a long way to go.

9. So often in business, managers and directors have a tendency to overlook those who are doing well because they find themselves spending so much of their time working with employees whose sales are low. I decided early that it was just as important to work with sales people who were meeting and maybe even exceeding their projections and expectations as it was to devote all of my time to teaching and training the underachievers.

Every second of my week was important. Every minute counted. But, at long last, my time would belong to me, and I had the sole responsibility of managing it properly. I did not realize it at the time, but looking back on 1970, I had become a perfect case study for Steven R. Covey when he wrote about time management in his best-selling book: *The 7 Habits of Highly Effective People.*

As he wrote: "*Urgent* matters are usually visible. They press on us; they insist on action. They're often popular with others. They're usually right in front of us. And often they are pleasant, easy, and fun to do. But so often, they are unimportant.

"*Importance*, on the other hand, has to do with results. If something is *important*, it contributes to your mission, your values, and your high priority goals.

"We *react* to *urgent* matters. *Important* matters that are not *urgent* require more initiative, more proactivity. We must act to seize opportunity, to make things happen. If we don't have a clear idea of what is *important*, of the results we desire in our lives, we are easily diverted into responding to the *urgent*."

Constantly reacting to *urgent* matters, he wrote, was dangerous. It could create stress, burnout, crises management, and always putting out fires.

That had been my life.

He explained that the heart of effective personal management dealt with things that might not be *urgent*, but are definitely *important*: things like building relationships, writing a personal mission statement, long-range planning, and preparation. Such an individual has vision, perspective, balance, discipline, control, and, as a result, faces few crises in either life or business.

As Covey paraphrased Peter Drucker, "Effective people are not problem-minded; they are opportunity-minded. They feed opportunities and starve problems. They think preventively." They are concerned with the *important*, but not the *urgent*, facets of their lives.

The *urgent* phase of my work with Tom James was behind me. My concentration while moving forward was now on the *important* aspects of maintaining a critical balance between my personal and my business life.

My goals were back in order.

God.

Family.

And Tom James.

It was a winning combination.

Takeaways from the chapter

- *Time can be used wisely or wastefully. It can be controlled or it can control us.*
  Jim realized that his time was the most valuable asset he had. Am I controlling my time or is it controlling me?
- *Who am I helping to become a leader? Who am I holding back as a leader? Why?*
- *Do I focus on the "important" first and foremost? Or do I spend my time reacting to the "urgent" around me?*
- *Jim's priorities involved not only his career but also having a vibrant and active family life. Balance is always the key. Too much of anything in life wreaks havoc. Am I practicing a balanced approach to work and family?*
- *Jim outlines his plan of action within this chapter regarding his work and family. What is my plan of attack going to be in this regard?*

CHAPTER 18

Choosing to Be a Manager

Looking back, a statement I made in 1965 before Spencer Hays ever opened the doors on his first Tom James store became the basis for a great twist of irony in my life. He had shared with me his idea for the company and found me a job in a Nashville men's department store so I could start learning about the inner workings of fashion and the clothing industry.

My manager was Gary Searles, and I told him one day, "There's one thing in life I never want to do."

"What's that?"

"Be a manager."

"Why not?"

"I don't like dealing with other people's problems," I said.

However, as I began developing strategies, day and night, trying to figure out ways to turn Tom James into a hundred-million-dollar-a-year company, Spencer and I both realized that I needed to give up my clientele in Atlanta, hit the roads, run down planes, and spend my days developing top-notch sales people. Train them. Support them. Listen to them. Help them resolve any conflicts that might be blocking their sales efforts. If they succeeded, then the company succeeded. The formula was that simple.

As I saw it, my assignment at Tom James was to travel the country and help sales people identify and overcome those problems that might stand in the way of their ability to sell a hundred thousand dollars worth of custom-tailored suits, sports coats, trousers, shirts, and accessories a year.

I had once said that I didn't want to deal with other people's problems.

Now that was all that I did.

It was a monumental change for me.

It was definitely worthwhile.

Yet, the change might never have occurred if I had not driven to South Alabama and stood as a young man beside my great grandmother's grave one afternoon and come to the heart-felt realization that she was still influencing me even though she had left us eighty-seven years earlier.

From that moment on, I realized that the influence of a single life could last far past a single lifetime. It could last forever.

I wanted my life to be like hers.

I vowed that I would do my very best to influence the lives of others in a positive manner while I was on earth and, hopefully, long after I had gone.

Maybe even for eighty-seven years as she had.

Maybe more.

As I walked away from her grave, I knew that I didn't know how.

I certainly did not have a game plan then.

I did now.

The problems of others would become my own, and having a hand in helping our sales people kick aside any distractions confronting them and reach their potential at Tom James became the most satisfying job in the world.

I had been on the phone several times with Steve and realized that he was earning enough money to take care of his basic needs. He and his family had a nice house, a fairly new automobile, fine clothes in the closet, and food on the table three times a day. Even their bills were being paid on time.

But still, I realized that something was troubling him.

Something was interfering with his ability to become a top sales person, and I knew that he had the ability to be one. I encouraged him. I talked with him about various ideas and techniques for closing a sale. I did my best to motivate him long-distance, but for some reason, I was not able to connect with him. I had done all I could do by phone. I asked him to fly from his office in Omaha to Dallas to spend the day with me.

We talked for awhile, mostly small talk and inconsequential, and finally I looked over the desk and said, "Steve, there are three questions I would like to ask you."

He leaned forward in his chair and waited for the first one.

"Do you know what your job is?" I asked.

"I do."

"Please describe it for me."

He did.

I asked, "Do you know how to do your job?"

"I do."

Steve gave me an adequate account of making phone calls, making appointments, making presentations, making sales.

I nodded. He had his job down – step by step. He could have been quoting from my textbook on sales if I had written one.

He smiled.

Then I asked the most important question of all. "Is there anything or anyone interfering with your ability or your desire to do your job, someone or something that is preventing you from seeing a bright future for yourself?"

The smile faded.

After a long pause, he said, "There is."

"Would you mind telling me what it is?"

The facts came tumbling straight from the heart. "I still have college loans to pay back," he said, "and my wife has a staggering amount of credit card debt. I've figured it up, and it will take twenty years for us to pay off our debt."

It worried him daily. It frustrated him. It depressed him.

A serious debt was hanging over their heads. They had three children, which were a handful, so his wife didn't work. She stayed home to care for the children. The couple faced that credit card debt every month. The bills came around like clockwork. It made him ill to even see the invoice lying in the mailbox, and he was only able to send in the minimum payment each month.

After a while, he admitted that his debt was around twenty thousand dollars. In his eyes, it was gigantic because it hardly ever grew any smaller. Interest rates were larger than those minimum payments, and he was doing the best that he could to break even, and the debt had him in a financial stranglehold.

It was, Steve said, wholly unmanageable.

Because I had been placed in charge of the sales force, I knew pretty close to what Steve was earning.

I was smiling.

He had no idea why.

"Let me ask you another question," I said.

"Okay."

"If you had your debts paid off and were worry free, what would you do that you can't afford to do now?"

He thought it over a moment and said, "I'd go see my sister in Arizona and spend a week. And I would take my children to Disneyworld in Florida."

"Have they ever gone?"

"Not yet."

"Take out a pencil and piece of paper," I said.

He did.

"Now let's do a little exercise and figure out how we can whittle the debt down."

Steve had no objections.

So I said, "Calculate what you would receive in commissions if you were able to sell one more suit each month."

He figured a moment and said, "After taxes, that would be about a hundred and fifty dollars."

"Now, let's apply half of that extra income directly to your debt and save the other fifty percent for a trip to Disneyworld."

He nodded.

"Now if you did sell one more suit each month, what would happen?" I asked.

"I could cut that twenty-year time frame in half," he said. His face brightened. "And I would be able to make that trip to Disneyworld in two and a half years."

We were making progress. "If you put your mind to it," I said, "do you believe you could make one more sale a month?"

He shrugged. "I could probably do better than that," he said.

I leaned across the desk, looked at him squarely in the eyes, and said, "Let's figure out what would happen if you were able to sell one more suit every week. If you put your mind to it, do you think you could do it?"

His smile had faded.

But the grin was back. "I think I can come close," he said.

"Well," I said, "if you did, it would allow you to quadruple your income. All you then have to do is pay half on your debts and save the other half for those vacations you have been dreaming about."

He now realized that, within only a few years, he could totally eliminate the debt that was hanging like an albatross around his neck, dragging down his hopes, ambitions, and plans for the future. With debt gnawing at him, Steve had decided long ago that his chance for a bright future had dimmed considerably.

Now there was a flicker of light again in his eyes.

Then I hit him right between the eyes with my last challenge. "Steve," I said, "if you buckle down and make an extra sale a week, as near as I can calculate, you can pay off your debt in about a year and still have the money you need to take your children to Disneyworld after only about six months."

I saw the fire start to burn in his eyes again.

It would be a steep climb, but Steve flew home and immediately began making the adjustments necessary to reach such a lofty goal. He had a security need, and now he knew how to live his life without the threat of mounting debt hanging over his head like a black cloud just before the storm.

He never left a call or a satisfied customer without receiving a few referrals. Those names were his lifeline. He seized every opportunity to network and meet the people who knew the people who probably needed a new wardrobe of Tom James suits.

Steve had been making a few calls a day. Now he was on the streets and on the road calling on as many potential customers as he could find. He knew what he needed to do, and he did it. Almost immediately, I saw his sales begin to double.

Steve wasn't able to break free of debt in a single year as he had hoped.

It took a year and a half.

The freedom that had suddenly come into his life – the freedom he had to spend with his wife and children, the freedom he found to face each new day without feeling suffocated by the tentacles of financial obligations and liabilities – was worth every effort it took him to make the climb.

Day after day, year after year, Spencer Hays wanted me to sit with hundreds of sales people, even go on calls with those who needed someone to show them the way, watch them, listen to them, ferret out the problems that had shackled their sales efforts, and do what I could to help them remove any interference or obstacle that had prevented them from becoming successful. Within the organization, it was not uncommon for ordinary men to realize that they could accomplish extraordinary things. Most all of them had the ability and, at least in the beginning, the determination to grow their sales.

All they needed was a little direction.

All they needed was a map.

Spencer Hays thought I had the map.

Heidi was a young lady, still single, who had cast her lot with the Tom James Company and seemed to be doing quite well. However, after a meeting one afternoon, she waited until I was alone, walked up to me in the corner of the room, and said, "Mr. McEachern, I have to talk to you. I'm desperate."

"What's wrong?" I asked.

"I have gotten myself in a huge mess, and I'm so embarrassed."

My muscles tightened. I did not know if I wanted to hear anymore. I was afraid that she would tell me she was pregnant. I held my breath and braced myself as I waited for her continue.

"I have a fifty-thousand-dollar credit card debt," she said.

I felt so relieved. I shouldn't have, but I even laughed.

Here was a problem I could handle. Here was a problem that could be solved.

"And you want to get out of debt?"

"It's killing me."

"All right," I said, "Do you trust anyone well enough to send him or her your whole paycheck every month?" I asked.

She frowned. "My mother," she said.

"Then that's what you should do," I said. "Let her cash your check, give you a weekly allowance for food and a little driving around money, and write the check each month to the credit card company. Give her your credit cards, too, or, even better, why don't you just cut them up and throw them away."

She breathed deeply. It wasn't relief. It was more like resignation. "I don't want to do that," Heidi said. "But I can."

"Tell your mother never to make only the minimum payment," I said. "Pay as much as you have left on the principal. Can you do that?"

"I can."

It was the same kind of problem I had heard time and again.

Bad debts.

Deeply in debt.

Wading in debt.

Can't figure out a way to get out of it.

I always had the same answer.

Why?

It always worked.

"I think you have the ability to increase your sales efforts each week," I told her. "See if you can prove me correct. Work even harder and try to make one extra sale each month, although it would be better for you to make an extra sale each week. Do you think that's possible?"

"It'll be difficult, and I may not be able to do it right away," Heidi said. "But it is definitely possible."

She went home, cut up her credit cards, had her paycheck mailed directly to her mother, learned the science of living on an allowance and a budget, and focused on sales instead of the debt that was stalking her. It freed her mind and let her concentrate on the strategies of increasing her referrals, her appointments, and her presentation. The growth of her sales were soon to follow.

Within eighteen months, Heidi was debt free. She had her paycheck back and discovered that she could live quite well and quite comfortably without the weight of those credit cards dragging her down.

One morning, I looked up and saw Jack had walked into my office with a worried frown on his face. He, too, was in a financial bind. He, too, was looking for a way out.

Jack had bought a new house.

That was fine.

He had paid twice what he should have paid.

That wasn't.

He had looked at his income and decided to buy a house he couldn't really afford. After all, he had spent years calling on business executives who lived in big houses, and decided that he wanted to be just like his clients.

There was one slight problem.

His clients were millionaires.

Jack wasn't.

"I only see one solution," I said after I heard his story.

"What's that?"

"It'll be difficult for you and your wife," I said.

"Tell me your idea."

"You need to sell the house and buy one that costs no more than half the price of the one you're living in now."

He sat stunned.

I was right.

It would be difficult for him and his wife, extremely difficult.

"Let's talk about freedom," I said, looking for the bright side of a sad equation. "If you downsize, you'll be free to eat out when you want to, take those vacations you want to take, and buy new clothes. As it is now, I'm afraid you wouldn't have the money to fix your hot water heater if it broke. Don't handcuff your finances and your family by wasting all of your money on a big house you don't really need."

The message was clear.

Pay attention to the little things.

That's part of life.

The little things in life are what real memories are made of. Jack could stay in the big, fancy house, remain buried by debt, and hardly ever have any memories at all. His family deserved better than that.

When I walked into the Atlanta office, I had already reviewed the month's sales reports, and one of the team members concerned me a great deal. I was worried about him, his confidence, and his success; not about the financial totals of Tom James. During the past week, he had not made any sales at all, which was highly unusual for any person working at the company.

I bluntly asked him, "Why do you think your customers failed to buy?"

He gave me a few reasons.

None were legitimate.

All were excuses.

I was convinced that someone should have bought. After all, I checked his list of prospects, and all were highly qualified. All were important business executives. All had the financial status to afford our brand of suits. "Do you think you might be doing something in your presentation that prevents people from buying?" I asked.

He shrugged. "I don't know," he said.

"Line up appointments with everyone you called on last Thursday," I said, "and, if you don't mind, I'll make the presentation this time."

"It's not necessary for you to do that."

"Why not?"

"I don't think it would be wise for you to make the same presentation to the same customers."

"Sure, it would."

"But they've already heard it."

I smiled. "Let's allow them to hear it again," I said.

The salesman had told his story to all five executives, and I'm sure he told it well. But for some reason, he had not connected with any of them.

"Where did these gentlemen go to college?" I asked the salesman.

"I don't know."

"Were any of them married?"

"I don't know."

"What kind of hobbies do they have?"

"I don't know."

"How many children do they have?"

He didn't know that either.

"When you go in for your appointment, check around you," I said. "Is there a college diploma on the wall? Does he have a photo of his wife and children on his desk? Does he have pictures of himself out playing golf, or fishing, or hunting? Ask about them. Let the man know you care about him and his importance as an individual, and then he will be more receptive to your presentation."

"You really think that works?" the salesman asked.

"It does for me," I said. "I'm going to give you a chance to find out."

As the day progressed, I talked about college football fortunes in one office, a deep-sea fishing excursion in another, a son's little league baseball team in a third, a daughter's wedding, and a beautiful antique car that had been restored. I had witnessed them all in large and small frames on his wall or on his desk.

My salesman had already told the Tom James story five times to the same set of executives.

I told it again.

And all five bought suits.

They didn't buy from Jim McEachern. They didn't even know me, and more than likely, they might never see me again.

It didn't matter.

They bought from someone who took the time to make them feel important. They bought from someone who cared about their lives, their hobbies, their families. If a sales person was willing to listen closely to stories about their lives, then they were willing to listen to whatever kind of presentation that sales person had to give them. My customers didn't always buy.

But they always felt good about themselves when I left.

As a result, they were always happy to see me again.

And sooner or later I walked out with an order.

I had always taught that sales were a numbers game. That has been the gospel of selling since the first merchant rode the countryside from farm to farm and found that he could do quite well peddling a product that someone else needed. The formula was two-fold. Make more appointments, and you make more sales. There was, however, a real flaw in that line of reasoning. Just lining up a bunch of meetings without qualifying the customers was a dead end that destroyed a lot of sales people's dreams. The secret was this: *Make more qualified appointments, and you make more sales.* It works every time.

In Houston, I rode with a salesman to an Electrical Supply company. He was excited and wanted to show off his first customer of the day. The building was quite impressive and must have covered an entire block.

Somebody was making a lot of money.

And now even I was excited.

We walked inside and turned into a bullpen that featured row after row of desks with at least twenty men all sitting in the same room. My salesman led me back into the far corner, and introduced me to his prospect.

The gentleman was wearing a stained shirt with a frayed collar.

It was wrinkled.

I'm not sure he had ever worn a tie, not to work anyway.

My salesman proudly folded his arms and motioned for me to begin the presentation.

I shook my head.

He motioned again.

I ignored him.

He shrugged with disgust and waded right into the presentation himself. He did a great job. When he finished, however, the man told him, "That really sounds great, and I'm sure you have beautiful suits. But, frankly, I can't afford your clothes."

I smiled, shook his hand, thanked him for his time, and walked quickly away. As we crossed the parking lot, my salesman was exasperated. He asked, "Why didn't you give the presentation? That's what we had agreed upon."

"I don't give presentations to people I know can't buy our clothes," I said.

"Why not?"

"He's a good man. He does a good job," I said. "And I did not want to embarrass or humiliate him by forcing him to say with everyone looking on and listening in that 'I can't afford your clothes.'"

The sale was never as important as leaving a prospect with his respect intact.

No one ever had to defy the kind of odds that had long faced Naresh Khanna. He had been born in India. His mother and father had been medical doctors in the military. Naresh attended school in England and acquired an MBA degree at the University of Indiana. So far, so good. For two summers, he was on the streets, selling books for the Southwestern Company, and it was only natural for Spencer Hays to bring him aboard Tom James. Spencer always kept his eyes on his book sales people. He knew who might be able to sell suits as well as books, and he quickly hired them to help build his clothing company. He had a lot of confidence in Naresh.

Spencer possessed more confidence in his ability than Naresh did. The young man struggled for at least two years to make a living, able to survive only because he had the courage to take a job delivering newspapers door to door every morning and evening.

"Don't worry," I wrote him, "someday, you will be a really great sales person."

He kept right on working.

Naresh and his wife had a tiny efficiency apartment with a dining table that was really nothing more than a folding card table. Their bookcase had been built with cinder blocks and planks of one-by-twelve lumber.

"Don't worry," I wrote him, "someday, you will be able to afford a nice house in the best section of Atlanta."

He kept right on working.

Naresh drove a dilapidated old Mustang with more than a hundred thousand miles on the engine even though it was always threatening to fall out from under him. The rust kept holding it together. It was a long-shot and a gamble every time he sat down behind the steering wheel and turned the key in the switch.

"Don't worry," I wrote him, "someday, you'll be able to buy the biggest, newest, fastest, most dependable car on the road."

He kept right on working.

I kept right on sending him letters, always reminding him what he needed to do in order to make success happen for him, always encouraging him, always letting him know that we believed in him and continued to believe that he would someday become a great sales person. My final message to him was always the same, get all of the referrals you can, use them to line up a full schedule of appointments each day, and tell your Tom James story to customers at least five times a day.

It was not a complex formula.

It worked every time.

It took Naresh Khanna several years, but one day I looked up and realized that he had become the number one sales person at Tom James.

It didn't faze him though. He wouldn't dare slack off.

He kept right on working.

For fifteen consecutive years, Naresh Khanna remained the number one sales person for the Tom James Company.

He had worked for it. He had fought for it. He had it, and he wasn't about to let go of it.

After ten years at the top, Naresh was asked to deliver the opening speech at our annual Tom James conference. The room was filled with sales people, some old hands, some just starting out, all wondering what had been the spark to drive Naresh Khanna to the top.

He walked across the stage, moved toward the microphone, and in a clear, direct voice, read a letter I had written him.

Then he read another.

He said quietly, "I saved every letter that Mr. McEachern wrote me. I read them over and over, time and again. He kept telling me I could be a great sales person. He kept telling me I could live in a fine house in the best section of Atlanta. He kept telling me that I could drive a big, new car. And after awhile, I began to believe them."

Times had been bad for him. They were often worse.

But Naresh Khanna kept right on working for one reason.

He had a company that stood behind him and believed in him when, perhaps, no one else would have given him the chance.

Takeaways from the chapter

- *Jim states: "I realized that the influence of a single life could last far past a single lifetime. It could last forever." Who am I influencing and is it for the better? How can I have an eternal impact on people's lives?*
- *One of the big lessons of life according to Jim is "Pay attention to the little things. . . . The little things in life are what real memories are made of." Have I so indebted my family that we can't enjoy going out to eat, taking a vacation, buying new clothes, etc.? If I have an income and can't afford to do these things then I'm overspending for my house, car and/or other big ticket items. Downsizing could be the very best thing to do in order to get back to enjoying those little things.*
- *Jim used letter writing to encourage people. Interestingly many people report keeping every letter Jim ever wrote them. What could he have said that so inspired them as to save those letters? It seems that belief, encouragement, and positive affirmation were some of the more important aspects. How will I communicate these ideas, hopes, and dreams to the people that I interact with?*

Chapter 19

Choosing to Guide Those Who Need Help

As we grew, expanded, and moved forward at the Tom James Company, I had two goals in mind. Nothing had changed. They were the same two goals that I had been carrying with me for years.

I wanted to see my sales people succeed.

I knew that if I could help each of them increase his sales to a hundred thousand dollars a year, then Tom James had a splendid opportunity to reach a hundred million dollars in sales and move into the heady, elite company of the *Fortune 500*.

The concept was with me during every waking hour.

I dreamed about it.

The thought consumed me.

I had sold myself on the idea. I had probably even sold Spencer Hays. He was at least giving me the chance to reach that goal. Now all I had to do was sell the scattered sales force at Tom James. It would take a lot of plane rides, early breakfasts, long days, and late-night dinners.

Top retail sales people in men's department stores across the country – and at Tom James as well – generally had sales of forty thousand and occasionally ninety thousand dollars a year, some years better than others and some years worse. Even drawing nothing more than a commission fee, those were enough sales for a man or woman to carve out a decent living. However, I wasn't looking for sales people who were content to merely earn a decent living.

I was shooting for the top.

I wanted a sales force that was willing to shoot with me.

The question was this: how could I convince someone who had never sold more than forty thousand dollars worth of merchandise a year that he or she was capable of hitting the hundred-thousand-dollar-a-year mark?

It had often been said in motivational talks that whatever you can believe, you can achieve. I had no doubt that it was true. But could I persuade my sales people to believe, as I did, that by working together we could actually build a hundred-million-dollar-a-year company? For most, it was an idea far off the charts.

They didn't mind following.

I had to figure out a way to lead them.

Through the business grapevine, I had heard about two sales people, both dealing with men's clothes, who intrigued me a great deal. Larry Tweed worked at Muse's in Atlanta, and Hop Reynolds manned the men's department for Thurman-Reynolds in Dallas. They were legends in the business. For some time, they had been able to sell at least three hundred thousand dollars a year, and sometimes they threatened to break the storied four-hundred-thousand-dollar-a-year target.

No one else from coast to coast, as far as I knew, was even close.

I decided that it might help us all if I visited the stores, met both men, and tried to discover the reasons why they dominated the curious and ambivalent world of selling. I walked through the door of Muse's wondering why Tweed was even agreeable to meet with a competitor in the business, much less let me pick his brain and pry loose any of his well-kept trade secrets. I shouldn't have worried. He was nice, personable, and talkative and seemed quite honored that I had bothered to come to see him.

It was easy to uncover Tweed's basic secret.

He always had customers.

He said, "There are certain times of years when it is easy to get people in the store: When the weather turns and they need to change to a summer wardrobe, and then when the weather turns again, and they need to change to a winter wardrobe. Of course, there are the holiday gift-giving seasons like Christmas. And everybody wants to look nice at Easter. Unfortunately, during the slow months, and there are a lot of them, most sales people stand around, wait for the doors to open, hope a customer comes in, and hardly sell anything at all. Without customers, I'm out of business."

"What do you do?" I queried.

"Well," Tweed said, "while everyone else is standing around, I'm on the phone calling my old and regular customers. I don't wait for them to come to the store. If it is more convenient for them, I get their permission to bring a bunch of suits to their office. I already have their sizes and a pretty good idea of the styles they prefer."

You can't wait for customers to find you, he said.

There are times when you have to go out and find them.

I'm sure that Hop Reynolds would have been just as accommodating as Larry Tweed. It's just that we never had a chance to talk.

He was too busy.

As soon as he introduced himself, he immediately had a customer looking for him. As soon as the man came through the door, Reynolds called him by name.

He turned to me and said, "Please have a seat, and I'll talk to you just as soon as I get the time."

I sat patiently and waited for two hours.

He never got the time.

Reynolds had a continuous parade of customers. Businessmen. Wives. Young. Aging. Some just out of college. Some ready for retirement. White collar. Blue collar. It didn't matter.

He knew them all.

He called them all by name.

He asked about their businesses, the organizations where they did volunteer work, their last fishing trip, their last golf game, their next vacation, their children, and the high schools where their children played sports. He knew their scores, their golf handicaps, and the names of their wives and their children. I heard him ask one gentleman about his daughter's horse, and Reynolds even knew the name of the horse.

After two hours, I no longer needed to talk with Hop Reynolds.

I had a pretty good idea of what made him so successful. It was clear to me that he was not just a sales person. He built customer relationships. His clientele over the years, maybe from the first visit, had become his friends, not acquaintances but real friends.

Both Larry Tweed and Hop Reynolds were practicing what Dale Carnegie had taught years earlier. They weren't merely selling clothes. They were, in or out of the store, winning friends and influencing people because both men had taken the time and devoted their lives to knowing those customers as well as they did their own families.

Carnegie had said, "The sweetest word in any language is a person's own name."

Larry Tweed and Hop Reynolds had honed it to a science.

The lessons I learned from talking to and observing those two men only confirmed that our training methods were solid, and those same simple philosophies of dealing with clients would soon become further entrenched in the culture of a Tom James sales person. In reality, a sales person should never consider his client as a customer. A customer walks into the store. A sales person rings up a sale. And the customer walks back out again. It's mostly, "hello," and "thank you," and sometimes "come again."

From now on, I wanted to impress upon our sales force that clients weren't and would never be merely customers. They were our friends – old friends, new friends, and friends we just hadn't met yet.

On Making Friends

One of Jim's trademark qualities was to make each person feel special. Many times we would meet for breakfast at a popular restaurant in Midlothian. Of course, practically everyone knew Jim and would speak to him as they entered. I was amazed at his ability to make others feel important without making me feel neglected. He had a way of making everyone feel as if he had arranged a meeting with his best friends so they could meet each other. I rarely left breakfast without making a new friend and feeling that Jim had arranged it. Rev. Nick Harris- Jim's pastor at the Ovilla Road Baptist Church

Developing a close, personal relationship with a client was not unlike finding a gold mine. As I told our sales force, "Sell him once. Make him feel important and worthwhile to you, and he will buy from you for the rest of his life. It is always easier to keep old clients than find new ones."

I also shared with them the passage I had read years ago in a book: "We will never achieve what we could achieve and never become what we could become unless we recognized our own mortality. We must develop a sense of urgency about making something of our lives."

I felt a genuine sense of urgency.

I hoped my sales people did as well.

My urgency was reaching a hundred million dollars a year in sales. In order to accomplish that goal, every sales person at Tom James had the opportunity to become comfortable, if not wealthy, for the rest of his life.

A few years earlier, I had been searching for my own recipe for success. When I read Frank Bettger's book, *How I Raised Myself From Failure to Success in Selling*, I knew I had found it.

From Bettger's words, I developed this game plan for myself and gave it to all of our sales people. It had helped me. I was convinced that it would help them as well.

1. Be enthusiastic. Act enthusiastic and you will become enthusiastic. If you double your enthusiasm that you put into your work and your life, you will probably double your income and your happiness. You can double your income and

happiness repeatedly. It had happened to me. It could happen for them. Every day of my life, I choose to think, talk, and act enthusiastically.

2. Make the calls. Set up a full schedule of appointments. Tell your story enthusiastically and persuasively to enough people. Tell your story to four or five people every day, and you can't help making good. This works. When I was selling, I made sure I told my story a minimum of five times a day.

3. Face and overcome your fears. Do this and you will develop self-confidence and courage. Personally, I was able to overcome fear and develop both confidence and fearlessness by doing what I fear, by going out and risking rejection and failure.

4. Set goals. Review and think about your goals and priorities every day.

  a. Do everything in order of importance.
  b. Have your time organized in order to do the important things first.
  c. Begin every day and every week with a full and detailed schedule of goal-oriented activities in order to get results. Have a specific time each week for developing your goals, your plans, and your detailed schedule.
  d. Give your leaders a copy of your goals, your plans, and your schedule. Keep them to yourself, and you may or may not get around to doing them. If you hand them to your leaders or managers, then you are fully committed. This works like magic.

5. Find out what people want and help them get what they want. You can have anything you want if you help enough other people get what they want. The most important secret in selling successfully is to find out what people want, and then help them figure the best way to get it.

6. When you show a person what he wants, he will move heaven and earth to get it. This makes selling fun.

7. Answer objections with questions. Questions get people to think and get them involved. Questions are the key to effective selling. Cultivate the art of asking questions.

8. Make appointments, at least five daily.

   a. Be prepared for each appointment.
   b. Find out what the key issue is, and then stay with it.
   c. Focus your presentation on the key issue.
   d. Prepare key word notes.
   e. Ask questions.
   f. Create confidence.
   g. During the presentation, replace "I" or "we" with "you" and "your."

9. Remember: asking questions increases sales effectiveness. Listed here are six things that questions can do for you.

   a. Helps you avoid arguments.
   b. Helps you avoid talking too much.
   c. Enables the other person to recognize what he or she wants. Then you can help them decide how to get it.
   d. Helps the other person crystallize their thinking.
   e. Enables you to find out the key issue which enables you to close the sale.
   f. Enables you to show respect for the other person's opinion, which will likely cause him or her to respect your opinion.

10. The main problem in selling is the failure to find the basic need or the main point of interest, understanding the key

issue and the failure to stick to it. Never stray from the key issue once you have discovered it.

11. The most important word in selling is; "Why, or why not?"
12. Find the hidden objection.
13. Become a good listener; show the other person you are sincerely interested in what he is saying. Being a good listener is the key. People appreciate a good listener in any situation, particularly in sales.
14. Don't be afraid to fail. The message to me was *never, never, never give up*. Keep pursuing your goals regardless of the circumstances you face.

For a long time, I had made it a point to ask each of my clients to give me the best advice that he could possibly give. Their wisdom, gleaned from years of experience in the hard, no-holds-barred world of business, had always played a significant role in my own sales efforts, and I quickly passed each of those nuggets on to my sales people. The advice I received may have had very little to do with the art of salespersonship. But it was indeed vital to their quest for life, liberty, and the pursuit of happiness.

The president of the Southwestern Company told me: "People are more creative if they are not operating under financial duress. Never buy a big house or a fancy car if it causes you to feel constant financial pressure. You should grow your bank account large enough to equal six months of your salary. Don't ever make short-term commitments or decisions if they undermine your long-term objectives."

And another executive told me in no uncertain terms: "Don't ever lose your family in the process of fulfilling your pursuit of profits or attaining your financial goals."

I happened to be on a flight from Dallas to Tulsa, and, as we boarded the plane, I overheard a flight attendant call Ross Perot by name. He had been standing in line right behind me. I was well aware that Perot was one of the wealthiest men in Dallas. He had built several highly successful businesses, and I wondered what kind of advice he might give me. I was determined to find out.

I was sitting in coach.

Perot was in first class.

As soon as the flight leveled off for its cruising altitude and the seat belt sign was turned off, I made my way up the aisle, knelt beside him, infringed as politely as I could on his privacy, and told him how much I admired his success in the business world.

He turned around, smiled, and began asking me questions.

Where did I live?

What did I do?

"What kind of company was Tom James?"

"How large was it?"

"What were my goals and ambitions for the business?"

It was one question after another. Rapid fire. And he was listening intently to every word I said. All the way to Tulsa, not once did Perot ever stop asking questions.

And we ran out of time.

The seat belt light came back on. I thanked him and returned to my seat. As the plane descended, it suddenly dawned on me that I had made a terrible mistake.

I had not asked Ross Perot one single question.

Then I realized that there was no need to ask him a question. Perot had given me his secret. He had learned everything he could about me. He had made me feel special. Someone as important as Ross Perot, in just a handful of minutes on a short flight, had done his best to make me feel important. He had a genuine interest in people.

Once again, the point was driven home.

Business was all about people.

It wasn't about clothes or any other kind of merchandise.

It was about people.

I was sitting in a businessman's home in Houston after I had delivered his suits one hot summer day. It was a big house, and we had retired to the den, which must have been fifteen hundred square feet. It served as both his office and his library.

I said to him, "You are very successful, and I am ambitious. I like to learn from people who have already achieved a great deal of success. Please give me your very best advice, whatever it might be.

He looked at me for a long time.

It must have taken him thirty seconds to answer.

I could almost hear the sounds of his thoughts tumbling around inside his head.

Finally, he leaned forward and said, "You're on the right track. Keep on doing what you're doing. Keep right on asking questions. Never stop learning. And make sure you keep on delivering me fine suits."

I kept asking questions. I kept looking for advice. I read every book I could find on salespersonship, selling techniques, motivation, and success habits. But most importantly, I never stopped working one-on-one with my sales people.

My goal was still to someday reach a hundred million dollars a year in sales. I planted that seed in the mind of every sales person we had working and every sales person we hired. On paper, all I wanted from each of them was a hundred thousand dollars a year in sales. To most, such a far-reaching goal, especially during the early days of Tom James had no doubt seemed implausible, improbable, and impossible.

It was a mythical number that always seemed just beyond everyone's grasp.

Not anymore.

One sales person dug deep, worked hard, took care of old customers, became friends with his clients, and sold a hundred thousand dollars a year. It was a groundbreaking and breakthrough moment. This impossible barrier was no longer the impossible. Tom James the sales person, appropriately enough, inherited my clientele when I became the company's sales manager, and he topped the barrier first. When James departed the organization, Jim Rawdon was given his clientele, and it vaulted him past the hundred thousand-dollar-a-year bar. Those customers were passed on to Aaron Meyers, who had joined me in Atlanta in 1967, and it didn't take long for Aaron to keep the streak alive. Those original customers had provided the company a strong foundation, which would forever impact our climb toward membership *in Fortune's 500* list of top companies.

It was much like the day Roger Bannister broke the four-minute mile. Track stars had tried for years, but none of them had been able to crack the impregnable mark. None believed they could accomplish it; so no one did.

Roger Bannister blazed past the finish line at 3:59.4, and only forty-six days later Australia's John Landy eclipsed the record with a mile run of 3:57.9. No one on the track was troubled by the four-minute mile anymore. The grueling and arduous mile run, which had long been a strategic race, was suddenly dominated by sprinters, and all of the elite runners were breaking the tape in less than four minutes with regularity.

The Tom James Company was no different.

As soon as we had someone finally crack past a hundred thousand dollars a year in sales, there was a mad rush to see who would reach that illusionary sales total next. Competition was fierce, and it wasn't long before sales people were topping two, three, and even four hundred thousand dollars a year in sales. The barrier had been shattered, and the impossible had become the standard. Now I had a sales force aiming even higher than ever before and actually hitting their marks.

Spencer Hays created a President's Club. Members weren't chosen or elected, and no one could pay an entry fee and join. The President's Club was designed to honor the best; open only to those who achieved four hundred and twenty-five thousand dollars a year in sales. In time, we would have more than a hundred and fifty members enshrined in a very exclusive club. One of our top salesmen, Steve Adelsburg, was sitting at the top and all alone. Steve Adelsburg had climbed well above two million dollars a year in sales and was averaging a minimum of two thousand dollars a transaction.

We weren't all the way there yet.

But we were coming closer.

And Tom James was becoming a force to be reckoned with in the business world.

Even though their yearly sales totals might exceed far beyond a hundred thousand dollars a year, sales people always needed someone to listen to their concerns, understand their problems, and help put their feet back in the right direction.

I made it a point to spend the day with Adam because I realized that, as far as selling clothes was concerned, he had hit the proverbial wall. He was a good man and an extremely competent sales person, but something was wrong, and I was determined to figure it out. His sales had leveled off, and I strongly believed that he had the ability to sell his way into the President's Club at Tom James. In order to attain this he would need to sell $425,000 a year for us, but Adam, year after year, always seemed to end up about a hundred thousand dollars short of the goal.

He and I didn't go to work that day.

We didn't make any sales calls.

I just sat back and decided that I needed to know Adam a little better. What made him tick? What were his dreams? What did he consider a good life? What could I do to help him achieve the sales he needed to earn his way into the prestigious President's Club? What kind of invisible barrier was blocking his path?

I immediately placed the challenge in front of him. "What were your sales last year?" I asked.

"Close to three hundred thousand dollars."

"What do you expect to do this year?"

"Probably the same, maybe a little more." Adam grinned. "I guess it depends on how slow the slow season is this year."

I nodded. I paused. I waited a minute as I thought over his answer, then I said, "What I'd like to do is talk to you about selling twice that much."

The silence lingered for a moment.

Then he asked, "Do you think that's possible?

"I believe it is." I smiled and said, "All you have to do is sell seventy thousand dollars a month."

"How long do you think it'll take for me to reach that number?"

"I think you can do it right away." I shrugged. "I think you can sell seventy thousand dollars worth of clothes this month."

"I don't know. That's a lot of sales."

"You've got that kind of ability."

"I don't think so."

"Why not?"

He laughed softly. "Well," he said, "for one thing, the month's already half over."

I nodded again. "That means you have fifteen more selling days," I said.

"That's not much."

"It's enough."

Adam sold seventy thousand dollars worth of suits in fifteen days, and he kept it up. Once a person believes he can accomplish something monumental, he immediately has the confidence it takes to reach or surpass the same goal again and again.

I was able to teach him the secret that had escaped so many sales people. Sure, it was vital to increase his number of transactions each month. But it was just as important to increase the number of sales during each transaction.

The gentleman buys a suit.

Maybe he needs two.

Maybe he would prefer a casual sports coat as well.

And slacks, of course.

And shirts.

Business.

And casual.

And ties.

And never forget the socks.

As I told my sales people, "A customer might be a lot happier if you allowed him the opportunity to buy more. You should never walk out of his office without at least giving him that chance."

I didn't have any magic.

I didn't have any hidden secrets.

But I was able to listen and understand our sales people's needs, to guide them along and let them come to the conclusions necessary to achieve a greater degree of success.

During my career, Spencer Hays told me, a large percentage of sales people had shown a fairly dramatic increase in sales after I spent the day with them.

I thanked him.

I appreciated the recognition, but I didn't need it.

Most all of our sales people were now registering sales of at least a hundred thousand dollars a year.

A lot of them were selling a lot more.

Together, they were the ones propelling the Tom James Company at full speed toward a hundred million dollars a year in sales. They were building a great company, and had made Tom James a household name in the business marketplace, a name that had become synonymous with professionalism, integrity, and quality.

And me? I was just doing my job.

Our sales people were the ones making my promise to Spencer Hays come true.

Takeaways from the chapter

- *Jim was clearly most influenced by the books he read and the people he met. Jim did more than read and ask questions though. He learned to take the information gained to the application phase. Am I "applying" the knowledge I glean from books and people of influence?*
- *Jim had a genuine interest in people. He made everyone he met feel special and he did this through asking lots of questions. Am I asking people enough questions to make them feel special?*
- *Jim and Spencer Hays built into the DNA of Tom James the importance of recognition as motivation. In what ways am I recognizing those who are serving with excellence? Could I do more? What can I do to make a "big deal" out of an individual's worthwhile efforts?*

CHAPTER 20

Choosing to Confront Adversity

"In our personal lives, in business, and in our careers, we all come to important crossroads so critical to our future. The way we choose to go is the most important decision we can ever make." Jim McEachern

I have always been deeply affected by the faith, the indomitable spirit, and the determination of three men as they came face to face with adversity in their lives. The genuine character of individuals is never judged by what they do or how they act when their endeavors are crowned with applause and success but how strong they stand when confronted with the fear of failure or defeat.

Even as a schoolboy sitting in my history classroom, I was intrigued with the achievements and the battles fought by Abraham Lincoln. He is remembered as a great President and the nation's great emancipator who, as much as anyone, believed that all men indeed were created equal and should be treated that way.

What struck me, however, was the number of times Lincoln fought back after suffering another stinging defeat. His losses were as great as his triumphs, but nothing was ever able to stop him. Defeat only spurred him on to try even harder. He refused to quit. Lose today, and he was back on the winning track tomorrow. As Lincoln always said, "I will prepare, and someday my chance will come." He was not judged on the number of times he failed but on the number of times he succeeded, and the number of times he succeeded could be dutifully measured in direct proportion to the number of times he failed and kept on trying.

In 1832, for example, Lincoln lost his job and was defeated for state legislature. The same year, however, he was elected company captain of the Illinois militia in the Black Hawk War.

In 1833, Lincoln failed in business, but was appointed postmaster of New Salem, Illinois, and deputy surveyor of Sangamon County. A year later, he was elected to the Illinois state legislature.

In 1835, his sweetheart died and, a year later, Lincoln was stricken with a nervous breakdown. He was undaunted, winning re-election to the Illinois state legislature while also receiving his license to practice law in Illinois state courts.

In 1838, Lincoln was defeated for the Illinois House Speaker but still managed to win his race to the Illinois House and serve as the Whig floor leader.

In 1843, he was defeated for nomination for Congress but, three years later, won his seat in Congress. Within five years, Lincoln lost his chance to be re-nominated by choosing not to run for Congress, abiding by rule of rotation among Whigs.

He was rejected for land officer in 1849, defeated for the U. S. Senate in 1854, defeated for nomination for Vice President in 1856, and again defeated for the U. S. Senate in 1858.

A scant two years later, Abraham Lincoln stood before his country as the newly elected President of the United States.

Adversity had knocked him down but never one too many times. Lincoln always got back up and tried again.

Every accomplishment in life, it seems, always begins with the courage and the decision to try one more time and, if necessary, one more after that. After all, as Vincent Van Gogh said, "What would life be if we had no courage to attempt anything?"

During World War II, Viktor Frankl experienced the kind of horror that no man or woman should ever be forced to endure. The Jewish psychiatrist from Vienna, Austria, was placed in a Nazi

Concentration Camp and fought against all odds to find a will and reason to live. Both parents died during the Holocaust. His wife died. His brother died. Most of his Jewish friends and comrades died. Frankl lived on. As he would write in his book, *Man's Search for Meaning*, every material thing on earth was stripped from him. He was told where to work and what to do. He was told when to eat and what to eat. But nothing, neither the brutality of the guards nor the evil Nazi doctrine, was ever able to control Frankl's attitude or his thoughts. Within human existence, he said, we are always free to choose our own thoughts in spite of the adverse circumstances around us.

He wrote of one night when he and a fellow prisoner were on an icy road as they were marched back to camp:

> *As we stumbled on for miles, slipping on icy spots, supporting each other time and again, dragging one another up and onward, nothing was said, but we both knew: each of us was thinking of his wife. Occasionally I looked at the sky, where the stars were facing and the pink light of the morning was beginning to spread behind a dark bank of clouds. But my mind clung to my wife's image, imagining it with an uncanny acuteness. I heard her answering me; saw her smile, her frank and encouraging look. Real or not, her look was then more luminous than the sun, which was beginning to rise.*
>
> *A thought transfixed me: for the first time in my life I saw the truth as it is set into song by so many poets, proclaimed as the final wisdom by so many thinkers. The truth – that love is the ultimate and the highest goal to which man can aspire. Then I grasped the meaning of the greatest secret that human poetry and human thought and belief have to impart: The salvation of man is through love and in love. I understood how a man who has nothing left in this world still may know bliss, be it only for a brief moment, in the contemplation of his beloved.*

We all search for the meaning of life. I had found it through the eyes of a man who had seen, who had lived, the worst that inhumanity could inflict upon mankind, and still Frankl was able to understand that *love* is and would always be man's first and his last hope.

Like Viktor Frankl, Admiral James Stockdale endured the horrors of a wartime prison camp. Flying over the Tonkin Gulf from the deck of the USS *Ticonderoga*, he was on a mission above Vietnam when he was forced to eject from his disabled plane, an A-4E Skyhawk and parachute into a small village occupied by the Vietcong. Stockdale was severely beaten throughout the day and dragged to the Hoa Lo prison where the admiral would spend the next seven years. He was locked in leg irons in a bath stall and tortured on a routine basis.

When his captors told him that the admiral – the highest-ranking naval officer held as a prisoner of war in Vietnam – would be paraded in public, he slit his scalp with a razor blade to purposely disfigure himself. He absolutely would not allow himself to be used for propaganda purposes. The Vietcong placed a hat on his head. Stockdale beat himself with a stool until his face was bruised, blooded, and swollen beyond recognition. When it was discovered that Stockdale might possess information that could implicate the *black activities* of his imprisoned friends, the admiral slit his own wrists. He was willing to die. He could not be tortured into a confession.

To pay for leading other prisoners in an all-out resistance against their captors, Stockdale and ten other prisoners were marched a mile away and thrown into solitary confinement and locked into cells that measured three feet by nine feet. A light bulb burned day and night. He was locked in irons each night.

Dying would have been easy.

It was a real testament to his will and courage to survive.

James Stockdale had once promised his father that he would try to become the best midshipman at the Naval Academy. He became one of the most highly decorated officers in the history of the United

States Navy, being awarded twenty-six personal combat decorations, including the Medal of Honor and four silver Stars.

After the war, when he was being interviewed by James Collins for his business book entitled *Good to Great*, Admiral Stockdale was asked, *How did you cope during your confinement in the prison camp?*

"I never lost faith in the end of the story," the admiral said. "I never doubted not only that I would get out, but always that I would prevail in the end and turn the experience into the defining event of my life, which, in retrospect, I would not trade."

Please tell me, what kind of men didn't make it out of the camp? he was asked.

"Oh, that's easy, the optimists," Stockdale answered. "They were the ones who said, 'We're going to be out by Christmas.' And Christmas would come, and Christmas would go. Then they'd say, 'Were going to be out by Easter.' And Easter would come, and Easter would go.' And then Thanksgiving, and then it would be Christmas again. And they died of a broken heart."

Stockdale paused a moment, then added, "This is a very important lesson. You must never confuse faith that you will prevail in the end – which you can never afford to lose – with the discipline to confront the most brutal facts of your current reality, whatever they might be."

His words would forever be described as *The Stockdale Paradox*.

The lesson personally and professionally was two-fold. In order to succeed, it is vital to cultivate your ability and your organization's ability to accomplish two very difficult things at the same time:

1. Stay firm in your belief that you will prevail in the end.
2. Confront the brutal facts around you.

In his groundbreaking book, Collins and his research team studied ordinary companies that had made the tough and determined transition to greatness. And in every case, he wrote, "the management team responded with powerful psychological duality. On the one hand, they stoically accepted the brutal facts of reality. On the other hand, they maintained an unwavering faith in the endgame, and a commitment to prevail as a great company despite the brutal facts."

At the Tom James Company, we had followed that same unwavering track as we moved steadily toward becoming a hundred-million-dollar-a-year company. We knew the facts, and they were often brutal. I knew that to reach my goal, I had to motivate our sales people to break down real and psychological barriers that only a rare few in the clothing business had ever achieved. But neither Spencer Hays nor I ever lost faith. I knew and he was convinced that we would prevail in the end. As Dale Carnegie had written: "Most of the important things in the world have been accomplished by people who have kept on trying where there seemed to be no hope at all."

The Stockdale Paradox works for large corporations.

It works for small companies.

It works for individuals.

At the time that we were racing toward the goal we had established in business, I had no idea that the Stockdale Paradox would one day play such an important role in my own personal life.

It was 2006, and I had noticed that it was becoming much tougher each day to draw a strong breath when I exercised vigorously. I wheezed a lot. I blamed it on my age. After all, according to my physician, I was in pretty good health. The CT scans had not revealed anything unusual, and neither had my last X-rays. The only problem I had was an occasional shortness of breath. I ignored it.

Somehow, however, the scans and X-rays had overlooked a mass on my trachea tube, better known as my windpipe.

Dr. Carlos Girod, a lung specialist, had asked for me to come in for a biopsy just before I was scheduled to catch a plane to London. Nothing to be concerned about, I thought. I wasn't particularly worried. After all, I still had work to do. I had long been retired from my position as chairman of the board, but my mind never left Tom James, not for an instant. Next to God and my family, the company was still nearest to my heart.

"How will you notify me with the results?" I asked Dr. Girod.

"Why don't you call me?" he said.

"I'll be in London."

"Call me," he said.

By Friday night, I was on my way to Great Britain. I landed, went to my hotel, and never got around to calling. There was after all a five-hour time difference. I was tired, but the day was still young in London. Besides, I had people from Tom James to meet, and they could re-energize me like nothing else.

It was eleven o'clock that night, and I was already asleep when the phone rang. Jet lag still gripped me. I opened my eyes and, for an instant, wondered where I was. Nothing seemed familiar. I shook my head, trying to clear the cobwebs and didn't reach the phone until it had stopped ringing.

The red light was blinking.

Nothing has ever been as ominous as a red light blinking on the phone in the middle of the night.

Something must be wrong.

I prayed that my family was still all right as I checked the message.

It was from Dr. Girod.

"Call back as soon as you can," he said.

I tried.

But the day had already ended in Dallas, and the switchboard was closed.

I called Arlene instead. "Have you talked to Dr. Girod?" I asked.

"I have."

"What did he say?"

"We'll talk when you get home," she said.

There was a nervous, frightened tone in her voice.

It didn't sound good.

"What's wrong?" I asked.

"James," she said softly, "I'm so sorry, but you have cancer."

Cancer.

It was, perhaps, the most frightening word in the English language. It was a word I never expected to hear associated with my own life.

The night in London was dark.

It became even darker.

I was suddenly overwhelmed with a foreboding sense of claustrophobia. It was as though I had been squeezed into a tiny box and could not get out. I had a sudden feeling of anxiety and desperation not quite like any I had ever felt before.

I hung up the phone and sat down on the edge of the bed.

I took a deep breath, cleared my head, and began punching in the numbers on my cell phone. I called each of my four children. I called my pastor. I called Spencer Hays. I called Bob Sherrer, who had replaced me as chairman of the board for Tom James. The seven conversations lasted over the next four hours.

They all assured me of three things.

They loved me.

God loved me.

They would pray for me.

I hung up the phone. The night was still dark in downtown London.

I no longer saw the darkness.

The panic left me.

So did the claustrophobia.

And any rising tides of fear had subsided within me.

After all, I thought, my situation was not nearly as desperate as Viktor Frankl's had been. I had a nice room. I knew where my next meal would be served. I still had my family intact.

The adversity I faced was nowhere near as severe as calamitous as Admiral James Stockdale had endured. There were no chains around my legs, and no one would come to beat me before morning.

Lincoln had come back from failure and disappointment and unexpected setbacks.

Who was I to let the simple threat of cancer ruin my life?

I waited for the dawn to strike the streets of London, dressed in my finest Tom James suit, walked down to a big ballroom, smiled my brightest smile, and made two speeches to a conference of Tom James sales people.

The news I had received the night before had been highly emotional, but I had a responsibility and an obligation to my company. Those sales people were waiting to hear something that would benefit them, and I believed that it was still my duty and obligation to help make their sales efforts in the future more successful and worthwhile.

My mind was clear.

My worry had left with the panic.

In a calm, matter-of-fact voice, I told them about the message I had received the night before. There was no sense for alarm, I said. I did not want anyone to be concerned or feel sorry for me. I was fine. Tomorrow was as bright as it had always been for both the Tom James Company and for me. I was proud of them and their past and future successes. I loved them, and I had faith in them, their commitment, their abilities, and their devotion to Tom James.

I thanked them.

And I walked out the door.

I had planned to stay a few days in London. Now I was on my way to the airport. The flight lasted eight hours and took me through Chicago before I was able to connect back to Dallas.

The closer I came to home, the closer I came to reality.

I thought of James Stockdale.

Face the brutal facts.

Never lose faith in the end story.

Believe that I would prevail.

Have the discipline to confront adversity.

On Sunday morning, I went to my home church in Ovilla, Texas, and at the end of the service, my pastor, Nick Harris, announced my diagnosis to the congregation and asked me to come to the front of the sanctuary.

I was not alone.

I never had been.

I was surrounded by those who had come to worship that morning. They prayed for me.

The facts did not appear as brutal as they had been.

My faith was intact.

I knew I would prevail.

Adversity did not stand a chance.

As the service ended, a lady came up to me and handed me a business card with the name of Dr. Michael Wait, Thoracic Surgeon.

"This is my son," Mildred said. "I'm calling him this afternoon."

"Don't bother him," I said. "This is Sunday. It's his day off."

"I'm calling him this afternoon," she insisted.

"I wish you wouldn't bother him."

"But I must," she said.

"Why?"

"Because he's the best thoracic surgeon in the country," she said. "He'll be ready to see you when you're ready to see him."

I smiled and thanked her.

On Monday morning, I was sitting in the office of Dr. Carlos Girod. "I've made an appointment for you," he said.

"Okay."

"We're fortunate that you can see him."

I nodded.

"He's the best thoracic surgeon you'd ever want to meet."

I nodded again. "What's his name?" I asked.

"Dr. Michael Wait."

I almost laughed out loud.

God had been watching out for me just the way I knew he would.

The shock, the panic, the fear, the anxiety, the sadness I had felt were all gone. They had disappeared in a single heartbeat.

I was in my fighting mode now. All I wanted to know was the best way to deal with the cancer. Maybe I could defeat it. Maybe not. At the moment, I just wanted to be able to deal with it.

I was seventy years old. The decisions I had made for the past forty years had served me well, and until that particular moment in my life, I had never given a thought to the fact that I might someday be ready to leave this earth. It was inevitable, to be sure, the next great passage in life. I had just never worried about it. I still wasn't worried.

As in business, I wanted to be prepared to face any set of circumstances that might arise, and I began to re-examine all of my beliefs about Heaven, hell, and the relationships I had built during a lifetime.

These might indeed be the last days.

If they were, God knew what was best.

He always did.

As was my custom, I sat down, considered the possibilities of life, and began to establish my new set of priorities and goals. As I said, goals are important even though they do have a tendency to change now and then. Mine were changing again. I pulled out a sheet of paper and wrote goal number one at the top of the page: *Get in touch with everyone I know: family, friends, Tom James people, clients, customers, any name I had on a business card. Let them know how much I loved them, appreciated them, and was grateful for the role they had played in my life.*

All of them had made a difference, especially those who had reached out to help me during the struggles I had experienced during my growing up years. My only regret was that so many of their names had faded with time. I could still see their faces. I would never forget their faces. I would never forget them. I began searching my memory bank. *If I had failed anyone or ever hurt anyone, I wanted to own up to my mistake and make it right.* There were, I decided, two great and profound sentences in the English language: *"I'm sorry. And I love you."* I wanted them all to know.

Viktor Frankl had been right.

In the end, as it was in the beginning, love was all that counted. With love, I found that anyone can have a happy, fulfilling, satisfying, and enjoyable life.

Dr. Michael Wait performed surgery in May of 2006, and during September and October, I had thirty radiation treatments, one a day for six weeks.

We prayed.

We trusted.

We waited.

The next CT scan was encouraging. The cancer, at first glance, appeared to be shrinking and maybe even gone. In late January of 2008, however, the unexpected news was dramatically different.

I knew what the oncologist would tell me as soon as I walked through the door and saw his face.

"How are you doing?" he asked cautiously.

I smiled. "I have a cough I can't seem to get rid of," I said.

He didn't respond.

He just sat there at his computer, deep in thought. No one dreads bad news like the bearer of bad news. At last, he pulled up the results of the CT scan and showed me twenty spots that had shown up on my lungs.

"What can we do about it?" I asked.

"Unfortunately, we won't be able to perform surgery," he said.

I nodded.

"And we won't be able to radiate twenty different spots," he said.

I nodded again.

"And there is no chemotherapy known to work on this kind of cancer," he said. The oncologist shrugged apologetically and added, "Of course, we could send you to a chemotherapy specialist and try a couple of treatments. But if they don't show some immediate and positive results, I wouldn't suggest that we continue them. They would drag down your immune system and leave you feeling bad all of the time."

That would have been something new for me. I didn't feel bad at the moment. I had never felt bad, not really, not even when times were tough and work was scarce. I had no intentions of feeling bad now.

"What other possibilities are there?" I asked.

The oncologist shook his head. "I wouldn't recommend doing any more X-rays or CT scans or radiation," he said. "They may cause the cancer to grow."

An awkward silence hung between us.

He was waiting for me to ask the question he knew was on my mind.

I didn't make him wait any longer.

I asked it. "How much time do I have?"

The doctor took a deep breath. "I've known people who have made it a couple of years," he said.

Most didn't.

I knew that.

There was nothing else that the oncologist could do. But there was plenty I could do. Besides, I was gratified to know that I might indeed be around with my family and Tom James for two more years. Only God knew how long the clock had left to tick. I was on his schedule now, and, in reality, I always had been. I decided without any hesitation that I would be personally accountable for my near- and long-term future, making plans and preparations to give myself the best chance I could to prolong my days and my life.

Abraham Lincoln had not quit even though he had every reason to simply walk away from politics and be content to occupy a dark corner in a little Illinois law office.

Viktor Frankl had not let pain, sadness, despair, or frustration get the best of him. He still had his mind and his attitude and his thoughts, and no one, not even the evils of the Holocaust could rob him of his undying spirit. Love became his last shield, and it was strong enough.

Admiral James Stockdale had defied all odds that had been stacked against him. He had endured and prevailed.

So would I.

Everyone in life, I realized, comes face-to-face with a never-ending array of trials and misfortunes, disappointments, struggles, and hardships at home and in their business. Some experience a sense of futility. Some finally realize that life does indeed come to an end. We are only promised a short time on earth, and it is our obligation to make every one of those seconds, minutes, and days count. We can never get them back. As with the life of my great grandmother, we must live our lives so we can positively influence others long after our time has ended.

It happens to many.

It was happening to me.

My only thought was: "How do I deal with it?"

Thank God for the Internet. I began to search out stories of those people who had survived incurable cancer. Practically every one of them had made a significant lifestyle change, including a strict diet to support their immune systems. If it worked for some, I believed it would work for me as well. I began eating organic foods, including a lot of red, green, and yellow vegetables, as well as a lot of grasses, such as alfalfa, oats, and wheat. It was said that diet could make a difference. I was willing to give the diet a try and build up my immune system to fight off the cancer cells.

It might be a losing battle.

Then again, it might not.

Early on, just before my surgery a couple of years earlier, Dr. Michael Wait had told me, "People who have something to live for and who have a positive attitude and positive expectations for life have a fifty to one better chance to survive."

I had a lot to live for. I had now spent seventy-two years maintaining a positive attitude, and my expectations were as bright as ever. For me, *Life was good even if I only lived it one day at time.*

Takeaways from the chapter

- *Jim realized that failure is to be expected within the process of gaining success. What am I failing at on my way to success?*
- *Abraham Lincoln said "I will prepare and someday my chance will come." What am I preparing for?*
- *Jim introduces the Stockdale Paradox in this chapter. This is the belief that in the end you will prevail by confronting the brutal facts of where you stand at the moment. How did Jim face the brutal realities of his goals in business and of his goals in fighting cancer? Do I have goals and/or a vision that embraces this viewpoint?*

EPILOGUE

"Today is My Favorite Day"

"Today is my favorite day, and right now is my favorite time." Jim McEachern

It seemed only fitting to start this closing chapter on the life of James E. McEachern with the above quotation. On July 12, 2011 he went home to be with his Lord when he succumbed to a heart attack. The last portion of this book will seek to provide the conclusion to his story that Jim was unable to write. It was composed after extensive interviews with family and friends and will seek to provide final thoughts on the life of this extraordinary man.

Jim resigned as the CEO of Tom James Company in 1998. He did so, as it seemed he did with everything in his life, with purpose and good motives. He had achieved his goal of building a "$100 million dollar company" and he wanted to focus more on building metaphorically a "$100 million dollar family." There should be no misunderstanding on this point; it was not that his family hadn't always been the second most important thing in his life (with God being number one) for all the years prior to 1998. They certainly were. It was just that he had a strong belief that with the addition of grandchildren to the equation that he needed more time to build into their lives as well as his adult children. The years of weekly travel and 60 hour work weeks were starting to take their toll. He had achieved within Tom James the legacy he wanted to achieve and he wanted to leave a legacy behind with his family that would last well into the future. He didn't want to travel anymore. He didn't want to be away from Arlene and his adult children and grandchildren anymore. He also believed Tom James was ready for new leadership and vision. He stepped down as CEO and thought seriously about completely retiring at that time. He certainly could have. He was a millionaire several times over but . . . he loved his Tom James family as well (and he did think of his friends and colleagues in that manner).

At that time, Spencer Hays and the Tom James Company offered him a job he could not refuse. Stay with the company. No travel. Instead of you going to see sales people and mentoring them at their locations, we will fly them in to see you. You set your own hours but don't retire from the company yet. This really was Jim's dream position. He was only doing the parts of his job that he liked and completely free of all the draining features of being the CEO of a large company. Since he had complete control of his schedule he was able to avoid conflicts with family activities, important life events, grandkids activities, etc. He could take trips, pursue other interests, and still be contributing in an important manner to the company that he loved so much. He could continue to help Tom James and do the part of the job he enjoyed most but he could also begin to invest more heavily into his family than ever before.

His oldest grandson was 14 at the time and he had fifteen other grandkids following in a trail behind. It was during this time and over the following thirteen years that he got into the fray of being a grandparent. Jim was never one to sit on the sidelines about anything. He recognized that his legacy extended beyond his own children and Tom James. He realized that he could become a powerful influence in the lives of his grandchildren. He knew this from the powerful impact that his own grandparents had in his life. He also understood that in doing this that his own children would "rise up and call him blessed." It was during this time that he began to not only become more involved with his adult children but with each grandchild. He attended his grandchildren's sporting events, their recitals, their plays, their awards ceremonies, and more. He would go to their houses and devote time to each child. He was "Poppa" to them all.

And to a person they all report the same thing. They knew that he loved them no matter what. He played with them, wrestled with them, jumped on the trampoline with them. He threw the baseball, football, softball, etc. with them. He would go to the batting cages with them. If the grandchild was interested in it, then so was he. Two of his grandchildren delighted to tell the story about the day Poppa took them to the batting cages in 2010 and could still hit fast balls from the pitching machine. He would wrestle with the grandkids at seventy and would often make the adult children and Grammy (Arlene) nervous that he was going to hurt himself.

He watched them run and jump and act and sing. There were many days during this time when he would drop a salesperson, who he had been with all day long, at the airport and then rush to see one of his seventh grade granddaughters play in a basketball game. With sixteen grandchildren all living in the same area, attending their events was quite demanding. He came, he watched, and he bragged to anyone who listened. He wasn't just there in body. He was there for their events with complete attention. His Pastor Nick Harris relayed the following story: "I think Jim loved athletics, but I know he loved to watch his grandchildren play sports. He rarely missed a track meet, ball game, or cross-country run. What impressed me was not the fact that he attended but that he focused on each one he had come to watch. At one cross-country meet he was approached by a man who just wanted to talk. Without being rude Jim said, 'I came to watch my grandson run, I can't visit right now.' He then involved the man in cheering for his grandson." All the years of attending events, of playing with them, of taking them on special outings to the zoo, the park, the batting cages; they slowly began to accumulate into influence. He endeared himself to them through love, affirmation, and encouragement. He talked to them about the importance of relationship with Jesus Christ. He gave them books to read, helped them set goals, and worked with them on projects.

All of the grandsons at one time or another worked on special projects with him. Projects like building fences or cutting down trees or other work projects around his ranch. It was only later that they each began to realize "yes he was paying me, but he was also teaching me. He was telling me his story and he was preparing me for the future." Every grandchild believed that he or she was Poppa's favorite. Melinda reported that he would regularly tell her that she was his favorite "middle granddaughter." She said once he told her that she was his "favorite granddaughter." She later reported this to her cousin Melanie and she said that can't be because he told her the same thing. The grandsons reported similar stories. The fact was for Jim McEachern every one of his grandchildren were his favorites. He could honestly tell them all that they were his favorites and not be deceptive. They all knew that he loved them just as they were and he believed that God had great things in store for them.

It was also during this time that Jim sought to have the best possible relationship with his own adult children. As much as he loved his children, he was not a perfect father and he knew it. There were wounds present that needed healing. He would begin during this period to seek complete and total reconciliation and forgiveness for his own inadequacies as a father. At the time he didn't know if he had 12 months or 12 years of life left but he wanted his family to understand that they were the most important pieces of his life and that it mattered to him a great deal that all of those pieces were assembled together in harmony when he did pass away. Worthy of note is that this was before he had been diagnosed with cancer by eight years. At this time, he was in relatively good health but, the point is, he didn't want to have any regrets about his relationships within the family. He wanted what Jewish people call "shalom." He wanted relationships that "were flourishing, whole, and filled with delight." This was his final life's project that he would begin in 1998.

Sometime during 2006 Jim was diagnosed with cancer. It was during this time Jim fully retired from Tom James Company to focus on his health and family. He realized early in his cancer treatments that without dramatic life change that his days on earth could be substantially shortened.

After a surgery removing the cancer cells and a prolonged recovery he became more and more convinced that natural health solutions would be more helpful than the treatments traditional medicine could provide. He would still use traditional medicine but he wanted to exhaust natural means of healing before procedures and medicines. He handled this problem like he had handled every problem in recent years. He researched, he read, he discussed, he planned, and he changed his entire lifestyle. He ate very little meat and avoided sugar. He did treat himself occasionally with what became a family favorite quote "Darling, I would like just one bite" (referring to a sugared dessert). It would usually end up being two or three bites which would make everyone laugh.

In the early days after his surgery it became clear that his voice box had been damaged and he could not speak above a faint and raspy whisper. It had been damaged during the surgery but the doctors told us that his voice would come back . . . eventually (six to nine months). This story brought a smile and even laughter to all the family in the room as this was recently recalled. Jim liked to listen but anybody who knew him also knows that he liked to talk. We would get together for family events and his voice could easily overpower any room but for a short while he was as "quiet as a mouse" much to his chagrin. He wanted to share but his voice wouldn't quite let him. This may have been the point that he began to get more serious about writing the very book you are reading. He realized one day that he would not have a voice any longer. At any rate, during his recovery he determined that his health issues were a drain on Tom James resources and that he would fully retire from the company at that time. He felt that they were paying him a lot and he could no longer in good conscience take the money since he was in such poor health and couldn't mentor salespersons like he had done in the past.

His recovery was slow and the later radiation treatments were painful. On the bright side, he joked, "I don't have to deal with the psychological crisis of losing all of my hair" (He had been shaving his head since his early forties). By early 2007 he had regained his strength and voice and was fully engaged with life once more. It was during this time that he slightly refocused his priorities. His first priorities at this time were God, family, and . . . health. This is not to suggest that this is all that he focused on. He served on the Howard Payne University board of trustees. He was a member of the Ovilla Christian school board. He served as an elder at the Ovilla Road Baptist Church. He also pursued what would become a late in life fascination with Longhorn cattle. He had property and would take anyone who would listen out to see his cows and, according to his grandkids and Arlene, would "talk for hours about those cattle." It was also during this time that he became intensely interested in genealogical studies. He researched his family tree all the way back to Scotland. He was fascinated by the connection to the past that we all have through our family tree. During this time he mentored his oldest grandson in the art of selling. He went into a real estate partnership with a firm that had a suite inside the ballpark at Arlington (a firm that his grandson would be a part of). He went to baseball games (his favorite sport) and on several occasions had the entire family and some friends attend games in the suite. All this is to say that he was a man of many interests.

When Jim McEachern finally fully retired in 2006 he had plenty of activities and relationships that were ongoing. He didn't retire in the way retirement is traditionally understood. It was more like he began a new phase of operations as a military leader might do who was shifting fronts. The difference now was that all of the fronts were of his choosing and he could participate in as much or as little as he chose or was able to do. He had a plan, goals, a calendar, and a schedule. He wanted to live to be one hundred years old. He would often ask his family members if we thought he could make it. It seemed to us all, that he might well achieve that goal too. He never presumed that he would but he was always planning as if he could. The day after he passed one of the family members who was at his house noted that his daytimer was opened and a schedule made for the next six months: "Meet with Jonny (grandson) about real estate business. Travel to Howard Payne to visit grandsons' in college. Meet with Caleb about the biography. Work on goals for real estate business. Travel to Mike and Lynda's (daughter) in San Antonio to visit with them and grandchildren. Work on adding fencing at property in Avalon. Take a vacation with Karen (daughter) and Jerald. Meet with Mike (son) and talk about goals. Etc." There wasn't a week that he didn't have a rough plan of what he wanted to do. He often joked that he was as busy in retirement as he was in professional life. There is no doubt this was true.

His relationship with Tom James after 2006 continued in a sporadic and tangential manner but nothing like it had been in the decades prior. He was pursuing different interests that he enjoyed and delighted in but he used them as venues for his greater mission, namely, influencing his adult children, grandchildren, and other people within his immediate sphere of influence toward success in every area of their lives. Lynda (daughter) observed in one conversation. "Dad would become aware of what was meaningful to each person he interacted with and then he would seek to discuss or do that thing with them. In my case, he knew that quality time was important to me. So he would come to San Antonio and visit with me and my family. He also knew how important it was for me to be outdoors when visiting so he would often suggest going places so that we could be outside and talk. He gave me quality time in the way that I desired it. He seemed to never be distracted and as if he had all the time in the world for me."

During that time, I (Mike) was taking philosophy classes in a PhD program. He then began reading books on philosophy. I am certain he did this so that he could intelligently discuss these topics with me. Some variation of the above story was repeated by several members of the family, fellow church members, school officials, trustees, former colleagues at Tom James, guys at the coffee shop, basically whoever knew him. He was the person who seemed to have an abundance of time for everyone he interacted with and who valued them and their journey as much as he did his own. He never missed an opportunity to provide a word of encouragement or inspiration to anyone who was attempting to achieve a worthwhile goal. This is part of what endeared him to so many and why he influenced so many who knew him.

He wrote many handwritten letters to family members during this time. He also used cell phones to stay in contact as well. Josh Snow (grandson) in recalling one of his many phone calls from Poppa gave this example of a typical Poppa phone message: "Josh. This is your Poppa. I'm proud of you. I love you." It was during these years that Jim recognized that communication devices were changing and he began adapting to these changes as well. All of his kids and grandkids texted. He learned to text. He would often be awake in the night due to the sleeplessness that sometimes accompanies age. During these times he would text briefly to various family members sometimes at 3am to tell them he was thinking about them, that he loved them and/or to affirm some quality that he saw in them. All of his kids and grandkids were on Facebook. He got one of the grandkids to help him set up a Facebook account and began making many friends through this venue. He got an iPhone and later an iPad so that he could keep up with what was happening with his family, colleagues, and friends in ways different than he ever had before. He became so adept at using these tools that Arlene would remind him that she needed his attention too. He would laugh loudly and say, "Arlene, you can have all of my attention that you want." It's worthy of note that he had avoided learning anything related to the entire computer technological revolution that preceded in the decades prior but now he had a reason to learn how to use these tools and when Jim McEachern had a reason to do something there was no stopping him.

Jim had always been interested in heaven but after 2006 he began studying everything that he could related to the subject. He wanted to be as prepared as possible for his future. As anyone who knew him would affirm, he read incessantly, and could repeat back most of what he read to you better than the author had put it. He particularly liked the book *Heaven* by Randy Alcorn and encouraged all of his kids to read it. He read this book through (about 400 pages) several times and listened to a series of cd's that read the book aloud. In 2011 just a few months before his passing he delivered a talk to the entire congregation of the Ovilla Road Baptist Church on his understanding and on how one get's prepared for heaven. The message that day, one of many that, at least, in the early days "the reluctant speech giver" gave is still requested at ORBC by people who know about that talk. One of the most surprising revelations both to people who knew Jim and to his own family was his revelation in this book about how fearful he was of public speaking as a young person. It is shocking to all the family because Poppa was famous for making a speech on every occasion he could. He would make a speech at Thanksgiving and Christmas, of course, Mother's Day and Father's Day, birthdays for anyone, graduations, weddings, July 4th, Labor Day, it didn't seem to matter when he always had a timely word. Speeches were one of Jim's/Daddy's/Poppa's trademark characteristics and the thought that he might have been fearful about this struck particularly the grandkids as difficult to believe. Since they had been little they had been listening to his speeches and squirming and not always understanding or appreciating everything being said. In all seriousness, his speeches were usually quite similar. He would speak of the blessing of family, love, and Jesus Christ and that he prayed for every family member to have a relationship with God and be with him one day in heaven. He would speak of the past and his own heritage. He would speak with gratitude about the many blessings that God had bestowed upon him in the present. He would speak of his love for Arlene and his gratefulness for her life. He would speak of his love for every member of our family. It would usually end with a prayer and for those of us who truly understood him a sense of awe and admiration.

It was during those years from 2006 forward that he began to focus like a laser beam on those things which mattered most to him. He didn't know when but he knew, as we all should, that unless His Lord returned that he had fewer days ahead than were behind. Jim had co-authored a book with prison minister Bill Glass in 1984 entitled *Plan to Win* on goal setting. In order to understand his point of view this passage will suffice:

"There is one thing of which we are absolutely certain. If we will focus our time, attention, ability, enthusiasm, and study to a few singular, worthwhile causes, we can multiply our power. . . Like the magnifying glass, focusing our energies can increase our effectiveness 100, 200, or 300 percent. It is one of the most important keys to living successfully."

After his bout with cancer he focused his energies more than ever on his family. He did this in a variety of ways but one way he did this was by taking trips with family members. Mike McEachern (son) who admittedly had a difficult time relating to his father during his teenage and young adult years was able (for the first time) to begin to understand "who his dad was and where he had come from" after a trip to West Texas in 2008. Mike said he understood at that time whatever shortcomings (in his view) he thought his dad had as a father that it was only a matter of his limited perspective. The more he understood about where his father had come from, he said it was amazing to him that he was as good a father as he was. "He came from nothing. He had nobody to help him in his young adult years. Everything he knew about anything important he read in books and learned 'on the fly.'" This watershed moment was life changing for Mike and Jim. Their relationship flourished in ways that had not been possible previously. Later Mike and Jim flew to Scotland to see the land of the McEachern forefathers. Mike reflecting on this event said that he realized later that his dad went on the trip secondarily for this purpose but that he mainly just wanted to be with him.

There were other important trips as well. In 2008, the family made the biggest trip of them all. Jim had taken all the adults on a ski trip some years before. On another year all of our families (adults and kids) went to the Disney World resort during one of the Tom James semi-annual meeting weeks in Orlando.

On this year Jim paid for every member of the extended family that was available during the week of his 50th anniversary with Arlene to take a week long all expenses paid Caribbean cruise. 23 family members were ready and available for such a venture. This was the greatest trip we ever had together. It was fun and we all spent a lot of time together. He celebrated his 50th anniversary with almost all of the people he loved most (a few family members couldn't come because of other commitments). The cousins still talk about this trip as the best vacation ever. On the night of his 50th anniversary we all had dinner together. After dinner we all gathered in a private room with a sitting area and he made one of his famous speeches. On this night, he had a letter that he read to his one and only beloved Arlene. In it he extolled her many virtues and among many things he said he thanked her for "saving him" and, tongue firmly in cheek, declared that when he had married her he had made a contract with her to stay married for 50 years with renewable one year contracts after that and that he was now hereby choosing to exercise that renewability option. It was an unforgettable evening and the best family vacation ever. We have many pictures of that cruise. Jim took lots of pictures and had lots of pictures taken of us and him with us. This is something that all of the family had noticed in the last decade of his life. Jim was interested in documenting everything but especially with pictures. He took many, developed many, and gave many of these to family members. He had hundreds of pictures of him, his adult children, and his grandchildren made. He gave pictures of himself when he was young man and of his parents and grandparents to his adult children. He wanted his grandchildren and later great grandchildren to all have photo records of his life. He wanted them to have pictures of him together with them.

In 2010 he went to Israel with the Ovilla Road Baptist Church. This was a trip that he had always talked about taking but for various reasons had never done. When Lynda and I (Mike) committed to going, then he and Arlene committed to going. There had been previous trips to Israel but this trip would include two family members so that was enough "to seal the deal" for him. We were in Israel for ten days and it was a strenuous walking tour but he was there and engaged every day. If he was tired we never saw it. It was so exciting to see where Jesus lived, ride on a boat across the Sea of Galilee, to see the empty tomb. We were all baptized together in the Jordan River. He was thrilled at all of this but, it is my opinion, what was more important to him than being in Israel and walking where Jesus walked was being in Israel with his daughter and son-in-law. There were a large number of us on the trip from the church, and as he always did he was engaged with everyone on the trip, including his pastor for over twenty years that he loved dearly but, at the end of the day, when there was a time for sharing a meal, he always sought Lynda and I out. He wanted to be at our table. He wanted to "break bread" with us in Israel. Even now as I am writing this I am feeling emotional. It shouldn't be misunderstood, he loved Israel but it was the shared experience of being in Israel with some of his family that made it so significant.

During that same summer, he and Arlene embarked on a driving tour with Karen (daughter) and Jerald Snow. It was just the four of them on a ten day driving trip around Texas. They stayed at the Hummer House in Christoval and enjoyed the outdoors and watching hundreds of hummingbirds near the cottages they stayed in. Since they were driving they would spend lots of hours riding together and, according to Karen, they were able to spend many hours on that trip talking. "I was so glad that we went. In the past, I had been in the throes of raising five boys and was often overwhelmed with juggling all of their school activities and life events. They were all grown up and it allowed for us to be with dad and mom in a way that hadn't been possible for me in the past. It was some of the most concentrated time I had with dad in years. I loved it. It was very, very different."

Jim took many trips over the course of his life. Anyone who knew what his goals were, knew one of his goals that he set as a very young man was to visit every state in the United States. He accomplished this and numerous other countries besides but he seemed to conclude after 2006, however, that trips for the rest of his life would be about shared experience and relationships. A vacation to some place was only significant if he could spend it with the people that he cared about most. He would enjoy taking trips but trips were just really good excuses for spending time with the people that he loved.

In late May 2011 Jim would take one last vacation with Lynda and I on a cruise ship. We had booked the cruise and invited him and Arlene to come with us. He was eager to join us. This time he also invited Frank and Louise Sharp, long time friends, from Brownwood who he knew through Howard Payne University. Frank and he had shared a common interest in longhorn cattle (Frank was an expert in the field since he had written a doctoral dissertation on the subject); and over the years he had helped Jim in his endeavors with cattle. They had become very close friends. Louise was like a daughter to him. They had known each other for many years through some good times and difficult times at HPU where he was a board member and she was a highly placed administrator. It was a sixsome and we all enjoyed the trip very much but afterward Lynda and I both talked about how her dad seemed to be less engaged and more tired than usual. He was seventy five years old though so we thought it was probably the ebb and flow of being a "senior saint." I was with him on his property in Avalon a week later in early June and thought to myself that he seemed stronger and healthier than I had seen him in a very long time. He was marching around on the property telling us about all that he would like to do with it in the future. Of course, looking back we now realize that he was in decline.

Arlene recalled that during Jim's last few months he seemed more tired than usual. During his last years he was very concerned with his health so he changed his entire diet and exercise regimen in order to extend his days. He once told Lynda that his main reason for wanting to live as long he could was so that he could see what happened with his grandchildren. He was intensely curious and wanted to see the difference each grandchild would make in the world.

He walked a lot but liked variety in his exercise. He bought a bicycle in the spring of 2011 and was riding it periodically around the neighborhood. Arlene reported that one day in June after being out for just a very few minutes he came back in the house and said he was just too tired to ride. She was surprised because he would normally not allow tiredness to interfere with his workout.

Ten days before he died Karen saw him at church and he told her that he was not feeling well. She knew that he had planned to attend the Tom James meeting the following week and was concerned about his well being. At this time he had been fully retired from Tom James for five years but over the last months he had become reengaged with the company. He was mentoring salespeople again and was in contact with the new president Todd Brown. Jim mentioned to me in June that Todd had discussed a desire for him to be a mentor to him in his new role. Jim was mentoring salespeople and future leaders once again. This time though he was doing it for free. There was no compensation for this. He wanted to help people from Tom James. He was once again reconnecting with people that he dearly loved and the company that he helped found. As a result of this he had committed to several people at Tom James that he would come to the semiannual meeting if at all possible.

On Sunday night, July 3rd Karen and Angie (who had subsequently heard from Karen that he wasn't feeling well and she was worried) went over to his house and talked with him. He told them he was not feeling well but that he wanted to be at the Tom James meeting because he had promised several people that he would be there. At this point, it was decided that if he felt able on Monday that Angie would accompany him to the meeting and monitor his activity and behavior. If there was any sign of difficulty she had his permission to remove him from the meeting.

In a conversation with Angie she rehearsed the details of that week. "I am very grateful that I had that last week with dad. The hotel was a very large resort. From one end to the other it seemed like it was about a mile walk. I remember us walking back and forth a few times and during that time I was trying to maintain the right balance between guiding him and supporting him. Letting him be the big strong guy that everyone knew him to be but also being ready to step in if necessary. My dad was determined to go that meeting. In many ways it was the 'cherry on top' for him. Since he had been retired from Tom James for several years there were many new people, they knew about him, that he had created the materials they used, that Tom James was formed in his image, but this was their chance to meet him. I can only compare it with the awe an employee might feel if Sam Walton returned to Wal-Mart or if Bill Gates to Microsoft after being away for a while. There was a real sense of him being larger than life. There were people there who when he walked into the room acted as if a living legend had just come into their midst. It was quite an honor to my dad and the events of the whole week were very powerful and meaningful to him. No one in our family has any regrets about him going to the meeting. I'm sure that week was one of the best in his life. Looking back on it, his health was definitely in a compromised state at the time but none of us understood just how compromised." Arlene agreed with this saying that he had a real urgency about going to this meeting and in a private conversation with her said, "I want to go. This may be the last one I get to attend."

He and Angie returned to Dallas on Saturday, July 9 and he was tired but happy. After all, he had been with a group of people that he loved and who loved him. He had seen the fruit of his labor flourishing. He woke up on Sunday still feeling exhausted from the trip. He didn't go to church that Sunday. He told Arlene that "if he wasn't feeling better he was planning to go to see the doctor next week". He went on Facebook on Sunday, July 10th at 10:12am and made what would be his final post/message to his family:

"I'm grateful for God giving me a wonderful family . . . Arlene, Karen, Mike, Lynda, Angie, Jerald, Mindy, Mike McD, Jeff, Jonathan, Robert, Katy, Josh, Dan, Caleb, Melissa, James, Melinda, Melanie, Michael S.. Michael T., Nathan, Mitchell, Micah, Mekaylee, Candace, Stephanie, Lylah, Tiffiny and Juan. My greatest desire is to spend all eternity with God, with them and with all our friends in heaven." This list included his entire immediate family, their spouses, his grandchildren, their spouses, and his great granddaughter.

On Tuesday, July 12th in the morning he told Arlene he still wasn't feeling well and that he was planning to go to the doctor on Wednesday. His oldest grandson Jonathan knew he wasn't feeling well and suggested they cancel their weekly scheduled meeting but his Poppa insisted so he came over to Jim's house in Waxahachie to meet with him. As Jonathan recalled, "One of the many things I will always remember about Poppa was his affirmations. He was affirming me from the first time I can remember until twenty minutes before he passed away."

During their meeting Jim reported a sudden feeling of nausea and then collapsed within a matter of seconds. At that time, James Russell (grandson), a college student who was making preparations for a career as a paramedic and fireman was in the front yard cutting the grass for his Poppa. Jonathan ran out and got J.R. who immediately came in and began administering CPR in a desperate attempt to revive Jim. The emergency personnel arrived within a few minutes after the event, but Jim McEachern had gone to be with his Lord on the morning of July 12.

In the aftermath there were many things to be grateful about in this event. Jim was with some members of his family (Arlene and Jonathan) in his last moment. Arlene was not alone during this event. There was someone there who knew CPR (J.R.) to try and resuscitate him. All that could have been done was done and so there was no reason for feelings of guilt in his passing. Jim had left this world in a manner that the family is sure would have pleased him. He never liked the idea of an extended time in a hospital or being sustained long term on machines.

When he passed from this life it was like fainting. He passed out in this life and woke up in the next.

The title of this chapter is one of Jim's core life philosophies. It was something that he repeated daily in his affirmations. It's a simple notion really and defined the way he lived his life. Jonathan his oldest grandson explained what Jim meant by this in the following way. "Poppa and I would often get together for meetings related to business, goal setting, etc. During these meetings I would ask him, "Poppa, are you excited about _____ (fill in the blank) in the next few weeks or months?" He would reply, "Yes, but I'm more excited about what I get to do today."

So ends the story of the life of James E. McEachern. His incredible legacy and influence, however, will continue to provide ripples into the lives of many well into the future.

"Whatever you vividly imagine, ardently desire, sincerely believe, and enthusiastically act upon . . . must inevitably come to pass." *Paul J. Meyer*

APPENDIX 1

The following is from Jim's Goal Setting Notebook:
Goal Setting Steps by Jim McEachern
Create the following lists:

1. Determine the character traits in my life I want to develop that will make me a better person.
2. Set professional and personal goals I want to achieve
3. Determine my savings/investment objectives
4. Determine my debt elimination objectives
5. Determine the material things I want to be able to afford
6. Determine the things I want to be able to do. . . travel, education, etc.
7. Determine the organizations and people to whom I want to give

   - The purpose for these is to clarify what I want. I can only accomplish what I want to accomplish. Here are series of questions to ask yourself about every goal that you set. Write down your answers to each: A. What do I want?; B. Why do I want it?; C. When do I want it? D. What must I do to get it?
   - Determine how much income you will need to earn to be able to afford 3, 4, 5, 6 and 7.
   - Determine the order of priority for each objective listed above.

Set goals based on your priorities.

APPENDIX 2

Some Habits I Deliberately Work On, by Jim McEachern

1. Reading the Bible every morning.
2. Praying with Thanksgiving.
3. Setting goals and reviewing them often . . . self-motivation.
4. Working to achieve my goals.
5. Eating properly.
6. Exercising daily.
7. Going to bed early.
8. Reading (instead of television).
9. Being a good listener.
10. Being friendly and kind.
11. Expressing love.
12. Being a cheerful giver.
13. Thinking right . . . with a good attitude.
14. Making wise choices.
15. Avoiding unnecessary conflict.
16. Being cooperative.
17. Being honest and acting with integrity.
18. Using my imagination to see the possibilities.
19. Being relentlessly persistent toward achieving my goals.
20. Maintaining balance (God, family, work, recreation, etc.)
21. Being frugal . . . saving money.

APPENDIX 3

Jim was a voracious reader. He traced this quality all the way back to his childhood and his grandmother's encouragement. He would often quote a famous speaker of some years ago Charlie "Tremendous" Jones (tremendouslifebooks.org) in support of this viewpoint. Jones said this, "You are the same today as you'll be in five years except for two things, the books you read and the people you meet. There are three keys to being successful: read, think, share." Jim would add to these three a fourth key "reread." He believed that it was more productive to read one book several times than to read several books one time.

He certainly followed this in regards to the most important book in his library, the Holy Bible. This was the single most important influence on him, without a doubt. He had several Bibles that over the years he had written notes in and even made notations reminding himself of what books of the Bible he had read and when. These are today treasured heirlooms in the family's possession since they contain notes and important thoughts he had regarding God, His will, and His work in the world. In one period noted in the Bible (between 2007-2009), he recorded having read the entire Bible in about two years. During those two years, he read through the New Testament five times.

This appendix will include a list of some of the *other* major influences on Jim's formation. Some are dated, but classics, and well worth the investment of time, if you can find them. They are by no means all the books in Jim's library, but they are books that he repeatedly refers to in his writings and communications with individuals over the years.

These are in no particular order.

Goals: How to Get Everything You Want Faster Than You Ever Thought Possible by Brian Tracey
What to Say When You Talk to Yourself by Shad Helmschetter
The Laws of Success by Napoleon Hill
Million-Dollar Personal Success Plan by Paul J. Meyer
The Feldman Method by Ben Feldman
How to Win Friends and Influence People by Dale Carnegie
The Greatest Salesperson in the World by Og Mandino
The Richest Man in Babylon by George S. Clason
Man's Search For Meaning by Viktor Frankl
The Awesome Power of the Listening Ear by John Drakeford
How I Raised Myself From Failure to Success in Selling by Frank Bettger
Secrets of Closing Sales by Charles B. Roth
The Common Denominator of Success by Albert Gray
As a Man Thinketh by James Allen
The Seven Habits of Highly Successful People by Stephen Covey
Good to Great by James Collins
The Essence of Success by Earl Nightingale
12 Choices That Lead to Your Success by David Cottrell
How to Win Customers and Keep Them for Life by Michael Le Boeuf